Sport

ANCIENTS AND MODERNS

General Editor: Phiroze Vasunia, Professor of Greek,
University College London

How can antiquity illuminate critical issues in the modern world?
How does the ancient world help us address contemporary problems
and issues? In what ways do modern insights and theories shed new
light on the interpretation of ancient texts, monuments, artefacts and
cultures? The central aim of this exciting series is to show how
antiquity is relevant to life today. The series also points towards the
ways in which the modern and ancient worlds are mutually connected
and interrelated. Lively, engaging, and historically informed, *Ancients
and Moderns* examines key ideas and practices in context. It shows
how societies and cultures have been shaped by ideas and debates that
recur. With a strong appeal to students and teachers in a variety of
disciplines, including classics and ancient history, each book is written
for non-specialists in a clear and accessible manner.

Ancients and Moderns Series

The Art of the Body: Antiquity and Its Legacy, Michael Squire
Death: Antiquity and Its Legacy, Mario Erasmo
Gender: Antiquity and Its Legacy, Brooke Holmes
Luck, Fate and Fortune: Antiquity and Its Legacy, Esther Eidinow
Politics: Antiquity and Its Legacy, Kostas Vlassopoulos
Race: Antiquity and Its Legacy, Denise Eileen McCoskey
Religion: Antiquity and Its Legacy, Jörg Rüpke
Science: Antiquity and Its Legacy, Philippa Lang
Sex: Antiquity and Its Legacy, Daniel Orrells
Slavery: Antiquity and Its Legacy, Page DuBois
War: Antiquity and Its Legacy, Alfred S. Bradford

Sport

Antiquity and Its Legacy

Peter J. Miller

BLOOMSBURY ACADEMIC
LONDON • NEW YORK • OXFORD • NEW DELHI • SYDNEY

BLOOMSBURY ACADEMIC
Bloomsbury Publishing Plc
50 Bedford Square, London, WC1B 3DP, UK
1385 Broadway, New York, NY 10018, USA
29 Earlsfort Terrace, Dublin 2, Ireland

BLOOMSBURY, BLOOMSBURY ACADEMIC and the Diana logo are
trademarks of Bloomsbury Publishing Plc

First published in Great Britain 2023

Library of Congress Control Number: 2022941029

ISBN: HB: 978-1-3501-4020-2
       PB: 978-1-3501-4021-9
       ePDF: 978-1-3501-4023-3
       eBook: 978-1-3501-4022-6

Series: Ancients and Moderns

Typeset by RefineCatch Limited, Bungay, Suffolk
Printed and bound in Great Britain

To find out more about our authors and books visit www.bloomsbury.com
and sign up for our newsletters.

Contents

Figures

Acknowledgements

This book has benefitted from a Social Sciences and Humanities Research Council Insight Development Grant, and the support of the University of Winnipeg Chancellor's Research Chair programme. Time, more than money, was necessary for the completion of this book, and I am grateful for teaching releases agreed on by the University of Winnipeg and University of Winnipeg Faculty Association.

My colleague and partner, Dr Carla Manfredi, read the entire manuscript, suffered through countless conversations about ancient and modern sports and deserves as much credit as possible. My thanks are also due to my friend Professor David H. J. Larmour who read the entire manuscript and added numerous insightful suggestions.

I would like to acknowledge with thanks the following institutions that provided images at little or no charge: the H. J. Lutcher Stark Center for Physical Culture and Sports, the International Olympic Committee, the DAI-Rome and the DAI-Athens. Dan Diffendale produced the maps at the last minute, for which I am grateful to him.

I wrote this book a little before but mostly during the global Covid pandemic, at the same time as I became a parent and Chair of the Department of Classics at the University of Winnipeg. It has been extraordinary, challenging and difficult. It has crystalized, for me, the fundamental and foundational importance of childcare workers in our society. These workers are care-givers of the highest degree, whose diligent efforts, especially as frontline workers during the Covid pandemic, have not been adequately recognized or rewarded. For my small part, I dedicate this book in solidarity to the daycare workers of the University of Winnipeg Students' Association Daycare and with all my gratitude. I simply would not have been able to work, teach, write or research without their labour.

Conventions and Translations

I use BCE (Before the Common Era) to refer to dates before the beginning of the Gregorian calendar's reckoning (e.g. 500 BCE) and I use CE (Common Era) to refer to events in that calendar (e.g. 8 CE). Dates without BCE or CE appended are CE.

I interchangeably use the terms 'sport', 'sports' and 'athletics' throughout without precision. These terms refer, in this book, to those practices which I define as 'sport' in the Introduction. Similarly, I use 'classical antiquity', 'antiquity' and the 'ancient world' without precision to refer in the broadest geographical and temporal sense to the ancient Mediterranean from the end of the Bronze Age (c. 1177 BCE) to the end of antiquity (c. 500 CE).

Unless otherwise noted, all translations are my own. I use an eclectic method of transliteration for names in ancient Greek. Those that have long been established in English, I leave in their familiar Latinized version, but for less familiar names, I retain as much as possible ancient Greek spelling.

Introduction: Which Ancient Sports?

This book examines the sports cultures of ancient Greece and Rome from their earliest beginnings to the end of antiquity, and their reception and resonance in the centuries thereafter. The period of classical antiquity was given extraordinary value among the peoples of medieval, early modern and modern Europe and their eventual settler colonies. Imagining themselves as the descendants or inheritors of these civilizations, Europeans held them up as the 'Classics', models for emulation or comparison. In this context, where ancient Greek and Roman literature and art were prized as exemplary, sport emerged in Europe that also looked back to the ancient Greek and Roman world and was often imagined as the rebirth of one of its practices. Therefore, across this book, the questions of value and meaning loom large: why are the sports practices of the ancient Greeks and Romans valued and imitated? How do later sports in Europe and across the globe imagine themselves in accordance with or in opposition to these so-called Classical models?

What are sports?

Sports are 'games that tire you'.[1] This definition encapsulates the fact that sports impose conditions that restrict the possibility of winning and these conditions are dependent on the human body. Even with this in mind, sports are hard to define. Foot-racing, wrestling and boxing seem to fit almost anyone's idea of sport. But, when we turn to sports that rely heavily on equipment or which use machines, it is not clear. Even less clear are e-sports that take place in a virtual realm, yet rely on the physical abilities of players. The winner of a race is obvious, but other sports rely on judges' opinions to crown their winner. Does sport require an objective criterion to determine victory, or does the nature of how victory is adjudicated play no role in its definition?

Sports and games have some relationship, in that each asks participants to accept conditions that limit their actions to those prescribed in 'the rules'.[2] What makes sport different from a game is the necessity of victory or defeat; sports require competition. The imposition of voluntary conditions of difficulty is intrinsic to sports since they make a victory harder by restricting just how one can achieve it. In sports, we see people strive to complete a task amid conditions designed to make it difficult: the overcoming of these difficulties in the best manner is the definition of victory.

Physical activity must have something to do with sports: games like chess or pool or video games require physical action, but they do not rely on the body as the medium through which success or failure is achieved. Sport uses the human body: if voluntary conditions of difficulty constrain how you may win, the limits of the human body constrain whether you will win. Speed, strength, agility, sight, hearing and every other aspect of the physical experience of living come to the fore and are measured in sports.

Other ancient sports

While this book examines the sports of classical antiquity, these cultures were not alone in granting physical abilities social and cultural importance. The evidence for other sports in the ancient Mediterranean is slight, especially since so few texts survive that discuss them. The interpretation of artistic remains is fraught with difficulty, but the evidence suggests that physical displays, though not necessarily competitive ones, existed and were valued across the ancient Mediterranean.

Ancient Egypt has seemed a natural place to search for other early sports, since Egypt's long and continuous civilization produced much artistic evidence. Evidence for ancient Egyptian sports privileges the elite, and it almost exclusively focuses on the Pharaoh. Demonstrations of physical ability, whether in running or archery, were important to the self-representation of the Pharaoh and indicative of his ability to rule.[3] Beyond the Pharaoh, there are visual representations of wrestling in ancient Egyptian tombs (e.g. in the graves at the village of Beni-Hasan, *c.* 2134–1991 BCE).[4] Despite this rich visual representation, there is no written source that discusses wrestling, and scholars have been puzzled by the Beni-Hasan images: are these competitions such as we know from the Greek evidence or is this military training of some sort? New Kingdom (1552–1153 BCE) images offer more certainty about competition, although the context, rules and meaning of wrestling in ancient Egypt remains mysterious.

When searching for the origins of Greek and Roman sport, many scholars have suggested the civilizations of the Bronze Age that flourished during 2500–1177 BCE, especially the Minoans, whose culture began on the island of Crete but spread across the Aegean. The best attested physical activities during the Minoan period are bull-leaping and boxing. Bulls were important to Minoan religion, and famous representations of bull-leaping in wall paintings have survived. It is, however, difficult to parse these scenes. What can we say about the 'sport' itself? Almost nothing, unfortunately. It is not clear that this is actually sport, instead of a sort of acrobatic demonstration; it is not clear there was competition (except, as some have glibly remarked, between man and bull). Boxing is better attested than bull-leaping, though our familiarity with boxing brings the danger of relying too much on later evidence. The famous fresco of boys boxing from the island of Thera (modern Santorini, *c.* 1600 BCE) shows two mostly nude boys hitting each other, but we are at a complete loss as to whether this represents training, sparring or competition – we cannot say that it represents any reality of boxing on Thera at all.[5]

Women and sport in the ancient Greek and Roman world

Girls and women appear throughout this book, but it bears mentioning at the outset that a complete history of women's sports in classical antiquity is impossible to write. Too little evidence survives to get a comprehensive picture. We have fragmentary evidence for the participation of girls at festivals (see Chapter 3) or as part of ritual activities (see Chapter 1). We know, from meagre evidence, that certain physical activities like ball-throwing were associated with women at times in antiquity, but our largely male writers do not record much of women's activities.

I have tried, in this book, to account for the appearance of women as audience members or participants. In this context, I am reminded of the salutary warning of Stephen Miller:

> whenever I have taught a course on ancient athletics, I have measured the amount of space given to different topics in the sports section of the *San Francisco Chronicle* … The average coverage, measured in square centimeters of print, over these years has been: advertising, 29.37 per cent; horse racing, 5.04 per cent; men's competitions, 64.10 per cent; women's competitions, 1.49 per cent. If two thousand years from now these newspapers are the only athletic records that survive, what will historians conclude about the relative importance of women's athletics today?[6]

This book begins therefore from the position that since there is evidence for women's sports amid fragmentary remains, they must have been more widespread. They were, however, largely invisible to the elite, male writers who shaped the artistic, literary and to a large extent documentary evidence of classical antiquity.

Between antiquity and modernity

The practices studied in this book sit at the heart of a contradiction: even in antiquity, sports were imagined as old practices decayed from some superior origin. In some way, sports – ancient and modern – sit between the past and present uneasily, perhaps because sports, relying on the body as the medium of competition, bring into focus mortality. Sports at the broader cultural level express anxiety over individual death through nostalgia and a focus on the past. Ancient and modern sports practices imagine themselves as ancient or position themselves against other older practices. In turn, this book's comparative analysis takes seriously these claims to antiquity at the same time as it critiques them. The book aims at the broadest level, to illuminate the various pasts, presents and futures that are alive in sports, from their supposed origins over 2,800 years ago to today.

Organization and aim

This book ranges widely in time and geographic breadth, from Bronze Age Greece to twenty-first-century North America. Its goal is not to be a comprehensive guide to ancient sports, but rather to focus on those aspects of ancient sports that have been reimagined or that resonate beyond classical antiquity. The first two chapters provide an overview of ancient Greek and Roman sport, in order that readers unfamiliar with ancient sports will be able to follow the arguments of the chapters about ancient influence and modern adaptation.

In Chapters 1 and 2, the book stresses its indebtedness to many scholars, since some aspects of ancient Greek and Roman sport remain debated and controversial among experts. History, the discipline that studies the past, differs from its subject, the past. While the past is unchangeable, history – the myriad interpretations of evidence that remains from the past – changes all the time. The book presents, therefore, one perspective on ancient sports, based on one reading of the fragmentary evidence that has survived to the present. The Notes and Further Reading provide references for those who wish to follow up on debates.

Chapters 3 through 6 turn to the reception of ancient sport, that is the influence and resonance of the sporting cultures of ancient Greece and Rome in the centuries following antiquity, mostly in the years after the Industrial Revolution. There are myriad examples of ways in which ancient Greek and Roman sport have been influential, even within such a short time period, and far more than could fit within the space limitations of this book. I have chosen, therefore, with an eye to novelty and interest: that is, the aspects of the reception and resonance of ancient Greek and Roman sport that have not been covered in past books about this subject and those which demonstrate the rich history of reception and adaptation of ancient sports from antiquity to today.

Sport in Greek Antiquity

A fragment of a chariot, horse and charioteer on a vase from the eleventh or twelfth century BCE begins my examination of ancient Greek sport (see far right of Figure 1.1). The vase depicts a racing scene like others from the same period. On the far left, however, is something new: a tripod cauldron or *krater* (a mixing bowl) next to an enthroned female figure. Vessels of this sort, and tripods, are prizes in ancient Greek sport from their earliest appearance in literature. Is this a prize for the chariot race that would have filled most of the scene on this vase?[1] If so, these fragments contain the first depiction of an athletic prize in ancient Greek art and are an evocative starting point for a discussion of athletics.

Figure 1.1 Collar-necked jar, Tiryns (*c.* 1190–1020 BCE). D-DAI-ATH-ARCHIV-GA-Tiryns-1977. Photographer: Gösta Hellner.

Athla – 'prizes' – are central to sports in ancient Greece. Athletics refers to the events and competitions that concern prizes, while an *athletēs* is a person who competes for them. Prizes are crucial to ancient Greek athletics, and there is no evidence of a competition where prizes are not awarded: to compete without a prize at stake is to have no competition at all. After all, this fragmentary vase suggests that the association of prizes with sport is over three millennia old.

Ancient Greek sport, more than any other sporting tradition from the past, has been the explicit source of inspiration for modern revivals. Even the history of scholarship and study of ancient Greek sport integrates with modern attempts at revival: the study of Greek sport ebbs and flows, at times, with the cycle of the modern Olympic Games, and the popularity and international scope of that modern competition ensures that the 'relevance' of ancient Greek sport is always, apparently, clear. This chapter provides an overview of ancient Greek sports and festivals – beginning with the central concepts of prizes and competition – but it also points to those elements that have been most influential in its reception in later revivals.

Prizes and competition

The earliest literary evidence for athletics in the ancient Greek world supports the notion that prizes were always critical. Homer's *Iliad*, a monumental song from a long tradition of songs, generally dated to around 800 BCE, includes a long episode featuring athletics. After the death in combat of Achilles' friend Patroclus, the heroes bury their comrade, and Achilles calls for Games to honour him. Commonly referred to as the 'Funeral Games of Patroclus' (*Iliad* 23.257–897), this episode indicates that Games and prizes were well known to audiences. In these Games, we see sports that are familiar (chariot racing, footrace, boxing, wrestling), somewhat familiar (weight toss, javelin toss), and unfamiliar (armed combat, archery) from later Greek sport. The Games on the island of Scheria (the 'Phaeacian Games' in the *Odyssey*) add the jump and discus (*Odyssey* 8.104–249). Across the Funeral Games of Patroclus and the Games on Scheria, the narrator almost never explains the rules of the contests or the conditions of victory, meaning that the audience of the epics was already familiar with Games and contests.[2]

Audience familiarity may be the result of a curious historical synchronicity. The codification of the *Iliad* and *Odyssey* into written forms (they were previously orally transmitted songs) similar to those we have today is contemporaneous with the period of a burgeoning interest in athletics, as evidenced by the growing size of the Olympics in the sixth century BCE and the establishment of the other important and regularly occurring athletic festivals in the same period.[3] The Homeric poems and the Olympics therefore developed hand in hand. Neither was in its fully developed form until at least the middle of the sixth century BCE, and they had a reciprocal effect on each another's popularity.

If athletic prizes are attested as early as the eleventh century BCE, and a sophisticated literary representation of athletics appears as early as the eighth century BCE, where and when did athletics come from at all? Writers and thinkers throughout antiquity were confused about the origins of sport, though they occasionally made the claim that athletics and warfare were related. Even if the origin of athletics in warfare cannot be fully substantiated, ancient Greek poets and intellectuals saw an affinity between the two on an ideological level (i.e. a striving for glory and fame by a single man) and the connection is repeated continuously.[4]

Vocabulary suggests some connections between sports and war. *Athlon* and related words may be used throughout the Funeral Games of Patroclus (and at other points in the *Iliad*'s narrative when competitive athletics are referenced) to refer to prizes. The ultimate etymology of this word is unclear, though evidence from related languages in the Indo-European family suggests a basic meaning related to fatigue. But *Aethlos*, 'a competition', may mean something like 'strenuous activity for a goal' at its root,[5] but it ranges much further in both epics. It emphasizes the similarity of 'contests' both martial and athletic. The broader scope of *aethlos* is clear when Odysseus uses it to refer to the generalized 'struggles' that he and Penelope have had to face (*Odyssey* 23.248, 261, 350), and in *Iliad* 3, when Helen is weaving the 'numerous struggles (*aethlous*)' (3.126) of the Greeks and Trojans onto her tapestry. So, even if war was not the origin of athletics, from a very early point, the two were seen as similar pursuits, so much so that they could be described with the same word.

The fundamentally competitive and physical aspects of *aethlos* corresponds well with another common ancient Greek word for contests, *agōn*. Derived from a root meaning 'to drive or lead', the noun, at least in its Homeric usage, often means 'assembly', though it is most frequently used of assemblies where competition takes place. *Agones* are those places where men assemble to compete as or to be leaders.[6] The idea of *agones* as places where men act or become 'leaders' is evident in the way that warfare and athletics are venues to come forth from a crowd and be named. In *Odyssey* 8, as the Games for the Phaeacians are organized, the spectators follow as a crowd (8.109–110); as the Games begin, in contrast, young men step forward and gain names and identities (8.111–119). The distinction between named hero and 'crowd' occurs frequently in battle scenes in the *Iliad*, when heroes step forth (e.g. 5.528, 12.49, 20.178) or meld back into the nameless crowd (e.g. 3.36, 8.94, 11.359). Through language, ancient Greek encodes some of the characteristic elements of their version of sport: prizes, effort and competition. Athletics from its earliest representation and in its etymology epitomizes the notion that identity and individuals are made through action. Action and strenuous effort, whether in war or sport, were key components of ancient Greek identity and, especially, masculinity.

While warfare and athletics share actual and lexical affinities, ancient Greeks told many other, more vivid, narratives of the origins of athletics. Most of them were located in the distant past of mythology and legend. Athletics were not given an origin story and rather the poets or writers who engaged with the history of athletics tended to tell stories about particular festivals. The poet Pindar (518–438 BCE), who wrote songs for victorious athletes, related the legends surrounding the beginning of the Olympics, and he alludes to other myths and legends of the origins of festivals like the Nemean Games. These stories were often obscure or contradictory already in antiquity, and like all myths and legends – often only related in oral form – they were changeable.

Since athletics in ancient Greece always took place under the auspices of a divinity, religious practice is part of their origin as well: at Olympia, for example, sacrifice and ritual predate the evidence for the Games; at Delphi, religious observances, especially prophecy, always took precedence over the Pythian Games. When later figures in antiquity (or today) try to make sense of these contradictory legends, actual religious practice and the continuity of athletic competition, they must make choices about which stories are 'believable' or which evidence is 'important'. These choices reveal as much about the scholars themselves as they do about the past.

If Games had no discernable origin to the ancient Greeks, it may be because their primary characteristics, a focus on the body and competition, were thought to be an intrinsic part of the cosmos. In *Theogony*, the early song of Hesiod (*c.* 700 BCE) that narrates the story of creation from the beginning of the universe, anthropomorphic gods strive to better one another often via physical exertions. The ancient Greek imagining of the gods as human-shaped must have influenced the origins of athletic competition, which also finds meaning in physical exertion. In the *Theogony*, generations of gods battle each other and conflict creates the situation wherein Zeus is able to gain control. After his ordering of the cosmos, conflict passes to mortals, where it remains an inherent part of existence. In *Works and Days*, Hesiod's other major surviving poem, he tells a story of the 'two types of conflict' (11–12): the good, Hesiod observes, prompts people to compete with each other and improve themselves and society (20). So prevalent is this type of conflict that 'potter vies with potter, craftsman with craftsman, beggar with beggar, and bard with bard' (25–6). Here, in two poems that concern themselves with the origins of values that structure ancient Greek society, the body, physical exertion and competition are central.

Origins and the search for the origins of athletics have been at the heart of modern approaches to ancient sports. Rather than imagine we can locate the actual beginnings of sport, distant as they are in time from the present day, our own and ancient searches for origins reveal a search for meaning, or the construction of meaning itself. Prizes and competition appear at the beginning of the historical record and occurred, according to the ancient Greeks themselves, at the beginning of the cosmos, at least metaphorically. Athletics' meaning was linked to the apparent necessity of competition to the structure of space and time – and to enduring social structures that emerged thanks to this cosmic order. The idea that competition is fundamental and athletics has value as such is found in modern ideologies of athletics, connected as they are to the emergence of industrial capitalism. If modern athletics, especially international competitions, emerges at the same time and in connection with nineteenth-century capitalist society, then athletics has value, at least in part, because it parallels the way those types of societies are imagined to work ideally: through a supposed meritocracy where each individual's striving can bring them success. The ancient Greek desire to locate origins in the fabric of their society or the universe is similar to the integration of sports and competition into the unquestioned ideologies that structure some societies today. In both cases, athletics are a cipher for the values that support certain social conditions and broader concepts of society altogether.

Athletics and festivals

Throughout Greek history, competitive athletics took place under the aegis of patron deities, in religious or civic sanctuaries, and cannot be disentangled from what is called religion today. Given the connection of the body and anthropomorphic deities, it is difficult to envision separate 'secular' and 'religious' athletic spheres. Participating in athletics was always a religious activity, and even for spectators, attendance at festivals could be like a pilgrimage, especially since regularly occurring festivals featured not only sports but religious offerings as well.

The main competitions were the so-called 'Crown' or 'Panhellenic' (all-Greek) Games. By the middle of the sixth century BCE, these were the Olympic Games, the Pythian Games, the Isthmian Games and the Nemean Games. Aside from the Olympics, the founding of which is traditionally dated to 776 BCE, the others were founded in what modern historians call the 'Archaic Period' (776–490 BCE). During this important time, athletics, along with other key institutions and concepts (the alphabet, coinage, democracy, philosophy, history) began. Regrettably for modern historians, while this period includes the beginnings of so many important phenomena, contemporaneous sources are, nearly, non-existent.

While the Olympics was the most famous ancient festival, the other Panhellenic Games were also important religious and athletic institutions. These contests were characterized by patron deities and prizes without monetary value; they also occurred on predictable and regular schedules. Later in antiquity, this set of competitions was recognized as something special – akin to the 'Grand Slam' in professional golf and tennis today – and to win each competition over the course of one's life permitted special recognition as a *periodonikēs*, a 'circuit winner', someone who had accomplished an incredible deed.[7]

The Olympics, held at Olympia every four years, were dedicated to Zeus Olympios, and offered an olive-leaf crown as a prize; the Pythian Games at Delphi were similarly held every four years, dedicated to Pythian Apollo, and offered a laurel crown as a prize. The two 'junior' Panhellenic Games, Isthmia and Nemea, mirrored the senior two to some degree: the Isthmian Games, at the important travelling and trade centre on the Isthmus of Corinth was held every two years, dedicated to Poseidon, and offered a pine-leaf crown as a prize (visible on the centre-left of Figure 1.2); the Nemean Games were held every two years at the sanctuary of Nemea in the Peloponnese (at least, originally), were dedicated to Zeus Nemeios, and offered a celery-leaf crown as a prize (again, originally; see far right of Figure 1.2).[8] It is indicative of the

Figure 1.2 Marble relief fragment depicting athletic prizes (*c.* 2nd century CE). 59.11.19. Metropolitan Museum of Art.

ancient Greek tendency to place human inventions in the mythological past that these contests, even though the Pythian, Isthmian and Nemean Games were known to have been established in 582, 580 and 573 BCE, respectively, were given their own legendary origins, often added later, as explanations of, among other things, the particular place, crown or deity with which the Games were associated.[9]

All four festivals offered similar contests, which were broken into two groups: 'gymnastic' (where the athlete and competitor were the same person) and 'hippic' or equestrian (where the competitor like a jockey or charioteer was not the athlete who could claim the prize; the owner of the horse or chariot was the winner). Gymnastic competitions include footraces, the distances of which were defined by the stadiums in which they took place: a *stadion*, one length of the stadium (approximately 200 metres), the *diaulos*, two lengths, and the longest race, the *dolichos*, perhaps 24 lengths (some sources say as few as 7). There was no longer race, and no marathon, in antiquity.[10] The *hoplitodromos* ('race in armour') was added to the Olympics in 520 BCE and featured competitors who carried a shield and ran two lengths of the stadium in bronze helmets and greaves (shin protectors).

The other gymnastic competitions were boxing, wrestling and pankration. Wrestling began with a *syntasis* or 'lock-up', and the object was to force your opponent to the ground three times. In boxing, which occurred without gloves or ear protection, but with leather thongs (*himantes*) tied around the fingers to prevent broken bones, the object was to knock out your opponent or cause him to admit defeat. The pankration, an almost 'anything goes' competition akin to mixed martial arts, was particularly bloody; only eye-gouging and groin punches were illegal, though we have records of violations of both rules. There were no rounds or time limits for any of these competitions, which took place in the stadium, under the sun, on a kind of square area of overturned dirt (the *skamma*). The last gymnastic competition was a multi-sport event, the pentathlon (the 'five contests'), in which athletes competed across five individual competitions: jump (likely a standing long jump), discus, javelin, *stadion* and wrestling. The first three, commonly called the 'field sports' of the pentathlon, were never staged separately, but were rather specialties of pentathletes who combined skill, speed and strength.[11]

'Gymnastic' brings to mind another of the fundamental aspects of ancient Greek sport, and one way in which the athlete was always marked, whether in reality or representation: nudity. The body was, for the ancient Greeks, in the athletic context, always naked, and almost always male. Nudity may be one reason for women's restricted access to athletics. Even in those instances in which women practiced sport, they generally were depicted or imagined wearing short tunics (not always: Spartan women may have competed nude. See Chapter 3). *Gymnastēs*, a synonym for *athletēs*, means, etymologically, 'to be naked', and related words like *gymnasion* (gymnasium) have the same root meaning. While nudity in public would usually be associated with humiliation or defeat, in athletics nudity signalled the primacy of the male body. Just as they were confused about the origins of sports, ancient Greek critics were baffled about the practice of athletic nudity. They knew it made them unusual and set them apart from their neighbours in the Mediterranean,[12] but in this way they simply assimilated nudity with competitive sport, since the latter was also thought by the ancient Greeks to distinguish them from their eastern and western neighbours.

In a dialogue from the second century CE, the Syrian-Greek satirist Lucian imagines the quasi-legendary Scythian (someone from the area north and east of the Black Sea) wise-man and philosopher Anacharsis who, during a visit to Athens, watches the activities in a gymnasium. The Athenian statesman Solon (a historical figure from the sixth century BCE) explains the exercises and competitions to the bewildered foreigner (*Anacharsis* 7). Anacharsis is astonished that Greeks strip naked, oil themselves up and compete all for the sake of a symbolic prize (*Anacharsis* 9). Solon is amused; the exercises, he says, strengthen the body and the soul; they prime the mind for politics and the body for war (*Anacharsis* 15). Anarcharsis' confusion is a clever literary trick that allows Lucian to explore some of the ways in which athletics were, clearly to Romans and perhaps even to some Greeks of Lucian's day, strange; nudity, needless to say, is one of these aspects.

> Solon, for what reason do these young men of yours do these things? Some trip each other up after they entwine themselves; some come close and throw each other and are mixed up whirling in the mud like pigs. But from the outset they stripped off their clothes – for I was watching – and then they anointed themselves with oil and scraped down each other peacefully in turn.
>
> Lucian, *Anacharsis* 1[13]

Lucian begins with nudity and oil – the 'costume' of athletics in Larissa Bonfante's influential phrasing – since it was undoubtedly the visual impact of naked bodies intertwined or on display that gave athletics some of its appeal or caused it to be confusing to outsiders.[14]

Nudity, however, cannot explain athletics, since athletics predates it (in the *Iliad*, for example, athletes do not strip down: e.g. 23.683, 23.711). Therefore, the suggestion that nudity evokes connections of athletics with prehistoric hunting or ritual initiation of youths, while enticing, are to a degree impossible to prove.[15] Even in antiquity, there was debate about the precise introduction of nudity to athletics and its meaning: a chance 'outfit malfunction' in the eighth century BCE by the runner Orsippos may have been so successful that subsequent athletes followed suit (Pausanias, 1.44.1). Notwithstanding the propensity of athletes in all times and places to copy each other, the Orsippos story, found in the geographer and historian Pausanias' work, seems more like the etiological stories characteristic of ancient Greek mythography. Another writer, the fifth-century BCE historian Thucydides, says that nudity is a 'recent' innovation (1.6.5–6), though he offers no further precision, and his ambiguity has vexed modern historians. Oil caused confusion in antiquity and continues to confuse: Lucian thought that it softened the skin and cooled it (*Anacharsis* 24), whereas modern scholars have focused on the connections among anointment, oil and divinity.[16]

In contrast to the gymnastic competitions, in which the competitor was the athlete and prize winner, hippic (equestrian) competitions featured horses or horse-and-chariot teams which were owned or hired by wealthy people. Equestrian competition permitted wealthy, though older, people (sometimes women) to continue to compete in contests, long after their physical skills had deteriorated.[17] Perhaps because of the involvement of wealthy and politically powerful competitors, equestrian contests were considered the top prizes at the Games. In the classical period, the main contests were four- and two-horse chariot races (*tethrippon* [for adult horses and foals] and *synoris*) and a race on horseback (*kelēs*). By the Hellenistic and Roman period, these contests had expanded even further, with a *synoris* and *kelēs* for foals at the Olympics. Such a continuous expansion of equestrian competitions must reflect the aims and desires of the wealthy elites who controlled sanctuaries and dominated sport: more competitions meant more opportunities to leverage the glory that came with victory.

Unlike the gymnastic events that took place in the stadium, equestrian events took place in the larger hippodrome. Distances raced differed from competition to competition: four-horse chariot races for adult horses spanned 12 rounds of the hippodrome at Olympia (maybe 10 km); in the single-rider horse race the distance was much shorter (approximately 1.2 km). Chariot-races for foals and colts (8 laps for four-horse; 3 laps for two-horse) and in two-horse chariots (8 laps) were shorter again. Equestrian competitions like the horse race and chariot race are familiar enough to modern spectators, but others were more unusual. For fifty years or so at the beginning of the fifth century BCE, Olympia hosted a mule-cart race (*apēnē*) and another competition called the *kalpē,* in which a rider jumped off his horse (always a mare) and ran beside her for a distance. At Athens, in the Panathenaic Games, we have artistic and literary evidence for another combined sort of equestrian sport known as the *apobatēs*: here, athletes would imitate Homeric heroes by leaping on and off speeding chariots.[18]

The leveraging of victory is likely behind another expansion of competitions at all four Panhellenic Games: the division of competitors, especially in gymnastic competitions, into age groups.[19] At the Olympics, where tradition reigned throughout antiquity, there were only ever two age classes, adult and boy. At the other Panhellenic sanctuaries, however, further age groups proliferated, so that by the Hellenistic period at the Isthmian Games, for example, there were men, *ageneioi* ('beardless youths') and boys.[20] The final category was adjudicated differently at each festival, so that from the third century BCE onwards, we hear of 'Pythian boys' and 'Isthmian boys'. Rather than having less meaning because they were associated with children – like a 'junior' competition in contemporary sports – victories in the younger age classes appear to have had the same allure and to have generated the same glory as victories in the 'adult' category. Again, it is likely that the same impulse that prompted the increase in equestrian contests is at play. More opportunities for more victory meant more possible victories to leverage for the wealthy and politically powerful groups who made up most of the competitors.[21]

Across Greece, various competitions focused on the bodies of men, boys and horses, where prizes were at stake and deities presided. One sanctuary may serve as an example for the ways in which architecture, religion and athletics came together. Nemea, located in the hinterland of Argos and Corinth in the northeast Peloponnese, was a site dedicated, exclusively, to the Nemean Games (see Figure 1.3; the stadium is to the

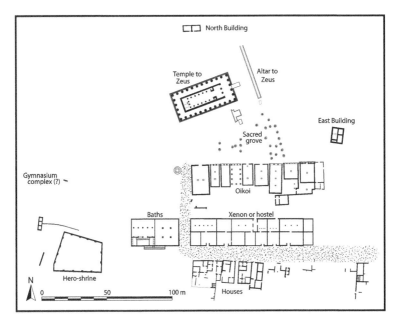

Figure 1.3 Map of ancient Nemea. Artist: Daniel P. Diffendale. After a map in S. G. Miller, *Ancient Nemea* (Archaeological Receipts Fund, 2004), figure 60.

north, off the map). Unlike the sanctuaries of Olympia, Delphi and Isthmia, Nemea was not an important religious or economic site in and of itself, and it was likely relatively empty except during the two weeks around the Nemean Games every two years. Even with this somewhat limited use, Nemea housed an impressive collection of buildings, some of which were related to the worship of the local, agricultural iteration of Zeus, and some which were designed for the participants and audiences of the Nemean Games. Nemea is unusual, because its buildings were used for a comparatively short time: the sanctuary hosted the Games until the end of the fifth century BCE, at which point they moved to Argos. The Games returned to Nemea – along with the extensive construction project – around 340 BCE, though they only took place at the site until, at latest, 250 BCE, when they were shifted – permanently – to Argos. Nemea offers a kind of 'snapshot' of the best in athletic and religious architecture in the early fourth century BCE.

The sanctuary is separated into the stadium, built several hundred metres to the north in a natural valley and the sanctuary proper on an open plain. The main entrance to the site was from the west, past the hero-shrine to the founding hero, a child named Opheltes or Archemoros. This small open area was enclosed by a low, five-sided wall, at which offerings were made to the hero, a child whose death supposedly prompted the foundation of the Nemean Games.[22] Shrines to 'heroes', that is mortals who retained power after death, were common at many sanctuaries, and a few athletes were worshiped as 'heroes' after death.[23]

The first significant structures that one would have encountered coming from the west were athletic. Although now covered by vineyards, the gymnasium-*palaestra* complex of Nemea was likely north and slightly east of the hero shrine; also, just east of the shrine was a bath complex, which is one of the oldest in the Greek world.[24] None of the other Panhellenic sanctuaries have evidence of athletic facilities of this complexity in the middle of the fourth century BCE. Nemea's reconstruction, when the Games returned in 340 BCE, may have been an opportunity to imagine a 'state-of-the-art' athletic sanctuary.

In the same vein, east of the athletic facilities was another first for a sanctuary: a *xenon* or 'hostel'. This two-story building was comprised of two rows of rooms on the north and south sides. Cooking material and evidence of hearths have been located in the southern rooms, so these rooms may have incorporated private or shared cooking facilities.[25] Given its relatively small size, the *xenon* was presumably for athletes or important guests. As at Olympia, which eventually had its own *xenon* called the Leonidaion after its dedicator (*c.* 330 BCE), most guests would have camped in tents outside of the sanctuary proper.

North of the *xenon* were the key religious and political buildings of Nemea: the temple to Zeus and a series of small buildings called *oikoi* by archaeologists that probably functioned as 'treasuries'. The latter were a feature of Olympia and Delphi as well; they were constructed and maintained by individual Greek cities and functioned at the site as a storehouse of valuable dedications given by the city (or *polis*) or its individual citizens to the deity. Immediately north of the treasuries stands the Temple of Nemean Zeus that still dominates the landscape of Nemea.[26] Unlike the Zeus worshipped at Olympia, Nemean Zeus was an agricultural iteration of the sky-god, and the site included few, if any, martial dedications. The temple itself was less impressive sculpturally than its Olympic counterpart: it seems to have included no architectural sculpture and was relatively unadorned. In front of the temple stood the altar at which sacrifices were conducted and a sacred grove of Cypress trees.

The stadium is located in a natural valley, which saved engineers the trouble of creating a slope for seating.[27] The grassy slopes today are authentic, since aside from some ceremonial seats and a judges' stand, the stadium, which could hold around 30,000 spectators, had no stone seating.[28] The length of the track was 178 metres, slightly shorter than the 192-metre-long course at Olympia, and it was surrounded by a drainage system which included water that was piped into basins, possibly for athletes or spectators to drink or to dampen the track to reduce dust.[29] Every 3 metres were distance markers – a first as far as we can tell at Nemea – which may have helped ancient runners time their bursts of speed for the final sprint in the various lengths of footraces.[30] The most prominent feature of the stadium is the entrance tunnel, carved through the hill in the southern side, which connected to the ancient *apodyterion*, a dressing room, now reduced to a few standing columns.[31] The fact that the tunnel is connected to the *apodyterion* indicates that it was for the use of athletes only. The engineering is impressive: over 2,300 years later, the arch of the tunnel still holds, and archaeologists only had to clear debris and dirt from the inside when it was excavated.[32] The tunnel shows that the spectacular entrance of athletes was important: at Nemea athletes would enter the arena from below the filled stadium seating area, passing from darkness into light at the moment they began the contest that would determine whether they were winners or losers. Moreover, excavations have revealed evidence, in the form of graffiti, for athletes in the tunnel: some inscriptions on the tunnel walls consist of athletes' names, adjectives describing them, their cities and claims of victory.[33] Here, we can be sure of the presence of ancient athletes, who congregated in the tunnel as they waited for their event to begin; they had already stripped and oiled up and now, like athletes in many eras, jostled elbows and exchanged compliments and insults with those who were momentarily to become their competitors in the stadium.[34]

While the Olympics and the Panhellenic Games fill the imaginations of modern scholars, students and even athletes, sanctuaries like that at Nemea were not the only place competitive athletics took place, nor were Panhellenic Games the most prevalent of venues for athletics in antiquity. Just like today, when the Olympics or other recurring festivals are high points on the athletic calendar but still far from the only competitions, many other ancient Greek athletic festivals existed. By the beginning of the classical period, at least 76 and perhaps as many as 155 festivals occurred with some regularity in the Greek world outside of the competitions of the *periodos*.[35] Some, like the Greater Panathenaia at Athens, were important and rivalled the Panhellenic Games (see far left of Figure 1.2 for an engraved prize vase from Athens). Others, however, have left almost no impression in the historical record beyond mention in catalogues of victories, inscriptions on stone or bronze plaques or on statue bases or brief mentions in other writers (at the centre-right of Figure 1.2 is a representation of a shield, the prize from a festival at Argos). Athletic festivals were not only for men, and we hear, at least in brief, of athletic festivals dedicated to women's sport,[36] like the Heraea at Olympia or the footrace of the Dionysiades (Spartan virgins) in honour of Dionysus at Sparta (on the Heraea, see Chapter 3).[37]

While famous athletes like Milo of Croton, Diagoras of Rhodes and Theagenes of Thasos fill the pages of history books and still encourage imitators today, ancient athletes were a diverse class of people beyond these larger-than-life figures. Some athletes continued the type of athletic life they had learned at the gymnasium as young men, while others became more or less professionalized – i.e. they pursued athletics as the main occupation of their life.[38] The latter group, by the early Hellenistic period, had formed associations – we might call them athletes' unions – to protect their economic interests and special statuses, and to provide for members in retirement or in case of untimely death.[39] Though we have no record of a figure like Marvin Miller (the powerful first executive director of the Major League Baseball Players' Association, under whose tenure salaries increased and players' rights expanded), it is clear that generations of athletes used these organizations to work for better salaries (in the form of prize money) and perks (in the form of, among other things, freedom from taxation). By the Roman period, the myriad number of associations had been made subject to a single supra-national group that was based in Rome – a type of umbrella organization for athletes' unions across the ancient Greek and Roman world. Not only do these organizations demonstrate the social and economic importance of athletics in antiquity, but they also demonstrate the collective self-identity of athletes.

The scope and breadth is incredible: many important sanctuaries to deities across the Mediterranean – wherever Greeks went – had athletic games associated with them. Athletics were appropriate to religious celebrations, funerals, city-foundations and military campaigns; they were the regular activities of boy, girls, men and women in countless cities. When Alexander of Macedon marched east, conquered the Persian Empire and brought ancient Greek culture – and political and military hegemony – to the Near East, athletics and athletic competitions marched along with him as central elements, as important as Homer, the phalanx and the *polis*, of ancient Greek civilization.

Celebrating victory

As the opening of this chapter made clear, prizes are central to the ancient Greek notion of athletics. Fittingly, then, prizes, whether in material rewards for success or more symbolic representations, formed the basis for celebrations of athletic victory.

By the middle of the sixth century BCE, victory monuments became normal in the ancient Greek world, and anthropomorphic victory statues followed soon thereafter (Pausanias, 6.18.7). By the third and

second centuries BCE, there were 90 statues leading up to the temple of
Apollo at Delphi[40] and 197 statues in the central area at Olympia.[41]
Victory statues are some of the oldest sculptures that represent human
beings, as opposed to gods. Statues were conceived as substitute (and
painted) people.[42] Inscriptions, whether in prose or verse, furthered this
identification, and together these two elements brought the monument
to life as viewers looked at it and read (or heard aloud) the inscription.[43]
Statues did not normally depict moments of drama within the contest
itself (though there are exceptions). Instead, post-victory rituals are
often the focus of victory statues, especially those at Panhellenic sites,
whether the announcement of victory, the presentation of the victory
crown or the dedication of the crown to the god.

The famous Charioteer from Delphi (see Figure 1.4) exemplifies the
focus on post-victory rituals. While today only the charioteer and some
fragments of reins, horses and chariot remains, in antiquity, the statue
would have been a complete chariot group, with four horses, a chariot
and the charioteer; the statue group would have been embellished with
gold and other metal decorations. Even in its complete form, however,
it did not depict the chariot race itself. The charioteer's clothes, which lie
still along his body, suggest a moment of calm. The ribbon around his
head indicates that the scene is after the race, though before the
presentation of the victory crown since these ribbons were an immediate
acknowledgment of victory. We might compare, today, the victorious
athlete in a footrace, who runs along the track with their flag immediately
after winning the race. Unlike the exhausted and jubilant modern
athlete, the charioteer's face shows evidence of neither exertion nor
pride. Most victory statues or other depictions of athletic victors render
a contemplative face with eyes often cast down in a show of modesty.
The athlete, at the moment of highest triumph, shows deference to the
gods who caused his victory and attempts to avoid the envy of those
watching.

Not only do statues and other material manifestations of victory
attempt to combine celebration and modesty, but song, particularly the
victory or epinician ode, similarly exalts the victor at the same time as

Figure 1.4 Charioteer of Delphi (*c.* 470 BCE). Archaeological Museum of Delphi. Photographer: Author.

the genre works to forestall jealousy. Victory odes were a short-lived and complex genre of song, but they appear to have begun in the middle of the sixth century BCE, and the last genuine classical song is likely that of Euripides for the Athenian elite Alcibiades in the 410s BCE.[44] The most famous singer of victory odes was Pindar, whose sometimes lengthy, allusive and deeply metaphorical lyrics became part of the canon of classical literature. Pindar's odes vary in structure, but they frequently praise by implication through long narrations of myths, sometimes obscure ones, which illuminate the values of athletics and the particular qualities of the victor. Athletes are often mentioned only briefly, at the beginning and the end of the ode, though these sparing references likely reflect generic and cultural concerns with hubris and envy. Victors, after all, commissioned these songs, so they clearly saw them as useful for popularizing their victory and leveraging the cultural capital associated with it.

Pindar's odes reflect ideologies of competition and victory that can be observed from Homeric epic onwards. In one of his most famous songs, *Olympian* 1, in honour of the horse-racing victory of the Syracusan tyrant Hieron in 476 BCE, Pindar enunciates a rationale for athletics, which, though couched in myth, resonates in ancient Greek culture for centuries. In the story that is narrated in the song, Pelops, the namesake of the Peloponnese and a foundational hero for the Olympics, speaks to the god Poseidon and explains why he chooses to face a mortal challenge to win the hand of a bride:

> Great danger does not take hold of a coward. Since all men are compelled to die, why should anyone sit stewing an inglorious old age in the darkness, with no share of any fine deeds?
>
> Pindar, *Olympian* 1.81–4[45]

The connection between the necessity of death and the desirability of glory is not an exclusively athletic concept. It occurs most notably in ancient Greek epic, in Achilles' choice of whether to pursue a long life of obscurity or a short life of fame (*Iliad* 9.410–20). While the *Iliad* may answer that glory trumps longevity, as early as Homeric epic, the certainty of this choice is questioned: when Odysseus meets the ghost of Achilles in *Odyssey* 11, he regrets his choice and observes that it would be better to be the servant to a slave than the king of the dead (11.478–91). Athletics, or at least its representation in epinician song, connects to this early debate on the value of mortal life and its remembrance after death. Athletic victory appears as an analogue to the martial glory of Homeric heroes and their memorialization in a tradition of song.

Another piece of ancient epic vocabulary is relevant here: *nostos* or 'homecoming' (connected, of course, with nostalgia). The *Odyssey* is the homecoming poem par excellence, and at its outset, it connects the need for a return home, or at least for a message to return home, to obtain glory. Odysseus' son Telemachus, in a house besieged by his mother's suitors, claims that it would be better that his father were dead and his death known than for him to wander unknown to anyone (*Odyssey* 1.239–43). Athletics also requires a journey out, a struggle and a return home; Pindar's songs refer implicitly and explicitly to the necessity for the victorious athlete to be reintegrated into a community that he has literally and figuratively left.[46] In these songs and in other representations of athletic ideology, we see arguments for the value of athletic victories to families and to cities. Athletics in antiquity is, in these representations, an activity with concurrent and intersecting individual and communal values.

Athletic success in the ancient and modern worlds, to some degree, runs parallel, despite the vast differences in political organization. Athletes in the contemporary world, especially Olympic athletes, pursue individual glory at international competitions and form bonds with athletes from other nations. At the same time, these athletes represent their nation and the vast state investment in Olympic sports demonstrates the belief that victory has a communal value as well. Pindar's odes may be more sophisticated than the proverbial Wheaties box, but both point to the necessity of transmitting victory beyond the confines of the stadium and finding in sporting success something more than success in a competition. In antiquity and today sports success is imagined to play an important role in the private and public world, a role important enough to require poetic and artistic manipulation in the past (and civic investment) and massive state-sponsored investment and marketing in the present (and artistic representation).

Gymnasium culture

Competitive athletics like those associated with festivals and sanctuaries were not the only way in which sport took place in ancient Greek society. From early beginnings in Athens, education and physical fitness were linked through the space of the gymnasium. Education, in fact, was almost impossible to imagine without physical fitness and training.

By the fifth and fourth centuries BCE in Athens, where sources are relatively plentiful, gymnasiums were prominent social and intellectual institutions.[47] Plato's Academy and Aristotle's Lyceum were both gymnasiums, where young men – at least freeborn young men with leisure time – could attend to physical and intellectual pursuits, ancient Greek *paideia*. These institutions remained voluntary, or private inasmuch as they were not administered by the state, until the Hellenistic period (323–331 BCE). Cities across the Greek world institutionalized a kind of public education through gymnasiums during this time, which included hiring free or using enslaved school teachers who were in charge of physical education.[48] Gymnasium personnel were often elected or selected in various ancient Greek cities, so that by the Hellenistic period, the gymnasium became an institution of the city, and the activities of the gymnasium were integral to civic identity and ideology.

By far the greatest amount of evidence for gymnasiums and their integration into civic politics is for the age group of young men (*epheboi*) and their specific training and schooling regimen (the *ephebeia*), though there is evidence for the paramilitary training of younger children as well.[49] *Epheboi* were adolescents, young men close to adulthood and citizenship. By the fourth century BCE, *epheboi* in Athens participated in institutionalized training operated by the state, the aim of which was to prepare young men for military service as citizens. Youths were enrolled, special trainers elected to supervise them, and they practiced military drills and some sports (Aristotle, *Constitution of the Athenians* 42).[50] Even if the aim was not athletic excellence, the *ephebeia* at Athens and in other cities demonstrates civic interest in what is recognizably physical education. The leisure for such activities was built on the back of enslaved persons, who were forced to perform much of the physical and manual labour necessary to maintain the city and economy in antiquity and who were forbidden – often by law –

from participation in activities like athletics, which were the mark of free citizens.

Athletics were not the only activity at the gymnasium in most ancient Greek cities. From almost as early as their appearance in Athens in the classical period, gymnasiums attracted those who were interested in having access to young, citizen men – mentally and physically. From the vantage point of the late sixth century BCE, after over a thousand years of gymnasium tradition, Isidore of Seville described the gymnasium as fundamentally about mental and physical training: 'a gymnasium is a general place for exercises. Yet, at Athens it was the place where philosophy was learned and the pursuit of wisdom was "exercised"' (*Etymologiae* 15.2.30).[51] The gymnasium was from its founding to the end of the ancient world, a place for mental and physical education.

In Athens, since access to gymnasiums was restricted to legitimate, freeborn, male citizens, the gymnasium could act as a stand-in for the citizen-body or city itself. These spaces attracted sophists, who, from their first appearance in Athens, claimed to be able to teach a variety of disciplines including rhetoric. As a place where 'training' occurred, the gymnasium was a suitable space for mental training as well. Sophists, who frequented the palaestra and who were sometimes athletes themselves, used athletic and especially wrestling metaphors to describe rhetoric and philosophy. Wrestling was likely suitable because it was a technical sport that required training, and one in which a well-trained, but physically smaller or weaker competitor, could defeat a larger or stronger one; in the same way, sophists claimed to teach a skill to 'make the weaker argument stronger'.[52] In the Athenian gymnasium, especially as the new discipline of philosophy developed (and was housed in gymnasiums), a nexus of educational practices came together that would be conceived of as integral to the development of citizens in the Greek tradition for the remainder of antiquity: training in music, rhetoric and athletics.

Training and the gymnasium go hand in hand with the ancient Greek practice of pederasty. Pederasty describes a sexual or at least erotic relationship between men of different ages; the exact parameters and the ages of each partner have been the subject of much modern debate. It is almost certain that there was a difference of status – perhaps a citizen adult and a boy prior to attaining the age of majority – but the age difference may have been slight in some cases. It is clear that the gymnasium could be tied to homoerotic relationships. A law attributed to Solon forbid the mixing of ages in some Athenian gymnasiums (Aeschines, *Against Timarchus* 9–12) and an inscription from Macedonia similarly concerns keeping age groups separate while they are nude in the gymnasium (*Supplementum Epigraphicum Graecum* 27.261).

If there was anxiety about the mixing of ages and the possibility of homoerotic relations in the gymnasium, pederastic relationships and teaching and training were nonetheless deeply connected. Plato's *Lysis* offers a vision of Socrates, en route between two of Athens' main gymnasiums, stopping to visit a new facility. One of his first questions on entering is to ask who is the most beautiful young man there (204b). His host, Hippothales, blushes, and the dialogue turns quickly to the object of his affection, the eponymous Lysis, with whom Socrates talks. Homoerotic liaisons may have been fraught with anxiety at Athens – at other cities we know far less of their pederastic practices – but the connection of erotics, athletics and education was consistent across Greek antiquity.[53] These sexual relationships could even be considered part of the training and education of young men, with the older man a tutor and guide for the young man.[54] Connections made through pederastic relationships in youth could, theoretically, be important political connections later in life.

Physical education's critical role in civic ideology and identity is most obvious in the case of the ancient Greek city of Sparta. Sparta institutionalized a distinctive system of physical education (the *agogē*) earlier than any other city. While the evidence is difficult to interpret because of admiration for Sparta among later ancient Greek and Roman (and modern) writers, Sparta seems to have put in place a more or less official education regime for youth by the late sixth century BCE.[55] Boys would embark on a course of physical education from as young as seven, when they were enrolled in training groups.[56] While early tutoring seems to have focused on the sports popular throughout the athletic circuit, once a boy reached adolescence, athletic training became more competitive, aggressive and connected to Spartan state-organized martial practices.

Sparta's long grip on hegemony in the ancient Greek world, from at least the middle of the sixth century BCE to the middle of the fourth, was predicated on its well-trained citizenry, or at least on other cities' perception that Spartans were the most physically well-prepared and formidable population. Only Spartans, they themselves claimed, were soldiers full-time, whereas other Greeks were farmers and artisans and therefore part-time soldiers. Physical fitness was central to this ideology and reality. Sports and dancing, especially since they were practiced in communal settings, generated the class cohesion and solidarity necessary for Spartan citizens to retain internal control over Sparta for generations.[57]

Beyond evidence for early institutionalized physical fitness, Sparta's *agogē* also offers a good example of the reception of 'ancient Greece' even within the time period of classical antiquity. Sparta was considered, by the late Roman Republican Period (146–131 BCE), an atavism, a place where people had 'lived for more than seven hundred years with one and the same set of customs and unchanging laws' (Cicero, *For Flaccus* 63). One important aspect of these 'unchanging' laws was the *agogē*. However, Sparta's system of physical education, by the end of the first century BCE, bore only some resemblance to the famous system that had propelled Spartan hegemony in the classical period. Rather, the Roman system was itself a revival of a revival, the first under the Spartan revolutionary King Kleomenes III (235–222 BCE) and the second after the dissolution of the Achaean League by Rome in 146 BCE.[58]

By the time of Cicero, Sparta had become a tourist attraction, which wealthy Romans and Greeks could visit to see a people supposedly unchanged by time. Like a modern archaeological site or, in some ways, like the modern revival of the Olympic Games, Roman Sparta's system of education claimed some connection with that which had led the

Spartans to greatness in the past even as many aspects were different. Revivals, in any time period, necessitate change, since they must accommodate new and changing conditions, so that even if the rhetoric of revival at Roman Sparta claimed the continuity of the *agogē*, it is clear that the Roman system was a creative and imaginary interpretation of the past.[59] The landscape and cityscape of Roman Sparta buttressed this revival, since tombs, monuments and memorials throughout the city evoked its ancient past.[60]

The vision of Spartan society as communal and physically active has been influential for over two thousand years, from Athenian Laconophiles ('lovers of Sparta') of the classical period, to Roman tourists of the early Empire. By the nineteenth and twentieth centuries, one of Sparta's main influences, beyond its still important reputation for military prowess, was on physical fitness and sport advocates, especially in the burgeoning world of 'physical culture' in the early decades of the twentieth century (see Chapter 4), and the world of professional and university sports teams.[61] The reality of Spartan sports and physical fitness must be divorced from its reception and romanticization in both antiquity and modernity: the Spartans were unusual in their early focus on sports, but their society, structured as it was on authoritarianism, terror and repression, is no model for contemporary advocates of physical fitness.

One of the most notorious aspects of Spartan physical education, at least to ancient writers, was its inclusion of women. While women were not permitted at the gymnasium in Athens, this prohibition does not reflect a lack of interest on behalf of girls and women in physical fitness or sports. Spartan women were well known enough for their physical education that one Athenian playwright, Aristophanes, lampoons Spartan female characters by having them be over-eager to physically conquer any obstacle (*Lysistrata* 78–83, 117–18). Young women danced in various ritual performances, often competitive, that were important religious activities but also opportunities to show their skills and talents and be displayed to potential grooms.

At Athens, some evidence suggests that athletics, in a tightly controlled ritual form, could be part of the initiatory practices of girls, though not in the gymnasium proper.[62] At the Sanctuary of Artemis in Brauron, about 40 km from Athens, we hear of rites called the *Arkteia*. The literary evidence is almost non-existent, but scraps of vases found at this and other sanctuaries show young girls of varying ages either nude or in tunics, in a position that seems to indicate that they are running. While some have understood this to be a competition, it may simply be a ritualized imitation of a hunt.[63] The *Arkteia* may not be competitive athletics of a type we recognize or the institutionalized athletic practice of the male gymnasium. Nonetheless, it points, like dancing, to physical activity as socially and religiously important to all sexes and part of normative development and integration into society.

The perceived connection between mental and physical development has been one of the ancient world's most enduring contributions to modern educational theory. Pierre de Coubertin's (1863–1937) dream, far before he developed an interest in the revival of the Olympics, was to introduce physical fitness to the French school system. The French system, to Coubertin, performed poorly in comparison to some British private schools (among others, Rugby College, made famous in Thomas Hughes' influential novel, *Tom Brown's School Days* [1857]) with their emphasis on physical fitness and competitive sports, an emphasis often generated through brutality that aimed to create group and class cohesion. From this initial interest, Coubertin moved to the revival of the ancient Games, but education never left his thinking: the Olympics were meant to prompt physical rejuvenation in the broader world, alongside a philosophy of sport and morality.

The belief that education proper includes physical fitness is, of course, normal in many school systems now, as is the belief that team sports in particular provide important developmental opportunities for children and adolescents. Contemporary society, especially in Europe and its settler colonies, is in sync with and indebted to the ethos that powered gymnasium culture in the Hellenistic period: a belief that the state has some role to play in the physical development of its populace, that training has some benefit beyond the physical, that 'fit' bodies are desirable sexually and morally. A spectre beside and behind these

altruistic motives and their contemporary commercial expression is the
Spartan example of physical fitness and martial preparation, a kind of
ancient eugenics that inspired mass physical fitness movements in Nazi
Germany and which still finds eager adherents in 'Spartan' fitness 'boot
camps' and the like.

While there was debate throughout the twentieth century on the
types of activities that best constituted 'fitness', some sort of physical
activity as part of health became standard in the USA in the decades
after the Second World War.[64] These activities could be conceived of as
necessary for the health of the nation[65] – especially its military and
reproductive capacities – or simply as individual pursuits that added to
personal and familial happiness,[66] both notions that the ancient Greeks
would have understood.

Other ideologies associated with ancient gymnasiums and sports
came to the fore in the fitness culture of the late twentieth century:
joggers conceived of their training as a pursuit in and of itself, often
with a religiously described 'runner's high' as part of the benefits.[67] In
contrast, the 'return of muscles' in 1980s' fitness brought an aesthetic,
rather than healthy aspect, to the shaping of the male and female body,
something that would be recognizable in classical antiquity.[68] By the
beginning of the twenty-first century, the 'fitness body' had emerged as
desirable and representative of moral and physical health for men and
women (what Eric Chaline calls a 'contemporary expression of ancient
Greek *sophrosyne* and *arete*').[69] This body, developed on an individual
level at the gym, was a product at a collective level of media and
commercial marketing of health and fitness as ends in themselves,
supporting, now, a massive consumer culture.

*   *   *

Prizes began this overview of ancient Greek sport because prizes are
one of its key aspects, and one which distinguishes it from the
participatory ethos of modern sport. Prizes are essential to ancient
Greek sport as physical manifestations of victory, but prizes and victory

lose their potency without a celebration of success. Athletics, inasmuch as it intersects with literature, history, gender, sexuality and identity, plays a major role in ancient Greek culture, but, except and unless a prize was won and made known widely, athletics risked futility and meaninglessness. The world of Greek sport as we see it is a world of victors and victories. Our vision of ancient sport, constrained as it is by limited evidence, mostly obscures the agony of defeat that must, for over a thousand years, have been the main experience of ancient Greek athletes. While today's athletic culture celebrates participation and honours best efforts, ancient Greek sports envisions a stadium where one prize makes athletic competition valuable, and to falter and lose, makes even the effort itself futile. In this key aspect, at least, lies one of the greatest gulfs between ancient Greek and modern sport.

2

Sport in Roman Antiquity

In the *Pro Sestio*, Marcus Tullius Cicero lists three places where the judgement and desires of the Romans may be found: 'in a meeting, in the assembly and in the crowds of Games and gladiatorial shows' (*Pro Sestio* 106). Along with the political settings of meetings and assemblies (where elections were held and laws were passed), he mentions Games and gladiatorial shows. These correspond to events at which political authority could be used by the Roman people, or harnessed by their representatives. Implicitly, the ideal audience for all of these events was the same: Roman citizens.

Audience is a key place to begin the study of Roman sport since seeing and being seen, and the distinction between performer and audience, was critical. Roman audiences, like many modern sports fans, were highly sophisticated consumers of Games, from chariot-racing to beast hunts to gladiatorial combat; they knew the intricate details of strategy and competitors' careers and they bought and displayed everyday items connected to the Games. The distinction between citizen and audience, the audience's ability to judge, discern and interpret, and the various attempts to subvert or reinforce distinctions lie at the heart of Roman sport.[1]

Roman sport has never been 'revived' in the same way as the sports of the ancient Greeks; nor has Roman sport served as explicit inspiration for modern imaginings of sport. There are many representations of Roman sport, usually in fantastical or speculative settings, but little direct re-creation. Instead, as this chapter makes clear, Roman sport *resonates* with the globalized sports of the twenty-first century. Like most modern sports fans, Romans themselves were not elite competitors, and the sporting culture of Rome privileges the audience and their experience over that of the competitor. Roman sport was about and encouraged fandom, celebrity and celebration. From the very venues in which these sports took place, to their integration into politics and society, Roman sport resonates with the large-scale spectacular quality of many contemporary sports.

Spectacle

This book uses the phrase 'Roman sport', because Roman competitions were sports by any reasonable definition. Still, many books refer to Roman *spectacle*, because the competitions seem to privilege audiences over what some conceive of as a 'pure' sports phenomenon focused on competitors.[2] Much of this distinction concerns modern self-representation and modern adoption of aspects of an imagined ancient Greek and Roman culture more than it does the ancient evidence. Nonetheless, there is *something* 'spectacular' about Roman sport that distinguishes it from its ancient Greek predecessors and contemporaries. It is undoubtedly the case that Greek sport attracted audiences and that athletes became 'celebrities'. But, this seems to have been a side effect of Greek sports' focus on the individual competitor. Moreover, individual Greeks – especially freeborn, citizen men – almost certainly had direct experience, if only as novices, in many of the sports they watched in large festivals. In contrast, Roman sport begins from a distinction between participant and observer. While there are, as we will see below and throughout this chapter, occasions when the boundaries between athlete and audience were challenged, Roman sport explicitly includes and expects audiences in its very structures.

This distinction appears even in the legendary origins of Roman Games. Chariot racing is connected to the foundation of Rome, or at least to one of its foundational stories, in a way that demonstrates clearly the connection with sport and the spectacular. In the traditional narrative, the city was founded in 753 BCE after a violent confrontation between Romulus and his brother Remus resulted in the latter being killed and the former giving his name to the new city. Romulus, however, had a problem: the city's population was all men, mostly criminals and exiles recruited from neighboring cities and tribes in Italy. He hatched a scheme to obtain women through the use of chariot racing and spectacle. He invited the Sabines, a nearby Latin people, to attend a festival to Neptune. Romulus used one of the festival's main attractions, chariot racing, to obtain the desperately needed women. When the chariot race was about to begin, all eyes, both Roman and Sabine, were on the chariots. At a given signal, Romulus and the Romans grabbed the Sabine women near them and ran to their homes (Livy, 1.9). The Sabine men were left staring at chariots, bereft of daughters – the Roman spectacular gaze in prototype form.

Of course, there is much to dissect in this story beyond its role as early evidence for chariot racing, especially the issue of sexual violence at the origin of Rome (a repeated element in Roman foundational legends). The connection between sexualizing women and chariot racing as a place to obtain women recurs in the poetry of the Augustan writer, Ovid (43 BCE–18 CE). Ovid compares the primitive conditions of theatres in the early days of Rome – specifically the imagined context of the Rape of the Sabines – with the more sophisticated audiences today. Still, he notes, shows and Games are ideal venues for the pursuit of women, at least in part because the mixed audience makes illicit (and unwanted) advances less conspicuous (*Ars Amatoria* 1.101-63). Needless to say, Ovid's writing and the Rape of the Sabines legend must be contextualized within the norms of gender and sexuality in Late Republican and Augustan Rome. But, it is also worth noting that our sources, mostly elite men, offer no women's perspective on these legends or male practice at the Games. No doubt modern opinions on the Rape of the Sabine women would differ significantly if any ancient woman's interpretation survived.[3]

There is, however, no reason to suppose the story of the Sabine women is true. While the legend was doubtless current earlier in

Roman history, the coherent narrative appears in Livy's *History of Rome*, which was written in the late first century BCE, some 700 years after the events.[4] The connection, historical or not, of chariot racing with the story of the Rape of the Sabine Women does reveal something key about chariot racing and spectacle in the Roman imagination. Sports attract and divert attention; audience, not competitor, are the key participants in the sporting experience at Rome.

Outside of legendary narratives and beyond chariot racing, other Roman sports reveal the centrality of spectacle in their very conception. Gladiatorial combat, for example, assumes an audience in its structure, since the victorious gladiator, when he had subdued, though not killed, his opponent, turned to the organizer for the provision of the *pollice verso* ('turned thumb'). This sign to kill or release the defeated opponent was given by the match's organizer, but he almost certainly took into account the audience's reaction. Individuals outside the scope of the match itself – organizers and audience – played a necessary role in the end of the combat. Since gladiatorial combat often ended in defeat, not death, the appeal to the audience and the provision of the *pollice verso* was theatre, not competition.

Gladiatorial bodies were certainly spectacular and meant to be seen, as the various armour and weapons worn by the different types of gladiators ('armatures', see below) make clear. While various pieces of armour covered the head and arms of different types, the torso and most of the body of the gladiator was nude. Here, in contrast to Greek sport, nudity did not convey an essential aspect of masculinity, i.e. independence and citizenship. Rather, the partial nudity of gladiators and the pervasive public display of them throughout the organization and preamble of the Games, points to nudity's other association with servility. The body of the gladiator was therefore not only that of an athlete and competitor skilled in his sport, but also an object of public curiosity and display – an element aimed clearly at the audience of Roman sport that explicitly demonstrates its intrinsic spectacular quality.[5]

Chariot racing

The story of the Rape of the Sabine Women places chariot racing at the foundation of Rome, but actual evidence for chariot racing comes much later. Early kings were credited with various innovations such as delineating a course for the races or with founding or reinvigorating festivals to the gods by adding races.[6] As with most events prior to 390–387 BCE (when the Gauls supposedly sacked Rome), historicity is tricky. The entire regnal era of Roman history is almost without contemporaneous evidence and many of the details, especially of the personalities and activities of individual rulers, must be, at least in part, the invention of later authors.[7] Even if this absence of sources makes the origins of chariot racing hard to determine, later authors are consistent in placing chariot races in Rome's distant past. Their association with legendary figures from Romulus through the kings of Rome, points to a later Roman belief that chariot races – unlike gladiatorial combat – were integral to the Roman state from an early stage.

The historical record for Roman chariot racing contests only goes back as far as 366 BCE, the first staging of the *Ludi Romani*, at which chariot racing was a mainstay (Livy, 1.35). Even with this reference, however, we are on thin ice, since the exact evidence Livy would use for knowledge of events 300 years before his time is unclear. Later iterations of the *Ludi Romani*, especially those put on by important figures like Scipio Africanus (in 213 BCE), have more evidence behind them since they would have been recorded by contemporary historians, even if their works are lost to us. By the late third century BCE, further public festivals were established, all of which feature chariot racing: the Plebian Games (216 BCE), Apollonarian Games (208 BCE), The Megalensia (191 BCE), Ceralia (202 BCE) and Floralia (173 BCE).

Chariot racing reflects the Roman geographical and cultural position between Etruscan civilization and the ancient Greek Italian colonies. Chariot racing had, of course, occurred in the Greek world from as early as the eleventh century BCE. When colonies were founded in southern Italy and Sicily in the Archaic period (776–490 BCE), sports followed, and we have records of chariot-racing victors from Italy and Sicily from the sixth century BCE. We can surmise that Romans would have been familiar with Greek chariot racing from almost the foundation of the city.

North of Rome, the Etruscans were voracious consumers of Greek culture, and, judging by depictions on paintings in tombs, they were extremely interested in Greek sports. But for the Etruscans, sport seems to have served a different purpose. Rather than perform as an athlete, Etruscan elites organized sports competitions or demonstrations for special events like funerals. Most of the wall paintings come from the Etruscan Archaic period (575–480 BCE) and from a very small proportion of the extant tombs, but many sports in these paintings are familiar from ancient Greek evidence (e.g. boxing, wrestling, running; two- or three-horse chariots).[8] One wall painting even shows a grandstand where elite Etruscan men and women recline and watch the activities of athletes.[9] While wall paintings depict a variety of events familiar from ancient Greek athletics, the competitors, unlike those in ancient Greece, are clothed. Public nudity was anathema to the Etruscans, just as it would mostly be to Romans.

Roman chariot racing mixes ancient Greek and Etruscan influences, along with specifically Roman practices. Like the Etruscans, Roman elites did not take part in the Games as competitors. Spectatorship and display were key, and the staging of Games brought glory to the organizer, and, in the Roman case, to the state itself. Despite these similarities to the Etruscans and Greeks, chariot racing developed Roman characteristics. One key aspect was the venue, the circus. Unlike ancient Greek chariot racing, which took place in temporary hippodromes that were erected for the event, and unlike Etruscan sports, for which no permanent venue has been detected, Roman chariot racing, from a very early period required a venue, the circus, located in the valley between the Aventine and Palatine hills.

Organization of the Games was particularly Roman. The staging of the Games may have been under the control of state magistrates, but the chariot-racing teams were separate entities altogether. Unlike in Greece, where individual elites paid for chariots and trained horses and charioteers, chariots and teams of horses were owned by *factiones*, corporate entities who also organized the Games.[10] Corporate groups controlling the organization of the Games as well as the participants and deriving profit from it resonates well with modern team sports, especially in professional leagues where the teams jointly manage the league, its schedule and games (e.g. in Major League Baseball). The Games in antiquity were complicated interactions between the Roman state – or, its representatives, magistrates – and Roman elites – the *factiones*; in the modern period, team sports are distinguished from state-controlled groups like national teams. Nonetheless, it is clear that even today, corporate sports bodies hold great sway over apparently non-corporate national sports teams. The participation – or lack thereof – of professional hockey players from the National Hockey League in the Winter Olympics speaks to this point: every four years a complicated set of negotiations precedes the Games, and the participation of professionals under contract to corporate sports bodies is not a given. The chariot games in Roman antiquity, therefore, like some sports events today, were negotiated settlements, both public and private, and are, in this way, uniquely Roman innovations in equestrian competition, and, indeed, in ancient sports altogether.

Factiones are attested from the fourth century BCE.[11] Four groups were prevalent throughout Roman history – the Reds, Blues, Whites and Greens – although their origins were as murky as that of chariot racing itself. Each faction operated across the Mediterranean to recruit or purchase charioteers (who were often enslaved persons). Internally, they trained and ranked their own charioteers, so that only the best could hope to become an *agitator* (driver) and drive *quadrigae* (four-horse chariots) in the Circus Maximus.

Most Roman chariot racing occurred in two formats: two-horse and four-horse. The former, using a chariot known as a *biga*, was a kind of 'minor league', where novice charioteers and horses honed their skills before they moved onto the four-horse variety. The *quadriga* was the main event at *ludi*, and these events attracted the greatest number of fans, the largest prizes and the most highly skilled charioteers. On a given day of Games, 24 chariot races might take place and modern estimates put each race at 8–9 minutes (chariots likely attained speeds of 35–70 kmph), so that racing might take up four hours.[12] Of course, the track would have to be cleared and prepared after each race, victors given their victory laps, and new teams of horses brought into the starting gates.[13] With all of this in mind, a 'day' at the Games was likely a long affair.

The day began with the *pompa circensis* (Circus procession), a procession with meaning that a Roman audience – especially those who had come to the Circus many times – would understand.[14] Dionysius of Halicarnassos (late first century BCE) provides a complete description (7.72): the state's magistrates organized the procession, at the head of which, representing the virility and fertility of Rome, were sons of citizens who were approaching manhood. Other officials and the charioteers were part of the procession as well, but most important were the images of the gods, which came last; these were imagined to be the gods themselves, brought to the Circus to watch over and enjoy the Games. Instead of being housed in a sanctuary, as in the Games of the Greek world, the gods processed from their temples to the Circus, which temporarily became a sacred space inhabited by deities or their surrogates.

While the procession focused on the competitors, elites and representatives of Rome's future prosperity, the Games required many support personnel who were not given pride of place in the procession. A myriad of technical titles come down to us from antiquity, some of which remain unclear to scholars today. Attendants and staff were critical to the most basic functions of the circus: *moratores* (delayers) were stationed inside the starting-gates to help control anxious horses; *tentores* (handlers) operated the levers to open the gates; *sparsores* (sprinklers) threw water on the animals as they ran; *hortatores* (encouragers) cheered the charioteers and their crews; and many more staff, both freeborn and enslaved, were central to the Circus' functioning.[15]

Chariot racing was a technical sport, and pure talent – on the part of charioteer or horse – was not enough to win; rather, strategy played a key role. Chariot races started quickly and noisily with a huge amount of dust kicked into the air as horses and chariots began to move. Chariots raced in marked lanes for the first 160 metres,[16] but as they reached the first *metae*, or 'turning-post', they could move freely across the track, jockey for position and attempt to turn as close as possible to the turning-post at the far end of the Circus (see far right of Figure 2.1 for the *metae*).

But chariot racing did not only mean racing as quickly as possible and, at least in fiction, tactics could cause trouble between drivers. In the *Iliad*, Menelaus chastises Autolichos for rash driving that threatened them both (23.466–8); in *Punica*, Silius Italicus' Atlas makes the same complaint of the youthful Durius (16.409–10). In reality, charioteers used almost any trick to gain an advantage over their opponents. While violence between charioteers was forbidden, violence against the

Figure 2.1 Terracotta relief showing a chariot race (*c.* 1st century CE). 1805,0703.337. British Museum.

opponents' horses was not. Charioteers could whip the eyes of horses as they rushed past, aiming to blind or maim their opponents' horses. They could try to destroy or damage the wheels of other chariots.[17] Violent crashes – called *naufragiae* (shipwrecks) by the Romans – were part of the appeal of the spectacle.

Romans were avid and informed fans of chariot racing and of different *factiones*. Not unlike 'armchair quarterbacks' today, they yelled advice and admonished charioteers who failed to follow their preferred tactics. The interest and knowledge in chariot racing is evident not only in these literary representations, but in the plethora of objects – many of them everyday objects – that depict chariots and charioteers (e.g. knife handles, lamps, even, perhaps, a toilet!).[18] Modern sports fans are, of course, familiar with the incredible variety of objects available emblazoned with team logos: glasses and mugs, holiday ornaments, bedspreads, candles, coasters, towels and more.[19] Today and in Roman antiquity, sports mania knew no bounds.

The fanaticism around chariot racing extended to charioteers. Despite their enslaved or lower-status origins, some charioteers became wealthy and famous. Of the more than 200 charioteers known from funerary inscriptions, we can ascertain that only one was a freeborn man; the remainder were enslaved people or freedmen.[20] The poet Martial recalls Scorpus, an especially famous charioteer of first century CE Rome, in several epigrams (10.50, 53, 74), but the best sources for charioteers are their own inscribed funerary monuments.[21] Diocles, who raced for twenty-four years, in 4,257 events, won 1,462 victories and hundreds of thousands of sesterces, is an exceptional case (*Corpus Inscriptionum Latinarum* 14.2884; an ancient equivalent of Tiger Woods).[22] Charioteers were criticized by Roman elites for the apparent contradiction of their low-status and astonishing wealth (see Juvenal, 7.105–14). As with other public performers, Romans both loved the raucous, larger-than-life personas and – at least some Romans – despised their ability to upset deeply rooted ideas of status.

Charioteer funerary inscriptions read like career records of modern professional athletes. All manner of special victories are labelled, clearly indicating to us that charioteers and fans alike took pride in special achievements:

> Crescens, driver for the Blue faction, Mauritanian by birth, 22 years old. First won with the *quadriga* in the consulate of Lucius Vispanius and Messalla. On Nerva's birthday came 24th with these horses: Circus, Acceptor, Delicatus, Cotynus. When Glabrio replaced Messalla as consul, on the birthday of the divine Claudius, he started in 686 races and won 47. Among these in races for single *quadrigae*, he won 19, in races for pairs 23, and in races for 3 he won 5. He won after being passed once, led through the whole race 8 times, won at the finish line 38 times. He took second place 130 times, third 111. He received prizes of 1,558,346 sesterces.
>
> *Corpus Inscriptionum Latinarum* 6.100050[23]

The funerary aspect is evident from the outset with the driver's name, *factio*, birthplace and age given pride of place to clearly identify him to readers. After these elements, however, the remainder of the inscription concerns his career. When he died, Crescens had been racing for nine years, and his first victory with the *quadriga* was when he was fourteen. His inscription distinguishes his victories in races when individual charioteers from each *factio* raced *quadrigae* alone and those races when members of the same *factio* could work together; the former seem to be especially significant. Beyond victories, Crescens' inscription demonstrates that method of victory could be important. Leading wire-to-wire was worthy of mention, as was winning after being passed, and winning at the last minute.

Except for the funerary aspect, Crescens' inscription compares well with monuments like the plaque of Hank Aaron in the National Baseball Hall of Fame and Museum:

> Hit 755 home runs in a 25-year career to become majors' all-time homer king. Had 20 or more for 20 consecutive years, at least 30 in 15 seasons and 40 or better eight times. Also set records for games played (3298), at-bats (12,364), long hits (1,477), total bases (6,856), runs batted in (2,297). Paced NL in batting twice and homers, runs

batted in and slugging pct four times each. Won most valuable player award in NL in 1957.

Aaron's career mirrors that of Diocles in some respects, since both his plaque and Dicoles' inscription emphasize special achievements and the vast number of games they entered (3,298 for Aaron, 4,257 for Diocles) across their 25- and 24-year careers, respectively. Crescens' inscription and Aaron's plaque demand special knowledge on the part of the reader, who must know the terminology ('races in pairs', 'slugging pct.') and the significance of numbers ('second place 130 times, third 111', 'had 20 or more [home runs] for 20 consecutive seasons'). Sports achievements, in both eras, focus on longevity, special accomplishments and the great impression gained by specific and large numbers. It is incredible that athletes separated by almost 2,000 years can have their career records listed in such evocatively similar ways.[24]

Long careers and success could bring charioteers fame and fortune. The large amounts of money available as prizes drove, at least partially, elite disdain. And, the prizes were great. First prizes could be 20,000–50,000 sesterces,[25] and charioteers, even while enslaved, kept a portion of their winning or could work towards purchasing freedom.[26] Some charioteers desired fame and money so much that they continued racing even after they became freedmen. Even second or third prizes, 7,500–15,000 sesterces depending on the event, were valuable: soldiers in the early Imperial period earned 900–1,200 sesterces per year, artisans up to 2,300. One second-place finish in an important race could provide the earnings of a decade of lower-class work; one victory might equal a lifetime's earnings.[27] For the most famous charioteers, their wealth, like that of some professional athletes today, was incredible: Crecens' 1.5 million sesterces would have more than met the wealth requirement of the Senate, while Diocles' 35 million sesterces was astronomical. These prize amounts compare quite well with today's prizes in professional sports. In golf, for example, a runner-up at the Farmers Insurance Open in 2021 (a middle-of-the-pack tournament in terms of prize money on the PGA tour) netted $456,375, over a decade of the median American income ($31,133 in 2019). The winner received $1,350,000, or about a lifetime's earnings for a median income earner.

The charioteers of whom we hear in literary sources or whose funerary inscriptions survive to the present must represent a minority. Most charioteers did not end up racing *quadrigae* in the Circus Maximus, most did not amass great fortunes. Like professional athletes today, the rich and famous are the exception: a good, but undistinguished career was possible but still an outlier. Many charioteers must have raced in obscurity, been injured or died early and left little trace in the historical record. One epitaph for Eutyches of Tarro makes this clear: 'in this grave rest the remains of a beginner on the racetrack, who nevertheless was far from incompetent in handling the reins. I already had the courage to try my hand at driving *quadrigae*, although I was still racing in *bigae*' (*Corpus Inscriptionum Latinarum* II 4314).[28] Surely, Eutyches' career was more common than those of Diocles and Crescens and his death points to the dangers inherent in chariot racing: charioteers sped at breakneck speeds, performed hairpin turns, tied reins to their bodies and had little chance of surviving a crash.[29]

Perhaps because of these dangers, charioteers were assumed to be lucky, sometimes preternaturally so, and they attracted all manner of amulets, spells and other magicks. One evocative source are *defixiones*, 'curse-tablets', that attempted to affect a charioteer.[30] One tablet found in Carthage calls upon a demonic power to restrain the speed of opposing factions, to cause their horses' feet to be caught in the reins, to be lethargic on the morning of the race and to cause the charioteers to fall, dragged grimly to their deaths.[31] Fik Meijer compares these tablets with the blessing of football players' boots.[32] The curse-tablets demonstrate that the irrational fanaticism of modern sports was alive and well in Roman antiquity, too.

Fanaticism, however, had its limits. Powered by the intense interest of fans, chariot racing was perhaps the last ancient spectacle to die out. As the centre of the Roman world shifted east to Constantinople, so did chariot racing. At Constantinople, races continued to hold their central place in the Christianized Roman Empire of the early medieval period

and were an extremely popular entertainment into the eighth century
CE.[33] Fans of rival *factiones* created one of the largest riots in Roman
history in 532 CE (the 'Nika' riot), when Greens and Blues rioted in
response to the rejection of their demand for clemency towards some
fellow members of their *factiones*. The riot expanded from this incident
to what amounted to almost insurrection: the Hagia Sophia was burnt
down and rioters marched through the city with impunity. Only the
harsh intervention of the emperor Justinian and an attack on rioters in
the hippodrome ended it.[34]

Chariot racing continued at Constantinople beyond the eighth
century CE, though its popularity waned with the waning fortunes of
the Byzantine Empire. By the seventh century, racing seems to have
vanished from everywhere but Constantinople, and into the twelfth
century CE, the emperors started favouring more aristocratic spectacles
that were emerging or being imported from the west, such as jousting.[35]
When these races finally died out in the 1100s CE, it marked the end of
a 2,000-year-long tradition of chariot racing in the Mediterranean
world, perhaps the longest continuously practiced organized sport in
human history.

Gladiators

While chariot racing was the longest-lasting sport in Roman antiquity,
gladiatorial combat has had the greatest impact of any spectacle on how
modernity has viewed the Romans, and how, in turn, modern peoples
have contrasted themselves and their own spectacles – inevitably to
their benefit – with Rome. Gladiatorial combat features in almost every
incarnation of ancient Rome in modern literature, art, cinema and
theatre. Often, the supposedly innate Roman lust for violence that was
epitomized in the arena is fodder for a moralizing narrative on imperial
decline, physical appetites and more. But, gladiatorial combat is much
more than lurid and violent spectacle – though it certainly *is* that – and
gladiatorial combat reveals much about the Romans. Even in antiquity,

gladiatorial combat aroused strong opinions and critics found positive and negative aspects to the compelling spectacle of men fighting, if not to the death, then with lives in peril, in the arena.

The first gladiatorial combat at Rome occurred in 264 BCE at the funeral of Decimus Junius Brutus (Livy, *Epitome* 16). The Latin word used for gladiatorial combats, *munus* (pl. *munera*), suggests the obligations attached to funerary rites: in origin it refers to a 'duty' to the dead. Eventually, the connection of the *munus* with funerals became strained as these types of Games gained in popularity and as politicians realized their usefulness. In this manner, as funeral Games, they connect with practices known from Etruria and from ancient Greek literature and history and hint at sports' enduring connection with mortality. Even in the *Iliad*, armed combat happens at the Funeral Games of Patroclus (23.784–825), though this event is unusual. Closer in time and geography to the Romans are Etruscan funerary rituals that included athletic display and Osco-Samnite tomb paintings that depict gladiators.

The Etruscans were connected with Games from an early point, supposedly having invented them when faced with starvation (as a distraction, Herodotus, 1.94); or, Roman grammarians thought that the Latin for games, *ludi*, was derived from 'Lydian' and referred to Etruscans (who supposedly emigrated *en masse* from Asia Minor to Italy, Tertullian, *On the Spectacles* 5.2). Nicolaus of Damascus thought the Etruscans had invented gladiatorial combat (4.153ff), though he was writing some 250 years after their first appearance. These ideas may reflect what happened (i.e. the past), or they were part of the way that Romans *understood* the Etruscans historically: that is as foreign to the lands they inhabit and as practitioners of games. Nonetheless, no tomb has a painting of a pair of armed fighters such as is described in the *Iliad* or as actually fought in first *munus* at Rome.[36]

Other scholars have looked to the Osco-Samnite people of Southern Italy for the origin of gladiatorial combat. At Paestum, wall paintings from the early fourth century BCE show pairs of armed men apparently dueling. The influential work of Georges Ville assessed the evidence for

Etruscan or Osco-Samnite origins. While the Etruscan evidence
prevailed among many Roman historians and Etruscans were seen as
the originators of gladiatorial combat in antiquity, to Ville, the evidence
has been stretched beyond recognition. The only absolutely conclusive
evidence for gladiators prior to 264 BCE are the funerary wall paintings
in Southern Italy.[37] It seems likely that the Osco-Samnites began the
tradition of gladiatorial combat which was then borrowed by Romans
and Etruscans. The belief by many scholars in antiquity that the
Etruscans were the primary precursor to the Romans and one conduit
(along with the ancient Greeks) through whom the Romans developed
their culture has likely contributed to the belief that gladiatorial combat
must have come from the Etruscans. Etruscan origins also satisfied a
nineteenth-century belief that the 'civilized' Romans could not have
come up with this blood sport themselves. Rather, those scholars
attributed it to the supposedly decadent Etruscans who were thought to
have an 'oriental origin'.[38] Such beliefs were extended by Nazi theorists
who attributed Roman acceptance of Christianity to Etruscan
influences.[39] Instead, we can conclude that Etruscan practices of
ostentatious funerary display and Samnite practices of armed conflict
at tombs come together in the Roman practice of gladiatorial combat,
just as Roman chariot racing reflects a creative synthesis of ancient
Greek and Etruscan practices. It may be that the Romans themselves
were responsible for the vast increase in frequency and complexity of
gladiatorial combat once it became institutionalized at Rome.[40]

Soon after the first combat, displays of gladiators became regular
and expected parts of funerals. Even though later Roman historians
single out specific Games, there is no reason to think that these were the
only performances. For example, when Livy discusses the Games for
the funeral of Titus Flaminius in 174 BCE, he says that 'many gladiatorial
Games' were given that year (41.28.11) – gladiators were, it seems, a
normal part of the Roman sports landscape by at least the 170s BCE.
The scale of Games during the Republic increases over time, tied,
perhaps, to increasingly brutal political competition. By the time of
Julius Caesar's funeral for his father in 65 BCE, gladiatorial performance

was the norm, though Caesar still increased the scale beyond his contemporaries. He offered 320 pairs of gladiators (Plutarch, *Life of Caesar* 5.9); and at the funeral of his daughter, he put on another gladiatorial show (Suetonius, *Life of Julius Caesar* 26). The Games for his daughter Julia were incredibly expensive and unprecedented. Not only were they held for a woman but they were also held years after the death itself. Caesar picked famous gladiators and trained new ones for the occasion. He realized the necessity to control *munera* in a way that others before him had not: one could not simply wait for an appropriate death to take place when it came to the provision of such politically powerful spectacles.

Caesar's understanding of the political utility of *munera* set the stage for their transformation in the early Empire. By the time Octavian had defeated Mark Antony and Cleopatra, finalized his control over the Roman world and obtained the honorific Augustus, the world of Roman politics – and the Games that were intertwined with politics – had changed forever. Augustus realized, perhaps from the example of his adopted father, how useful gladiatorial shows were politically, but how dangerous they could be as well.[41] Unlike chariot racing, which was restricted to the regularly occurring festivals and under control of the Roman state, gladiatorial shows were private. They held the possibility for individual Roman elites to establish alternative bases of political support beyond the patronage of Augustus himself. Augustus seems to have enacted a specific policy on Games that conceived of them as intensely political. He offered Games eight times in his name or those of his sons or grandsons with 10,000 participants. He used them for political ends: by sharing the hosting of Games with his adopted sons and grandsons, he could introduce them to the populace and concentrate all the prestige of a *munus* in the Imperial family (*Res Gestae Divi Augusti* 22).[42]

Along with using *munera* for his own political ends, Augustus introduced regulations to prevent others from doing the same. The *munus* was changed from a private to a state affair, with strict controls over how much could be spent and how often Games could be held, especially for those high-ranking officials who might pose a threat to Augustus' consolidation of power. *Praetors*, a higher-status magistracy, took over the running of public festivals and *munera*, and they were not permitted to spend their own money enhancing these contests, to give a *munus* without senatorial decree, and they were limited to 60 pairs of gladiators (Cassius Dio, 54.2.3–4).[43] Whereas previously, the increasing size and lavishness of *munera* was a primary means to gain political favour with the populace, Augustus' reforms ensured that the state – or the emperor – was the primary recipient of praise for well-organized Games.

Augustus' reorganization, with some changes over time, became the norm in the Roman Imperial system that followed his death. Roman state investments in *munera* became more and more lavish, culminating in the Flavian Amphitheatre, often called the Colosseum, which was inaugurated in 80 BCE by the Emperor Titus. At this inauguration, massive Games were held, including huge numbers of animal hunts and gladiatorial matches (Suetonius, *Life of Titus* 7.3). When Trajan returned from his conquest of the Dacians, he offered 123 days of spectacles that included 10,000 gladiators (Cassius Dio, 68.15). These Games now took place in the Flavian Amphitheatre, in which 50,000 spectators could sit, and which was conceived as the centre, not just of Rome, but of the world that Rome ruled.

Attending a *munus* in such a venue could unify the disparate Roman populace. The podium wall that distinguished the seating area and performance space in an amphitheatre similarly distinguished citizens from non-citizens. When one gladiator struck another, spectators cried, '*habet, hoc habet!*' ('he's got it!'), and were a part of the victorious performance.[44] For lower-status Romans, this could be extremely alluring. Moreover, since gladiatorial types (through armour and weapons) at least partially imitated enemies of Rome, audiences could experience unity as Roman citizens and as rulers of the world.

Whether organized by a leading politician as part of an election campaign or by the emperor or his proxies as the celebration of a military conquest, the *munus* was, like chariot racing, a complex event.

Long before the gladiators took to the sands of the arena in Rome, they had been purchased or selected, trained and practiced on provincial circuits, before heading to the 'big leagues'.

Gladiators were almost always enslaved, though their specific origins were diverse: some were criminals condemned *ad ludum gladiatorium* ('to a gladiatorial school') for an ever-changing list of crimes.[45] Some, especially in the Republic, were prisoners of war sold to be slaves, whose unique fighting styles and panoply may have influenced the 'types' of gladiators that developed in the Republic and became standard by the Imperial period. Some were born enslaved and selected to be gladiators. Alongside unfree gladiators, a small but important contingent of free people volunteered. These men, known as *auctorati* (sing., *auctoratus*), were relatively few in number but stand out in the ancient and modern imagination.[46] *Auctorati* were almost certainly impoverished Roman citizens, whose choice to pledge themselves to a gladiatorial school for a number of years was likely an act of desperation in the face of financial ruin.[47] Some, however, have suggested these might be ancient 'excitement-seekers' who were looking, like extreme sports' participants today, for thrills.[48] In any case, whether enslaved, prisoner or *auctoratus*, gladiators suffered legal penalties for their participation in the Games of the arena through Roman legal strictures called *infamia*. By agreeing by oath 'to be burned, to be bound, to be killed by the sword' (Seneca, *Letters from a Stoic* 37.1), gladiators were imagined to have accepted penalties beyond those inflicted on Roman citizens.[49] Most gladiators would not have truly sworn *voluntarily*, but the notion that gladiators had agreed to their roles was an important aspect of Roman ideologies surrounding gladiatorial combat.

Beyond the *auctorati* were the truly unusual: elite Romans, often of senatorial class, who chose to fight in the arena on one-time contracts. These were not, as in the case of *auctorati*, acts of desperation, but rather acts that demonstrate to us the multifaceted and complex meaning of gladiatorial combat. Despite the danger of the arena and the potential social penalties for acting as a gladiator, Roman authorities had difficulty prohibiting elites from competing. If extant laws are any guide, Roman elites were eager to compete: in a period of twenty-five years, three bans were enacted by the Senate (46, 38 and 22 BCE). In fact, the ban was lifted in 11 CE because senators and equestrians (the top tiers of Roman social status) continued to break the law. A further ban followed in 19 CE, but elite access to the arena floor, despite the desires of the Roman administration, continued.[50]

In contrast to their depiction in many modern renditions (notably *Spartacus* in 1960 or *Gladiator* in 2000 and the TV series *Spartacus* in 2010–13 and *Spartacus: Gods of the Arena* in 2011), gladiatorial combats were not a blood bath, nor did gladiatorial matches regularly end with death. Gladiatorial combats were complex displays that combined political and social meaning for the presenter of the match (the *editor*, usually an elite Roman), the audience and the competitors. There is no doubt that blood was expected and the potential of death part of the attraction. But, our best evidence suggests that death as the *intended* endpoint of a match was rare. Some evidence indicates that fights to death (*sine missione*, 'without release') may have needed permission in the Imperial period. In fact, a *summa rudis* (a referee) is often depicted intervening when a gladiator raises his finger to indicate submission.[51] Deaths may have occurred in one in ten matches with similar chances for death across a career; the chances of dying likely increased in the early Imperial period.[52] So, while rates of 'to the death' matches increased with time, for its entire history, death as the intended endpoint of matches remained unusual. One reason was the value of gladiators and the amount of capital expended to train and equip them.

Gladiators trained in schools (called *ludi* or *ludus* in the singular) that were a combination of dormitory, athletic training facility and prison. A school was operated by a *lanista*, who may have also owned the school and gladiators or simply operated it on behalf of a wealthier owner. The *lanista*'s close association with gladiators and the fact that he depended on them for his livelihood made him a deplorable figure, akin to a pimp, who derived his own living from the bodies of others.[53] Like the gladiators whom he managed or owned, the *lanista* suffered the legal penalties of *infamia*, a loss of many civil and political rights for those whose professions were considered shameful by the Romans.[54]

Knowledge of life in a *ludus* is limited, especially since only a few *ludi* have been excavated even partially, and written sources come from elite members of society who would not have lived in a *ludi* and could only transmit second-hand or semi-fantastical imaginings of the gladiators' barracks and dormitory. Basic questions like the freedom of gladiators within the *ludus* are difficult to answer with certainty.[55] Nonetheless, we should not imagine the sort of filthy prison-like conditions that often populate modern, cinematic visions of gladiatorial schools. Likely, conditions varied. Plutarch says that the *lanista* Lentulus Batiatus, from whose *ludus* the revolt of Spartacus began, held gladiators in an unjust way (Plutarch, *Life of Crassus* 8.1), but he also remarks that this was unusual. *Ludi* were multipurpose complexes, with food preparation, training and dormitory areas; they were the home for, in some estimates, hundreds of gladiators, but also the workspace for a wide variety of staff, some likely enslaved and some free.

The partially excavated *Ludus Magnus* at Rome offers some evidence, though the facility was built on an unusually large scale. It was opened during the reign of the Emperor Domitian (81–96 CE) and was connected to the adjacent Flavian Amphitheatre by a tunnel. The *Ludus Magnus* was centred on a large amphitheatre of its own, capable of holding up to 3,000 spectators. Around the arena on all four sides were perhaps three tiers of *cellae*, small rooms that likely acted as sleeping quarters for 4–5 men. If so, the *Ludus Magnus* may have been home to 1,000 gladiators in addition to other support staff.[56] In the *Ludus* at Pompeii, there are also *cellae* on all four sides of a training area (with room for maybe 250 gladiators), separated by a shaded colonnade. There, we can see other communal areas like kitchens and more specialized locations like a prison (identified by the sets of shackles found on the ground).[57]

The proximity of the training (and sometime performance) arena to living quarters exemplifies life for gladiators – enslaved and free – in the *ludus*: the entire structure and life of the gladiator was based on training for excellence in the arena. One of our only literary sources from inside the *ludus*, the physician Galen, who worked as a doctor at a gladiatorial school, remarks on the gladiator's diet – of barley water and broad beans – that is intended to make them 'fleshy' (*On the Properties of Foodstuffs* 1.19). Beyond diet, the *ludus* and the life of the gladiator revolved around training. Likely soon after they arrived at the *ludus*, gladiators began to train for a specific type of gladiatorial type or armature.

In the Republic, the types of gladiators varied and new types were established and old ones died off. By the early Empire, the various armatures were formalized around eight major types that, judging by the visual evidence, were standard across the Roman world: *Eques*, *Murmillo*, *Thraex*, *Hoplomachus*, *Provocator*, *Retiarius*, *Secutor* and *Essedarius* (see Figure 2.2, a *murmillo* distinguished by his large-crested helmet and large shield).[58] Gladiators not only trained with a particular armature, but each type would only face a certain type or types in combat: *Equites* fought each other; the *Murmillo* could face *Thraex* or *Hoplomachus*; *Provcatores* fought each other; and, finally, the *Secutor* and *Retiarius* fought each other. The last pair – *Secutor* and *Retiarius* – demonstrates most clearly that these pairings were about complementary armour and weapons and tactics. The *Secutor*'s conical helmet, which completely covered his head except for two very small eye holes, was balanced with the long-reach and thin, sharp points of the *Retiarius*' trident. The former could move close, with helmet and large rectangular shield, on the relatively unarmed *Retiarius*, while he, with the long reach of the trident and net and the speed afforded by being relatively unarmoured, could stay out of harm's way and attack from afar. Other pairs show similar complements, such as the small shield of the *Thraex* and *Hoplomachus* and the large shield of the *Murmillo*. In other respects, they were equally matched, so that the defensive and offensive possibilities of the shield types were critical to each armature's tactics.

Doctores, ex-gladiators who worked as instructors, specialized in the different armatures,[59] and the matched pairs of the arena squared off with one another in training matches. Since gladiators of the same

Figure 2.2 Bone figurine of a Murmillo, Colchester (*c.* 1st or 2nd century CE). 1899,1010.1. British Museum.

school were often hired to fight each other in matches, they were probably well versed in the tactics of the school and their opponent's abilities. Such practice meant that gladiators could draw out fights and work to entertain the audience with complex displays.[60] Training at the *ludus* was regimented, with gladiators being assigned to a hierarchal ranking of training skill based around the *palus* (or 'pole') on which they trained.[61] Movement up and down this system may have brought privileges in the *ludus* and, regardless, would have brought prestige. It was not only gladiators who knew tactics and training methods: regular citizens were well versed in gladiatorial tactics from their attendance at the arena. The *Thraex*, *Hoplomachus* and *Murmillo*, for example, attracted fans based around their equipment: fans of the first two were called *parmularii* (small shields) and of the latter *scutarii* (large shields).[62] Crowds yelled at gladiators who simply followed the standard moves and at other times they offered advice,[63] like modern sports fans in the stadium, who call out tactical advice to their favourite players and teams.

A last type is perhaps the rarest: a few literary sources mention female gladiators. Some upper-class women fought, likely against their will, in the arena under Nero (Cassius Dio, 61.17.3–4),[64] but these were extraordinary circumstances. Although female gladiators were likely never common, the emperor Septimius Severus banned women from participating in gladiatorial combat, though Cassius Dio, the historian who reports the ban, say that the status, not gender, of female performers was the main issue (76.16.1).

A marble relief from Halicarnassus in modern-day Turkey and now at the British Museum depicts two female gladiators named 'Achilleia' and 'Amazon'.[65] 'Achilleia' alters the name of Achilles and transforms the hero of Homer into a fantasy female version; 'Amazon' connects the gladiator with the famous female warriors of legend. An inscription above them reads 'they were released' (i.e. obtained *missio*). The monument seems to memorialize an actual gladiatorial combat between women which both combatants survived. The relief from Halicarnassus indicates that those who staged combats with female gladiators wanted the event to be remembered, probably because of the novelty involved.

When Roman audiences watched gladiatorial combat, they watched a highly stylized and orchestrated event with which they were very familiar. Nonetheless, it held the possibility for novelty each time and the end result was ultimately unknown. In this way, especially with its stylized types and stage names, gladiatorial combat compares well with professional wrestling; in the sense of technical skill and training combined with brutality, it compares with boxing or mixed martial arts. Performance and display were key: the entire *munus* began with a *pompa*, a procession in which the gladiators appeared in their brilliant armour; the day before the *munus*, the *cena libera* ('open meal') was a banquet held for the competitors so that the public could watch the gladiators and– especially important for gambling – size them up.[66] Gladiatorial combats were by any definition a sporting event of technical skill and competition, aimed at an audience who understood the Games and their rules well, and performed by competitors who were trained and who had practiced to win within the confines of rules and conventions.

Despite being enslaved or prisoners of war, and despite the dangers inherent in gladiatorial combat, there is evidence to suggest that some gladiators took pride in their abilities and their successes. The rewards for an enslaved gladiator could include freedom,[67] and the financial rewards, for all types, could be lucrative. It is worth noting, however, that we have little evidence for the second-rate or provincial gladiator, whose life may have been brutal and short. From the evidence of funerary epitaphs, it is clear that, unsurprisingly, success bred wealth – and pride.

> Flamma, *secutor*, lived 30 years, fought 34 times, conquered 21, received *missio* standing 9 times, received *missio* 4 times, Syrian by birth. Delicatus erected this for a deserving fellow-fighter.
>
> *Corpus Inscriptionum Latinarum* 10.7297[68]

The inscription gives pride of place to Flamma's name and armature. It also provides evidence for the lengthy career of a successful gladiator, his won–loss record and unusual or extraordinary accomplishments.[69] Moreover, the last line demonstrates the camaraderie of gladiatorial troupes, developed through long hours of training and living together.

By taking the oath, gladiators were imagined to have transformed the involuntary to the voluntary, imbuing their actions with a sort of honour and masculinity that was similar to the ideals and ideology of the Roman army.[70] Roman response to the disastrous Battle of Cannae (216 BCE) may ultimately lie behind the dual nature of gladiators who are both abject and admired.[71] After that battle, in which Hannibal decimated a Roman army and the Romans imagined the sack of Rome was shortly to follow, Livy reports that slaves were enlisted in the army to offer an example of valour to Roman soldiers (22.57.9–12). Roman martial expansion and the expansion of gladiatorial combats at home parallel one another. The particular appeal of gladiatorial combat may come from the spectacular quality of violence and punishment, something that both arena and army shared.[72]

Through the combination of martial skill and voluntarily placing themselves in danger, gladiators were imagined, especially by philosophers, as models of Roman *virtus* (martial masculinity). Seneca, for instance, saw the gladiator as a model for Stoic virtues that suggested one accept what one cannot change, especially in the case of pain and death (*Letters from a Stoic* 30.8). Some have argued, following Keith Hopkins, that gladiatorial combat became a way for Romans to engage with traditional masculine values even as political and martial participation weakened in the early Empire.[73] However, the extensive evidence for gladiatorial combat in the Middle and late Republic suggests that gladiatorial combat may originally have grown hand in hand with Roman Imperial and military expansion.[74] If so, and ironically, martial *experience*, not its absence, prompted the growth of an institution that would become, in the Imperial period, a substitute for participation in the Roman army. Gladiatorial combat, we should note, involves over 500 years of evidence; it is hardly surprising that its meaning changed with time.

The effect of gladiatorial spectacle on men was to reinforce and reflect (in the Republic) or encourage and instill (in the Empire) a sort of martial courage. Women, however, were another issue altogether. While women attended chariot racing events, gladiatorial combat and the amphitheatre were imagined as dangers to Roman citizen women. Male politicians and writers believed that gladiators could arouse women and make them prone to give in to sexual temptation, even at the risk of their social status. Laws such as the *Lex Julia Theatralis* (passed between 20 and 17 BCE) sought to restrict women's attendance at *munera*, or at least to force them to sit in the upper echelons of amphitheatres (Suetonius, *Life of Augustus* 44.2).[75] If male literary sources are to be believed at all, even from these seats, women were still at risk in the presence of gladiators, whom they could find sexually appealing (see Juvenal 6.81–110). Gladiator sex appeal is a well-used trope in modern renditions like *Spartacus* (1962) and the *Spartacus* STARZ television series (2010–13). Although women were imagined to have no interest in the martial 'lessons' of the arena, the erotic appeal of gladiators was rooted in the quality that most closely aligns them with the Roman masculine ideal: their display of *virtus*. These laws and literary sources point to *male* anxiety about masculinity and male control of women, more than they tell us almost anything about the actual erotic desires of Roman women.

It was not only women who were imagined to be interested in gladiatorial bodies, or rather gladiatorial bodies had meaning across genders. The gladiator's body was fetishized across society and assumed many meanings based around its exposed physicality. Gladiators were surely popular with the elite classes, at least in part, because of their assumed physical abilities and their visual appeal. As the opening section of this chapter explained, gladiatorial nudity was emblematic of servility, but at the same time, gladiatorial bodies were, as a consequence of training and diet, sexually desirable and appealing. Roman ideas of sexuality diverge strongly from many modern notions, especially the strong – modern and Western – demarcation between heterosexuality and homosexuality. Rather, Roman men seemed to have conceived of desire in a more fluid manner, connected to power and status (at least publicly) instead of sex.[76] The masculine man was in control of his body and the bodies of others, and he demonstrated this control publicly.[77]

One armature, the *Retiarius*, is emblematic of these contradictory impulses. One ancient writer, the satirist Juvenal, considers it the most disgraceful of gladiatorial types (8.199–210). This disgrace may have something to do with the *Retiarius*' weapons – a trident and net – which lack the obvious sexual associations of the sword.[78] Perhaps just as important, however, is the unique armour of the *Retiarius*: he is the only gladiator without a helmet, and thus his face and full identity are exposed to the crowd. This relative nudity in comparison with his counterparts seemed to have tainted him, so much so that to elite

Romans, at least in the literary evidence (some graffiti suggests the sexual proclivity of *Retiarii*!), the *Retarius* became associated with divergent, likely homosexual, sexual practices (Juvenal 2.143ff). By virtue of the exposure of body and face, and perhaps because of the lack of a phallic emblem, the *retiarius* could be read as a 'passive' homosexual.

Despite – or perhaps because of – its deep-seated connections with Roman urban and military culture, gladiatorial combat eventually declined. We hear of gladiatorial shows far into the Common Era, and the new dominance of Christianity in the fourth century CE may have actually increased the frequency and violence of the *munus*. While some writers condemned shows as pagan pleasures, many emperors and officials saw no irony in their continued use of an entertainment that had included public executions of Christians who refused to recant.[79] Changing mores and religions may have had less to do with the decline of gladiators in the Empire than economics and logistics. As supply of gladiators or beasts became more challenging, travel more treacherous and urban centres less densely populated, the scale of the traditional Games could not be maintained. Rather than an edict that sentenced ancient spectacle to death,[80] gladiatorial combat petered out over time and, by the fifth century CE, had disappeared or transformed entirely.

Gladiators in the Greek East

The evidence of over 250 amphitheatres attests to the great interest on behalf of inhabitants of Rome and the western Empire in gladiatorial Games. For some scholars in the past, the lack of purpose-built amphitheatres demonstrated that the events of the *munus* were less popular or absent from the eastern, Greek-speaking parts of the Roman world. Greek-speaking populations were supposedly not interested in the blood-sports of the arena that represented a decadent Rome, in contrast to the more 'civilized' sports of the stadium and hippodrome. As Mark Golden writes, it is critical to the modern distinction often drawn between ancient Greece and Rome, that 'the Greeks shared our own revulsion at the spectacles of slaughter we imagine when we think of gladiatorial games'.[81]

Louis Robert's *magnum opus*, *Les Gladiateurs dans l'orient grec*, assembled a vast array of literary, visual and epigraphic evidence to demonstrate the popularity and importance of arena spectacles in the ancient Greek world.[82] Greek acceptance and enthusiasm for Roman spectacle may be compared to their participation in the Roman Imperial system more broadly since gladiatorial combat only appears in the east from the first century CE onwards.[83] Greek-speaking people in the Eastern Empire demanded *munera* and must have understood some meaning in them, and found them entertaining and socially valuable. The *munus* was almost certainly closely associated with the imperial cult in the east (i.e. the worship of emperors as gods), but even if this association is correct, *munera* were shaped by the providers and consumers of spectacle.[84] Games were Roman in origin (to the Greeks), but when presented in the east, Greek values could be found in them.[85]

Meaning is, of course, critical, since if gladiatorial combat was deeply connected with the specifically Roman understanding of military prowess and courage, *virtus*, and implicated with Roman interpretations of sex and gender, then the ancient Greek adaptation of *munera* must take these concepts into account. Gladiatorial combat, especially the granting of *missio*, implicitly brought along the connection between death, life and *virtus* wherever it went. But, different audiences could interpret things differently, and Greek-speaking peoples may have seen in *munera* an extension of the types of Games they already liked and an extension of the brutality that was part of everyday life across the ancient world, whether in the quotidian punishments doled out to enslaved people or cock-fighting and other blood sports.[86] Still, we cannot detach the importation of *munera* into the Greek-speaking world from its military subjection and political control by Rome.

Other imperial histories demonstrate that sport may be one of the tools of empire, or at least a practice that is carried along and may persist even after the end of empire; the overlapping of interest in cricket with former British colonies and baseball with former American colonies (or areas of more or less official control) are cases in point.[87] In the British case in particular, sport was a weapon of cultural power used to further the aims of Empire. Games and sports were seen as a uniquely British modes of education that offered moral lessons that in turn justified British rule.[88] Over time, these sports were appropriated and adopted outside of colonial officials and local elites and became truly popular.[89] Turning back to the Greek world, as always we have paltry evidence, but the frequency of these Games, epitaphs for popular gladiators and the modifications of stadiums must point to a popular appeal beyond the desire of Roman authorities and local officials. Presumably, Greek-speaking populations took to these Games and made them their own.

At the elite level, even if gladiators were absent from the literary record, they were integrated into the important system of euergetism (good works) of the Eastern Empire. That is, they were one of the public goods that citizens or foreigners could give to cities, and which would be rewarded and remembered through grants of citizenships and monuments. Public buildings figure greatly in euergetism, but athletes and athletics are also core components; gladiatorial combat was a natural addition to this system of competitive charity.[90] Incorporation did not mean complete acculturation. The vocabulary of gladiatorial Games is indicative: aside from *monomachoi* (gladiators), the technical language remained Latin, albeit represented in Greek letters.[91] Greek-speakers in antiquity rarely use Latin terminology, so it must be taken as evidence that despite their enthusiasm for *munera*, they saw them as distinctively and emphatically non-Greek.

To understand the meaning of the Games of the *munus* in the East, we can turn to the words of gladiators themselves. And, in this regard, we have plentiful evidence. Epitaphs for gladiators are found across the Eastern Empire, written in ancient Greek, and understanding the Games and their competitors as having meaning in their local context. Gladiators participated in what they called *agones*, the same word used for athletic contests. They competed for prizes (*athla*), using the same words that described ancient Greek sports.[92] Ancient Greek gladiators saw themselves as athletes, and they participated in a self-representation that led back to the *Iliad* (where, it is worth noting again, armed combat *does* take place). Claims to glory occur in their funerary epigrams that compare well with those in athletic epigrams and inscriptions. One gladiator, whose epitaph is lengthy, compares his work with that of Heracles and even boasts a thirteenth labour to best the legendary hero.[93] More modest epitaphs make claims to epic glory,[94] while in others the gladiatorial matches are given divine quality as the 'quarrels of Ares' (the ancient Greek god of war).[95]

Despite a modern, moralizing narrative that identifies gladiatorial combat with decline and decadence, and distinguishes Roman and Greek and immoral and moral, the evidence from the ancient world is, in fact, more complex. Ancient Greek cities adopted many Roman practices in their own right or to reinterpret them. Gladiators and the remainder of the events of the *munus* retained some Roman values, especially as they connected to the Emperor, but they were also mutable enough that audiences could locate in the person of the gladiator their own athletic identities and ideologies.

*   *   *

Roman sport – even the term is contentious – has provided one of the central moral lenses through which to view Roman society and civilization. Early Christian writers paraded the Games, especially but not only the *munera*, as exemplary of pagan debauchery and decadence. In the modern sports world, self-consciously influenced by ancient Greek festivals imagined as idyllic sports paradises, Roman 'spectacle' is the dark mirror to Greek antiquity. Roman sport, despite close connections with the brutal systems of slavery and imperialism that shaped all aspects of life in classical antiquity, does not necessarily reflect an essential brutality to Roman culture. And, certainly, arguments about morality and decline, and ancient Greece or the present in contrast, reveal modern preoccupations and preconceptions. In many ways, through sports fandom, a massive audience, the intertwining of sports with politics, empire, everyday life and religion, Roman spectacle resonates well with the global sporting culture of the late twentieth and early twenty-first century, in spite of – or because of – its close connection with the staging of pain and mortality.

The Ancient and Modern Olympics

By the beginning of the 252nd Olympiad, in 229 CE, the Olympics had been held continually for over 1,000 years. The Games and athletics were at their height in this period.[1] Around the same time, the philosopher Philostratus wrote a work on athletics called *On Athletic Exercise* that focuses on athletic training and trainers.[2] His argument from the outset is that athletics is a kind of 'wisdom' like philosophy (1). But, to prove this point, he embarks on a history of athletic events that makes them at first glance seem unnecessary in the present.[3]

For Philostratus, history and the idea that athletics is a type of wisdom, and therefore teachable, can combat what he perceives as decline in his own times, not in the nature of people, but in the methods used to develop natural ability (*On Athletic Exercise* 2). Virtue, he writes, may be possible again through the lessons of the history of sport and by comparing and connecting ancient and modern worlds.[4] Despite the apparent distance between the past and present, athletic history provides insights that have relevance: for example, he links past and present through comparisons of contemporary and ancient athletic stars.[5] Philostratus suggests that athletics has a role to play in his present, a role that may be discovered only by a return to the past.[6]

This chapter begins with Philostratus' perspective on the value of sport as a way to frame the most influential of the revivals of ancient sports in the modern period, the International Olympic Committee's (IOC) Olympic Games. Like Philostratus, the modern Olympics founder Pierre de Coubertin argued for the utility of sport, both on the basis of its perceived cultural continuity with antiquity, but also because of its ability to build character and contribute to the production and maintenance of a good society. His foundation of the Games was an explicit turn to the past for the needs of the present and evinced a strong belief that history had modern relevance, even in the face of those who thought sport was an anachronism. The modern Olympics, like the ancient ones, style themselves as a 'renewal' even as they stress their suitability for the present. In the case of the IOC's Games, the emphasis on renewal creates potential conflict since they imagine an impossible merger of antiquity and modernity.

Starting with the origins of the ancient Games, we move from the world of the ancient Olympics through the rediscovery of the ancient site to the IOC's Games. While the modern Games purport to be a rebirth of antiquity in the modern period – and one which continues to entrance a postmodern world – as this chapter makes clear, the contradiction of antiquity and modernity at their core has yet to be resolved. By narrating the history of the ancient Games, the birth of the modern Games and their connection with antiquity, their troubled relationship with class and gender and modern sport, this chapter demonstrates that nostalgia and a 'return to the past' is perhaps the most characteristic – and troublesome – of Olympic qualities, ancient and modern.[7]

Athletics and nostalgia in the ancient and modern Olympic Games

In the first century CE, the historian and geographer Strabo cautioned his contemporaries about believing in the ancient tales of the Olympics' foundation: 'For such things are variously reported, and not entitled to much credit' (8.3.30). Strabo was right: there were *many* origins of the Olympics current in antiquity, and these accounts were (and are) difficult to square with one another.

Pausanias, writing a century or so after Strabo, attempted to incorporate many of the tales of Olympia and the Olympics' founding into his own geographical and historical survey of Greece. His Olympics begin in legendary times, and he connects them to Zeus' predecessor and father, Cronus. He attributes the foundation of the sanctuary and Games to the somewhat obscure Daktyloi of Ida, in Crete, who protected Zeus when he was born (5.7.6). One of these Daktyloi, called Heracles (confusingly for modern and ancient readers alike), established a race for him and his brothers and crowned the winner with an olive-leaf branch (5.7.7). These initial Games were explicitly called 'Olympic' and set to recur every four years (5.7.9). From here the story involves even more obscure figures, but Pausanias' narrative nonetheless emphasizes that the Games were forgotten and resurrected several times: by Klymenos the son Kardys, who lived after the great flood (5.8.1), by Endymion who drove Klymenos from his throne (5.8.1), by Pelops who gave his name to southern Greece, the Peloponnese (5.8.2). After Heracles, the son of Zeus, organized the Games, and then Oxylos, another King of Elis (5.4.5), they were said to have fallen into abeyance.

Even after these myriad figures, Pausanias has not reached the generally agreed upon historical founding of the Games in 776 BCE. When he finally gets to Iphitos, a legendary figure supposedly contemporaneous with the Spartan lawgiver Lycurgus, he claims that he re-established the Olympic festival (5.4.5). For Pausanias, Iphitos' re-establishment of the Games is not just the founding of a festival with the same name as the prior one. Rather, it is an active process of memory: 'people had still forgotten the old days; little by little they remembered, and whenever they remembered something else they added it on' (5.8.5). Pausanias offers a narrative of the supposed development of the Olympics – from an initial footrace only in 776 BCE to a more or less full program by the early fourth century BCE – though it is not presented as the historical record of innovations in sport and competition, but rather proof (as he puts it: 5.8.6) of the recollection of the past and its implementation in the present.[8] Nostalgia, here an active force that recalls the past and transforms the present through recollection, is central to Olympic foundations which are, in fact, always refoundations.

For some modern scholars, Pausanias' connection of past and present is on the right track. Gregory Nagy suggests that at the most basic level ancient Greek athletics is a kind of re-enactment of the past exploits of heroes.[9] And not only Pausanias incorporates past and present with sport. Several of Pindar's songs use nostalgia and memory to suggest the transformative power of the past, inasmuch as ancient and modern athletes can be tied together, across eons, by the bodily action of sport.

Pindar's *Olympian* 10 was written for Hagesidamos of Western Lokroi, the victor in the boys' boxing competition at the Olympics of 474 BCE (some 600 years before Pausanias was writing). The poem is the earliest history of the Olympic Games and though set firmly in a legendary past, it is nonetheless fixed in the landscape of Olympia. Olympia's past, it turns out, begins in the further past – no surprise when we consider Pausanias' Olympic history above. Heracles founds Games by the already 'ancient tomb of Pelops' as a tribute to a military victory over the King Augeas. Following immediately after his destruction of Augeas' army, Heracles measures out the space of the sacred Altis – the heart of the sanctuary of Olympia – and he honours the Alpheus River and the other gods. Next, Heracles names the previously unnamed hill the Hill of Cronus. Old places gain new names or new recognition as Heracles, in Pindar's telling, works to establish the geography of Olympia.

Pindar then turns to the games themselves. He runs through the results of six contests: footrace, wrestling, boxing, four-horse chariot, javelin and discus. The list of contests seemingly contradicts Pausanias' careful evolutionary history, until we recall that Pindar's account is set in the legendary times, before Iphitos and later Greeks 'remembered' the contests of the past. Pindar mentions those contests that Pausanias explicitly attributes to the recollections of Iphitos and those who followed him after the final refoundation of the Games in 776 BCE: the footrace at the first Games, pentathlon and wrestling in the 18th Olympiad (708 BCE), boxing in the 23rd Olympiad (688 BCE) and chariot racing in the 25th (680 BCE). There are some differences, of course, since Pindar's athletes do not compete in the *diaulos* (double *stadion*, 724 BCE) or *dolichos* (long footrace, 720 BCE) – though a footrace may stand in for them – nor are javelin and discus in his account staged as part of the pentathlon. Pindar may follow a different tradition than that of Pausanias, but it is also possible he chooses these events not only for their association with early Olympic revivals. Rather than only an attempt to imagine the Olympics' past, Pindar also evokes the great contests of epic literature, which included a similar selection of contests: in the Games for Patroclus' funeral in Homer's *Iliad*, for example, chariot racing, wrestling, boxing, footrace, weight-toss, archery, javelin, armed combat. The Olympics, as far as Pindar represents them, are, from their inception, a more-or-less complete set of contests to compete with any epic event. As Pausanias would later conceive of it, these Games, epic and complete, were forgotten, and only 'remembered' in Iphitos' Olympic renaissance.

Following the competitions, the scene turns momentarily to the evening, during which the moon lights up a festive night, full of victory songs. The presence of songs like his own at the first Olympics is an anachronistic touch since the earliest epinician songs barely predate Pindar himself. As soon as he finishes the sentence that evokes the songs that follow victory at Heracles' Olympics, Pindar connects past epinician song with present: '*even now*', he says, 'we will follow the first beginnings' (10.78). Pindar's song, then, is the key that connects the past and present and the way in which the past can be transmitted to the present and to the future: eternal repetition, in the form of athletic contests *and* song, ensure the continuation of tradition. Poets and singers, in fact, were key parts of the preservation of memory and truth (as Pindar makes clear *in this poem*: 10.1–6). Pindar's song, like Pausanias' recollections, can re-establish the past in the present.[10]

It is not only in poetry and history that Olympia and the ancient Olympics blend the past and present. The very landscape of the site is marked by the continuity of religious activity of which athletics are a key component. Olympia in antiquity, as today, is bounded by the natural features of a river valley landscape: The Alpheus and Cladeus rivers on the south and west sides respectively, and the Hill on the north. Landscape features were associated with divine and legendary qualities: The Hill of Cronus was supposedly named by Heracles after Zeus' father. The Alpheus and Cladeus were recognized by Heracles, but were also imagined as river gods in their own right; the former supposedly fell in love with Artemis and as such followed her to Sicily (Pindar, *Nemean* 1). Even at this basic level, then, geographical features are incorporated into the legendary past and stand as testaments to the continuity of the past into the present.

When we turn to the built environment of Olympia, the various altars, temples, and facilities, we see the same the imagined – or actual – continuity of past into present (see Map of Olympia, Figure 3.1). While the site as it is reconstructed today represents a kind of ahistorical time, with older and newer structures visible, in the actual past, new building at Olympia took time.[11] In the Archaic period, i.e. the first 200 years after Pausanias' last 'refoundation', the only major structures were the Temple to Hera, treasuries, the prytaneion (a building for use by officials) and the council house. By the end of the fifth century BCE, even though more structures had been built including the walls around Pelopion, a shrine to Pelops and the great Temple to Olympian Zeus (*c.* 457 BCE), there were still no guest houses for visitors or even a

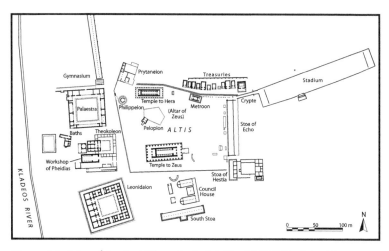

Figure 3.1 Map of Ancient Olympia. Artist: Daniel P. Diffendale. After a map in N. Kaltsas, *Olympia* (Archaeological Receipts Fund, 2009), figure 14.

fountain to provide reliable water (The Leonidaion, a large guest house was constructed in the 330s BCE). Stoas, multipurpose structures that could be used as gathering places, appeared by the end of the classical period (South Stoa, Stoa of Echoes, Stoa of Hestia). Athletic training facilities, however, were slow to appear: the gymnasium and palaestra complex, probably accompanied by baths (using the water of the Cladeus River), were constructed in the Hellenistic period (323–331 BCE). Other structures and monuments were added over the centuries that Olympia remained an important site such as the Theokoleon (perhaps quarters for priests, *c.* 360 BCE), the Philippeion (a circular temple erected by Philip of Macedon after his defeat of an alliance of city states in 338 BCE) and the Metröon (a temple of the Mother of the Gods built around 400 BCE).

While new structures were only slowly added, structures or objects that were supposedly connected with the legendary past were retained and still visible, even when they were dilapidated. For example, the foundations of the house of Oinomaos, a legendary king, which was destroyed by a thunderbolt from Zeus (Pausanias, 5.14.7), were visible as if they were an ancient archaeological site, even covered with a roof to protect them (Pausanias, 5.20.6). Other buildings accrued meaning as time went on. When the Temple to Zeus was finished and the statue of Zeus, sculpted by Pheidias and considered one of the great wonders of the world, was installed, the building called the Workshop of Pheidias where the artist worked on the statue was preserved, so much so that Pausanias recognized it almost 600 years later (5.15.1).

One altar in particular is significant for its ability to capture the physical manifestation of continuity at Olympia: the ash altar to Zeus. This altar, located somewhere near the middle of the Altis, was supposedly founded far in the legendary past. Unlike a stone altar, it was constructed from the ash leftover after burning sacrifices of bulls to Zeus (Pausanias, 5.13.8). The scale was massive. Pausanias reports a first step on the altar that was 125 feet around; the next step 32 feet; and the whole thing 21 feet high with stone steps leading to the summit (5.13.9–10; these are measurements in ancient Greek feet, i.e. 308mm, slightly larger than than the Roman and Imperial/US foot). The ash altar would have been impressive: not only in its scale, but also in what it represented – the record of unbroken religious sacrifices to Zeus on that very spot. As the sanctuary is laid out today, the ash altar's significance is lessened. In earlier periods, the stadium was further west and probably abutted the eastern side of the altar; the spatial continuity of sacrifice and athletics would be strikingly clearer.

Athletic continuity was part of the Olympic landscape and the past of athletics part of the present of competition in a way that is mostly foreign in contemporary sports. The stadium at Olympia, even when it was moved to its present location connected to the sanctuary by a covered tunnel, remained primitive in comparison to other stadiums in Greece: it never had much stone seating beyond a ceremonial 'box' for priestesses of Demeter; the north slope of the stadium seating was the Hill of Cronus. Old monuments for martial victories may have dotted these slopes even when they became seating for the stadium.[12] The athletic field was integrated into the ritual and religious geography of the sanctuary.[13]

Most prominently, athletic statues date to early in Olympic history, when the stadium would have been in closer proximity to the sanctuary's core. Statues, for the ancient Greeks, were not, as for many modern peoples, simply *representations* of people but rather they could be conceived as *replacements* for absent people. When athletes competed in the stadium, they competed not only with the eyes of their contemporaries on them, but also with the sculpted forms of rivals and peers from across time. By the classical period, Olympia was home to dozens of statues of athletes, which dated to the middle of the sixth century BCE. Athletic statues worked like the great ash altar of Zeus, as manifestations of a chain of unbroken ritual – in this case, athletic victory – that stretched back into the past and, through the bodies of those competing, into the present and future as well.

One Olympic tradition that makes clear the mixture of past and present in the form of athletics are the Olympiads. A four-year period beginning with the Olympics, an Olympiad could be used to reckon the times of the other main Panhellenic festivals. Moreover, Olympiads were integrated into the timeless and unchanging celestial sphere, since they were based around the cycles of the moon. The *ekecheiria*, the 'Olympic Truce', during which no spectator or athlete heading to the Games could be attacked or waylaid, began at the first full moon after the summer solstice; the Games took place at the time of the second full moon after the summer solstice, and an interval of 48 or 49 full moons made up an Olympiad.[14] The Olympiad could be named by number, i.e. counting from the first Olympiad which was reckoned as 776 BCE. But, the Olympiad could also be referred to through another practice, by naming the athlete who won the *stadion* race, the short-distance sprint at the Games. In this way, athletics and victory, the phases of the moon and movement of the heavens and the Games were tied together and could be imagined moving, in step, backwards and forwards in time.

Even as athletics became, at least according to some scholars, less associated directly with ritual and religion, the core of the site remained: by the late antique period, in the later third and fourth centuries CE, there is less evidence for the Games, though they almost certainly continued to be held regularly. When a fortification wall was built during the late third century CE, it incorporated the temple of Zeus, since it contained valuables,[15] including the famous statue.[16] Earthquake damage during the reign of Diocletian (284–305 CE) was repaired, and so the site was clearly still an important centre.[17] Continuity continued in the form of athletic competition, as a bronze plate discovered in 1994 makes clear: it records victors at the Games and runs – though fragmentary – from 28 BCE (the 188th Olympiad) to 381 CE (the 290th Olympiad).[18] Even when the Games died out, likely due to the fragmentation of the cultural and economic world of antiquity,[19] rather than a decree from the Emperor Theodosius in 393 CE,[20] the Olympiads were remembered as a method of reckoning time into the early Medieval period.[21]

With the end of the Games, Olympia's fate seemed sealed: a slow decline from disuse and lack of upkeep. Nature, however, had other plans, and the sanctuary was likely destroyed rather suddenly, covered, it seems, by catastrophic floods resulting from tsunamis that destroyed its buildings and the after-effects of which caused a massive layer of sand and sediment to accumulate up to 8 metres deep. Memories of Olympia and the Olympic Games lived on, as can be seen in etchings and woodcuts by imaginative travelers and the appearance of the Games in literature during the medieval and early modern periods.[22] In Greece, folk traditions and festivals preserved the spirit of the Panhellenic Games: athletic competitions on a cycle where competitors anointed themselves with oil were associated with religious feast days throughout the premodern period.[23]

The first true history of the Olympics appeared when Gilbert West published his *Dissertation on the Olympick Games* in 1749 alongside a translation of Pindar. Like my own work, West's began with a survey of the foundation myths of the Olympics and an outline of the religious setting, though Olympia itself remained unexplored by, at least, Western European scholars.[24] When Richard Chandler reached the site of Olympia in 1766, hoping to draw (or collect) specimens of ancient monuments and temples, he and his group found a river valley infested with gnats and almost devoid of monuments.[25] The French Expedition to the Morea (1828–33) excavated a little at Olympia (and brought part of the Temple of Zeus to the Louvre), and it was their initial investigations that concluded the ancient site was buried deep under sediment.[26] By the early 1850s, with Olympia still unexplored by Western Europeans, German philologist Ernst Curtius pushed for Prussia to excavate. While impressed with Greek antiquity, as were most German scholars of the nineteenth century, Curtius connected archaeology with the modern nation state's duty to scholarship and science, and he thought that the function of archaeology and museums was to enhance national prestige.[27]

Curtius' arguments for excavation as a project central to Prussian civilization eventually won over Frederick William IV (1840–61), who gave him permission to negotiate with the Greeks. However, negotiations were to prove fruitless initially thanks to the German insistence on bringing monuments from Olympia back to Berlin. Finally, Crown

Prince Frederick – the future Kaiser Frederick III – visited Greece in October 1869. While there, he condemned Lord Elgin's pillaging of the Parthenon and opposed all efforts to transgress the Greek ban on exporting monuments. Wilhelm I and George I signed an excavation agreement in 1873.

The excavations were a paradigm of positivism (i.e. to know the past 'the way it really was') and a prototype for scientific archaeology.[28] They began in 1875 and were soon central to the German national cause and to international political competition.[29] The excavations ran for six years, and the sheer number of finds surpassed all expectations: in 1879, the director reported that the previous four years had brought forth 1,328 stone sculptures, 7,464 bronze finds, 2,094 ceramics, 696 inscriptions and 3,035 coins.[30] In a major innovation, yearly reports were published as the excavations went on, and the excavation volumes yield much information on architectural monuments, sculptures, bronze and inscriptions, though one searches in vain, perhaps, for the *meaning* of these objects to late nineteenth-century Germany. While the forward to the first volume names Curtius as the one to have enacted Johann Winckelmann's dream of excavating Olympia, the eighteenth-century art historian would have been at pains to find, in the official reports, any of his 'countless beautiful monuments' of the Greeks[31] or comments on the contemplation of beauty and unity or art.[32] Scholarship had developed and become part of the state and its ambitions. Whatever relevance archaeology had for the present day was bound to its ability to catalogue, categorize and describe in detail.

The success of the German excavations and its broader appeal may be measured by the *Baedeker Guide to Greece*, first published in German and English in 1889. By this point, the excavations had ceased for the time being, and Olympia, equipped with a museum, had become an attraction for railway and steamship tourists.[33] Included within was a site plan to be consulted by the avid tourist, while the Guidebook detailed the architectural details of each ruin; the museum received a separate section where even the minor bronzes were described in summary. While occasional Romantic flourishes persist, historical details dominate. Although Olympia yielded few full sculptures, the Guide reads, 'a flood of light was thrown upon ... topographical and architectural matters'.[34] Hardly the stuff of philhellenism and aesthetics,[35] nor the resurrection of the past of Pausanias and Pindar's Olympic memories.

By 1894, when he visited Olympia for the first time, the site had been so excavated and reconstructed that Pierre de Coubertin could say that 'one can ... move through the holy site where Pausanias served as a guide'.[36] While Coubertin writes as if he were a Thomas Cook tourist to Olympia, his encounter with the ancient world was more complex than that of an itinerant traveler and less precise than a historian or archaeologist. Coubertin was aware on his visit of the German efforts, an honour for which he believed the world was indebted,[37] but his interest in Olympia was not located in the technical details of the excavation's official reports. While he trumpets the results of the German excavation and the sight of the ruins, he fears that scholars understand detail and scientific reconstruction, but not the true meaning or effect of the sanctuary. Rather than trust to Pausanias, Murray's Guide or a Baedeker, Coubertin states: 'I spent the whole morning wandering among the ruins'.[38] He returned to Olympia in 1927 for the unveiling a monument in honour of the restoration of the Olympic Games. He 'repeated' the tentative explorations of his first visit in pursuit of 'the grandiose scenes of another age'.[39] In a telegraphed letter from Olympia, he urged young people to maintain his work; the Olympics, he declared, were not revived, 'in order to be a subject for film or an object in a museum', but to be the emblem of a 'religion of sport such as that of their grand ancestors'.[40] The audacity of this message, from the site that helped give birth to scientific archaeology and mere steps from a museum dedicated to the objects excavated from Olympia, lays bare Coubertin's exploration of Olympia not as a place for scholarly research, but as an idea. Olympia did not consist of the 696 inscriptions, 3,035 coins and the rest – dead relics – but was a living monument – a sacred landscape – of ancient Greek culture and sport.

Coubertin wrote little about the ruins of Olympia that did not evoke this vision. In a lecture given in Paris in 1929 he specifically rejected a discussion of the details of the excavations.[41] For him, the ruins of Olympia had meaning only insofar as they represented the ancient Greek cult of beauty and balance and only insofar as that ideal had meaning for today.[42] He found the ruins more sublime than the completed monuments would have been, since with the 'patina of time' they act as prompts to a nostalgic vision of the past rather than as indexes for a scientific reconstruction.[43] He asks his audience to imagine they were speaking at the foot of Mount Cronus, with the ruins of Olympia around them. In a semi-somnambulant fantasy, he and his audience walk as if in a dream, while the Olympia of the past comes to life in sounds and vision. 'Olympia,' concludes Coubertin, in contrast to all the other ancient Greek sanctuaries, 'is alive', since the real meaning of these ruins, not the items sitting in a museum, has been transmitted to the world.[44] We are not far from the 'even now' of Pindar's ode for Hagesidamos or the resurrected memories of Pausanias' Olympic history.

Coubertin's fascination with the Olympics began from his interest in the educational potential of sport.[45] Throughout his life, even as the Olympics became successful, the moral and educational aspects of sport remained central to his aims. He thought of the nineteenth century as particularly amenable to his aims and understood the rebirth of physical culture as an almost messianic mission.[46] Nonetheless, in the midst of this historic mission, Coubertin recognized what to him were the signs of imminent decline by the closing years of the century: specialization, a mercantile spirit and unbridled ambition.[47] In the face of imminent decline, Coubertin decided that the way to forestall sport's inevitable corruption and to 'purify' it was to place athletics under 'The patronage of Classical Antiquity!'[48]

Coubertin unveiled his purified festival of sport only slowly, and, as he admits in retrospect, by subterfuge.[49] Much of Coubertin's writings create a narrative of his singular struggle to revive the Games, a task that, though aided by many, he credits almost exclusively to himself. His voluminous writings, over a long life, look back on early episodes and recast them as part of a story of Olympic revival in which he plays the role of Heracles, Pelops or Iphitos. His work, as much as that of ancient Greek poets and writers, demonstrates how nostalgia and memory, at the personal and communal level, contributes to a sense of what makes the Olympics important, or valuable, across different time periods.[50]

In a lecture at the Sorbonne in 1892 entitled 'Physical Exercises in the Modern World', Coubertin lauded the universal human impulse that leads to sport – and this impulse, he claimed, was sport's true virtue, not health or preparation for war, but the love of effort itself.[51] Coubertin's Hellenism and his understanding of sport was anything but antiquarian, and his interest in the Olympics far from that of a historian. Rather, he saw nineteenth-century athletics as particularly modern, especially in its democratic and international character. Coubertin believed that athletics would also further international cooperation and peace.[52] Democracy, internationalization and peace – the benefits that *modern* sport had to offer the world – coupled with the social and moral benefits of the pursuit of effort for effort's sake – the benefits of a universal and unhistorical vision of sport – these, Coubertin believed, were central to the survival of the world, a fusing of antiquity and modernity, tradition and innovation.[53] At the end of his speech at the Sorbonne, to rabid applause,[54] he called on his audience to restore the Olympic Games.[55]

Over the course of the next eighteen months, Coubertin and the nascent IOC would convince the Greek government to host the Games, invite scores of athletes, find the money to stage the Games and work out the logistics of what was the first major, international sporting event. Others played crucial roles, especially the first IOC president, Demetrios Vikelas, whose work in Athens on behalf of the Olympics was integral to them happening successfully and, indeed, at all.[56] The Greek royal family, especially Crown Prince Constantine, and Greeks abroad, especially wealthy Egyptian Greek Georgios Averoff, who singlehandedly paid for the restoration of the Panathenaic Stadium,[57] were critical. But, so, too, was the Greek press, almost uniformly positive about the idea, and the people of Athens, who hosted athletes and welcomed foreign visitors, journalists and diplomats with aplomb throughout what was, by the end of the Games, lauded as a highly successful event.[58]

Coubertin, in fact, disappeared during some of the organization of the Games (he got married during the lead-up to the Games, took on a political role in France and started a new project on French history),[59] though he was determined that his role as the central figure in the revival of the Games be maintained.[60] Despite some differences, his co-organizers on the IOC saw him in this light: Vikelas called him a 'messiah'.[61] Coubertin was keen on this role, perhaps because he saw himself at the end as a reformer, who had championed physical education and the 'physical renaissance' for years. His fusion of modernity and antiquity, however, aimed at modern and mutable restoration, not slavish imitation. Like Pindar and Pausanias, who locate in athletics an art that transcends time, Coubertin imagined athletics – in particular the revived Olympic festival – would transcend historical change and time as well. On envisioning the response of French athletes arriving in Athens for the 1896 Games, imitation and modification is on Coubertin's mind: despite their schoolboy Greek failing them, he writes, the French will recognize the connections between ancient and modern Greece in athletics.[62] The past's utility lay in its versatility as a model imbued with a remoteness and primordialism that can be equal parts inspiration and lustrous veneer.[63]

Coubertin's view of the past and sports merges a specific time in which restoration of the Olympics was necessary with the ahistorical, universal vision of sports that he sees in the French athletes arriving at Athens. In his analysis of the physical effort and consequences of sport, Coubertin, the champion of the historical sciences, the stubborn modernizer of his restored Olympics, is at his most unhistorical. In his vision of sporting effort, then, Coubertin's writing hearkens back to the epinician of Pindar, the song that transformed the historical athlete into epic hero, and fused time into an eternal present of universal values and importance. Consider, for example, his discussion of the first audience

of the 1896 Games as they enter the Panathenaic stadium. Coubertin is
at pains to describe the architectural marvel of the stadium. Stadiums,
he claims, are unfamiliar because they were lost, whereas Greek temples
and porticos formed the architectural inheritance of Europe. Despite
the unfamiliarity, the 'living stadium' will soon fill with crowds; despite
the strange surroundings and the pageantry of a revived pagan rite, the
people know how to react and the spectacle of athletics revives antiquity
in modern times.[64] Here, the physical landscape of athletics dismisses
time and change and fuses itself with the past; where Coubertin sought
'grandiose scenes' in the ruined landscape of Olympia, the living
stadium manifests the past in the present and centuries of time are
dismissed through the energies of sport.

The Panathenaic stadium figures in the clearest evocation of a
timeless sporting present to which Coubertin returned in his second
trip to Greece in 1927. Flush with the success of his project and with a
hero's welcome at Olympia, he envisioned the world continually
recreated along the lines of ancient Greek or Roman civilization. On
receiving an inscribed seat at the Panathenaic stadium, he watches an
English university team compete and notes differences but sees, still,
reborn, an eternal athlete, especially in the physical practice of sport.
Coubertin spies one of these student-athletes as he prepares to leave the
stadium:

> I saw one of them raise his eyes to the divine Acropolis still bathed
> in the last rays of the setting sun while the shadows spread fast around
> us. The student, full of the joy of living, his body suffused with the
> voluptuous glow that comes only from healthy tiredness induced by
> sport, and fired with youthful hope and ambition, seemed, with his
> fixed stare, to be imploring Minerva and paying her homage. He was
> like a sculpture representing neo-Olympism, the symbol of future
> victories awaiting Hellenism—still very much alive, and eternally
> adapted to human circumstances.[65]

Here, then, Olympic revival is driven by a kind of culturally shared
recollection: Coubertin's past audiences meld and transform into
present audiences and the spectators of sporting events, it seems, are

ahistorical and eternal: the universal regard of 'the joy of living' collapses the distance between past and present and disturbs Coubertin's modern vision for the Games.

Coubertin's nostalgic vision, like that of Philostratus, aims at the utility of the past for the betterment of the present. As such, his Olympic revival *is* a revival, not necessarily of the Olympic festival, but of sports' supposed function in antiquity and the deep connection of sports, whether ancient or modern, with visions of past glory and present decline. Whether, or how, this revival reconciles antiquity and modernity, however, remains an open question.

Making antiquity modern

Coubertin claimed that it was necessary, desirable *and* possible to recreate the Olympic Games 'suited to the conditions of modern life'. But, an ancient religious festival dedicated to a pagan storm god and celebrating the masculinity of a slave-owning society seems to have, at first glance, little to do with modernity. From the outset, Coubertin's vision for the Games was complicated by his insistence on the modern and international character of the Olympics. And, after the Games were founded, the modern world intruded in other ways that Coubertin had not considered or of which he actively disapproved: should the Olympics be open to all social statuses? All countries and peoples? All genders and sexual orientations? The antiquity of the Olympics imbues them with some sort of importance. However, antiquity, especially tradition and continuity, also disturbs the professed modernity of the Games.

Basic elements of the modern Olympics were disputed almost from the outset: location, sports and stadiums. Greece organized the first modern Games, and King George I's opening of the Games was seen by Coubertin as a direct refutation of the Theodosian decree that supposedly suppressed the ancient Games.[66] For the Greeks, the Games were a duty to their ancient past and an opportunity to demonstrate that Greece was a modern, successful, European nation.[67] Coubertin fought with American Olympians, the Greek press and organizers and the King for his vision of a mobile, international Games.[68] The argument about whether the Games should remain in Greece was the first evidence of the IOC's monopoly on antiquity: why, some asked, did this committee in Paris hold authority over sports events called Olympics?[69] A compromise saw Games scheduled for Athens every two years, though, in the event only one of these so-called 'Intercalated Games' took place in 1906.[70] Coubertin in fact wanted the Games to move as quickly as possible to the other 'great centers of sport', namely Rome and London.[71] The conflict over internationalism was reconciled later, especially as Olympic rituals like the Oath, parade of nations and above all the torch-lighting ceremony and relay became prominent after the First World War. Greece, though never the permanent host, became a kind of permanent 'home' for the Games as the source of tradition and ritual.[72] Even the IOC's focus on cities is a strange ancient and modern conflation: the main organizing principle for modern sport is the state, but ancient athletes were imagined, at least in part, as representatives of their city states.

The sports of the Olympics were also supposed to be modern, or at least ancient with modern adaptations: 'the bicycle at the foot of the Parthenon';[73] fencing instead of the 'brutalities of pugilism';[74] and one of the most discussed modern sports, the Modern Pentathlon. One of the most peculiar mergers of antiquity and modernity was the so-called 'Greek Discus', where athletes had to stand atop a pedestal and throw a discus explicitly in the style of the famous *Discobolus* of Myron; the sport was staged in 1904, the 1906 'Intercalated Games' at Athens and in 1908 before being abandoned.[75] Even the beautiful setting of the Panathenaic stadium in 1896 was a temporary nod to antiquarianism since Coubertin preferred the open fields of English, French and American sports venues.[76]

But modernity did not mean a complete break with the past for Coubertin, nor unfettered secularism. He argued for the philosophical and moral foundations of the Games as a *religio athletae* (religion of the athlete), a core philosophy of modern Olympism. Olympism remains central to the Games' self-image as something more than world championships. They are, in Coubertin's words, a 'cult of athletics'.[77] One aspect is their cyclical nature: like the ancient Games, which were based around a lunar calendar, the modern Games' Olympiads provide a cycle, and, within the Olympic community, a time-keeping mechanism. Olympism continues to be a force in the Olympic movement that implicitly connects with antiquity by making sport, as it was assumed to be in the past, about more than simply winning.

The connection with antiquity through a perceived philosophy or religious basis to sport is not so far-fetched. Sport in ancient Greece was *always* religious, and something like Coubertin's 'aristocracy of the muscles' would not be foreign to the dominant strain of ancient Greek masculinity.[78] The modern Games' separation of sport, religion and politics, however, would feel foreign, as would the assumption that 'fair play' was essential to athletics. While cheating was illegal at the ancient Games, and, at least on occasion, cheaters were forced to erect statues of Zeus as punishment (the Zanes that line the entrance to the Olympic stadium that begin in the fourth century BCE, see Pausanias, 5.21.2–8), cheaters faced few other moral or legal penalties, and in some cases kept their victory even if they were found to have cheated. Other elements of Olympism, especially those embodied in Coubertin's Olympic credo ('The important thing in life is not the triumph, but the fight; the essential thing is not to have won, but to have fought well') would be totally foreign to the ancient Greeks.

The question of universal Olympic sport – something Coubertin championed, at least with respect to ethnicity, nationalism and race – has, from its beginnings, been difficult.[79] Universal access is imagined as being modelled on the ancient Games, which were, with limitations of gender, open to 'all Greeks' without formal restrictions on social status; the prohibition of non-Greeks in antiquity may even be a mirage.[80] The modern Games' attempt to extend this universalism to an international and open festival, and in the face of a twentieth century where human rights were formulated and legally established, has been complicated at best.[81]

The most contentious issue for the early Olympics was the notion of 'amateurism', which was tied, specifically through its condemnation of training and wage-earning, to social status and class. Athletes, in this ideology, ought to compete only for the sake of sport itself, not for money, whether through actual wages or endorsements. Some earlier amateurist ideologies even excluded those who worked for a living in any capacity. David Young offers a detailed exposition of the prehistory of amateurism, and its ties to the very birth of the modern Olympic Movement.[82] Its connection to the elite British public school system is well attested, as is Coubertin's manipulation of the ideology of amateurism, both to garner aristocratic support for his revived Olympics, and as a way to connect (falsely) the modern Games to those of ancient Greece.[83] Early proponents of the Olympics and amateurism claimed that ancient athletes were also 'amateurs' who competed for nothing but symbolic prizes. In the ancient Games, while there may have been structures that implicitly restricted access to wealthy individuals, there was no formal status restriction beyond, in one late source, being a 'free-born Greek man'.[84] And, in fact, most competitions offered valuable prizes and most competitors participated in both 'crown Games' that gave symbolic prizes and 'money Games' that offered prizes of material value. There was, to be brief, absolutely no such concept as an 'amateur athlete' in classical antiquity.

Class has not been the only stumbling block to a universal Olympics. National identity, race and ethnicity have threatened the IOC's claim that the Olympics are an avowedly non-political area or that race and identity should not play a role in sport. The 'Fundamental Principles of Olympism' secure the rights to Olympic participation without any discrimination on the basis of, among other things, language or race or 'colour',[85] but these principles have been at odds with the internal workings of many nations and many Olympic Games.

The 1936 Games faced potential boycott because of concern about German treatment of Jewish athletes, especially after the institutionalization of anti-Semitism with the Nazi rise to power and enactment of the Nuremberg Laws in 1935. Many Jewish athletes spoke out and, in the end, decided against participating, though, the eventual decision by the American Olympic Committee[86] to participate drew most *national* (not individual) calls for a boycott of the Games to end. Individuals and other groups, however, did boycott the Games, though these actions were on a small scale. Today, of course, the Berlin Games are remembered most for the athletic triumph of Jesse Owens in the face of Nazi racial ideology. Owens' performance – gold in the long jump, 100 metres, 200 metres and 4x100 metres – is rightly legendary. Moreover, his competition with German long jumper Lutz Long, not only an incredible competition between two athletes, has been set down in Olympic lore as emblematic of the ability of Olympic sports to transcend racial and political difference. At a crucial moment, after Owens fouled on his first two attempts to jump, Long advised Owens to back up his run-up mark for the jumping pit so that he made the qualifying distance and continued in the competitions. Long sealed his fate, since Owens would best him later in the competition, but he obtained a place in a pantheon of sports heroes whose commitment to the principles of Olympism and 'fair play' outdo their desire for victory.

Racial politics like these, originating on the field of play and representing Olympic sports' supposedly transcendent values are, in the eyes of the IOC, acceptable. Politics and race, however, are different. Olympic sport in antiquity was completely enmeshed with politics, so much so that warfare occurred during the Games, at least once in 364 BCE (Xenophon, *Hellenica* 7.4.28–32), and the site of Olympia was home to competing military monuments from the earliest periods. Nonetheless, sport as apolitical has been fundamental to the modern Olympics' self-conception: section 50.2 of the modern Olympic Charter imagines an apolitical world within the Olympic site, where 'no kind of demonstration or political, religious or racial propaganda is permitted'.[87] When Tommie Smith and John Carlos stood on the podium and raised their fists to protest the economic conditions of African-Americans in 1968, they violated, in the eyes of the IOC, the supposed neutrality of the space of sports, which should demonstrate excellence through competition, not protest. When Damien Hooper stepped into the

Olympic boxing ring wearing a shirt depicting the Aboriginal flag of
Australia, he was penalized, and thus the Olympic *political* preference
for the citizenships of settler states over Indigenous ones was brought to
the fore.[88] By purporting to make a space politically neutral, the modern
Games reveal themselves at their most political.

The IOC's record on race is not strong enough to merit such assumed
neutrality. While Coubertin desired that the Games be open to all
nations and never insisted on a race-based criterion for entry, individual
Olympic committees were free to include or exclude as they wished.
Perhaps most notoriously, at the St. Louis Games of 1904, so-called
'anthropological days' took place, where colonized peoples participated
in athletic competitions against one another. Coubertin did not
approve,[89] but these noxious displays of racist bigotry *were* and *are* part
of Olympic history.

One of the most critical exclusions in the first decades of the Olympic
movement was of women. For decades during Coubertin's tenure as
head of the IOC, the modern Games were designed to celebrate male
athletic achievements.[90] As late as 1912, Coubertin wrote that the
Olympic Games were a way to celebrate male achievement in sport on
the international level, with 'the applause of women as recompense'.[91]
He even tied this apparent role of women to antiquity by claiming that
women had acted as appreciative audience at the ancient Games[92] – a
complete falsehood.

Ironically, the exclusion of women from the modern Games is one
aspect that does *not* find strong support in antiquity. While women
were probably forbidden from the Olympic sanctuary during the
festival (Pausanias, 5.6.7),[93] this formal prohibition does not reflect a
lack of interest in sports on behalf of ancient women as participants or
spectators, nor a lack of debate about the role of athletics for women.[94]
Our evidence is sometimes slight, but women were participating in
athletic contests across ancient Greek and Roman history. Even at
Olympia, Pausanias tells us, a contest called the *Heraia* took place, likely
close to the time of the Olympic Games. Like the Olympics, this contest
was held every fourth year, featured a foot race, oaths and judges. A

key distinction was that girls were divided into age categories and competition seems to have ended with marriage (5.16.2–7). Other evidence suggests that girls' sports could occur with some frequency, even in highly masculine spaces. One inscription from the first century CE at Delphi celebrates the victories at the Pythian, Isthmian, Nemean and other Games of Tryphosa, Hedea and Dionysia, the daughters of Hermesianax (*Sylloge Inscriptionum Graecarum*, 3rd edn, 802). Another inscription for the victory of Seia Spes survives from Italy: she won in a footrace held for daughters of the members of the *boule*, or council, of the city.[95]

Even after they were married, we still occasionally hear of women competing: the Spartan princess Cynisca won two chariot victories at the Olympics in 396 and 392 BCE. While male writers argued about her motives and who 'convinced' her to participate, Cynisca's victory monument speaks for itself and claims eternal glory *because* of her singular victory as a woman (*Carmina Epigraphica Graeca* 820). Other women followed, and chariot racing in particular became a sport of Queens, including various Hellenistic monarchs, especially the Macedonian queens and princesses of Egypt.[96] In fact, when Berenice I won the Olympic chariot race, she commissioned a short epigram that boasted of having *taken* Cynisca's glory (Posidippus, *Posidippi Pellaei Quae Supersunt Omnia* 87), since she, too, had now won at the Games. With such trans-historical competition taking place between women, it is impossible not to imagine that competitive sports were of interest across ages and social groups.

Beyond competitive athletics, girls' exercise and informal sports is also widely attested. As early as the *Odyssey*, girls can be imagined to find joy in ball games: Nausicaa, the princess of the Phaeacians, is represented playing with her friends after washing laundry on the beach when an errant throw wakes up the sleeping Odysseus (6.85–126).[97] Ball games, in fact, could be conceived of as especially feminine, so much so that an elusive fragment of the poet Anacreon seems to depict girls throwing a ball to one another instead of an old man to make an ironic and erotic point (*Poetae Melici Graeci* 358). The most famous of women who exercised in antiquity were those of Sparta. Lycurgus was reputed to have instituted exercise for women on equal terms with men for the sake of creating strong offspring (Xenophon, *Constitution of the Lacedaimonians* 1.4). Girls and boys paraded nude in front of adults and there were contests in speed and strength for girls. To be fair, these practices seemed odd to some other Greeks, especially Athenians (see Euripides, *Andromache* 595–601). Still, evidence for women's interest in physical exercise goes beyond the activities of young women: in the Hellenistic and Imperial periods in Greece, women were involved in running gymnasiums, offered benefactions to cities that included athletic facilities and may have, at times, gained access to the physical activities of the gymnasium.[98]

Women's cross-historical interest in athletics, despite the combination of derision and erotic objectification by male writers, demonstrates that sport in antiquity was not gendered specifically male. Rather, male authors took little interest in female sports as they took little interest in women's activities altogether. With this context for the evidence in hand, and the example of ancient participation and its relative exclusion from the historical record, it is important to note that the early exclusion of women from the IOC's Olympics was similarly not representative of a wide-ranging formal prohibition on women's athletics, or a lack of interest on the part of women. While many observers in the late nineteenth and early twentieth centuries considered women's sport contrary to a 'moral physiology' that regarded physical exertion in opposition to maternity,[99] feminist activists worked for the inclusion of women in the IOC's Olympics from their inception.[100] A skewed and reductive version of antiquity, where women were imagined as ancient cheerleaders, was used to lend the misogynist vision legitimacy.

A few women participated in the Games prior to 1928; since the organization of events was up to individual Olympic committees, not the IOC, for the first five Games.[101] In any case, such minimal and restricted participation was, clearly, to female sporting enthusiasts, not sufficient:[102] in 1922, the Fédération sportive féminine internationale (FSFI) formed, and subsequently staged a separate 'Women's Olympic

Games' in Paris; another followed in Sweden in 1926.[103] When the IOC guaranteed women more access to their Games in 1928, the FSFI agreed to suspend their staging of Olympic Games. The IOC argued for a renewed prohibition of women's athletics because of the 'horrific catastrophe of the women's 800 metres event' in 1928. The catastrophe was that women athletes could be as fatigued as men after competing at a high level.[104] It is noteworthy that one threat of the FSFI was to challenge the IOC's self-realized monopoly on antiquity. The suspension of the Women's Olympic Games was not without controversy, since the agreed-upon gender equality was not achieved (women competed in only five events in 1928), and the English Women's Amateur Athletic Association boycotted the Games in protest.[105]

The writing was on the wall, however, and as a result of the Great Depression, the Second World War and the increasing commercialization and corporatization of sport,[106] the FSFI disintegrated and left women's sports at the international level in the hands of the male-dominated IOC.[107] The results are apparent: while the FSFI had encouraged long-distance running, the IOC did not institute long-distance races for women until 1960; the FSFI had staged women's basketball championships in the 1920s and 1930s, but the IOC did not stage them as part of the Olympics until 1976. Even by 2020, at the international and Olympic levels, women run shorter hurdles distance (100 metres) and walk a shorter racewalk (only 30 km). Of course, women only compete in the seven-competition heptathlon at the Olympics in contrast to the men's decathlon. Much of this relative equality is recent: even pole vault for women was not included in the Olympics until 2000 and many other events were added at the 1996 Atlanta Games.

Even with women participating in Olympic sports, women's presence remains tentative and open to challenge. Assumptions about the appropriate appearance of female athletes lie behind some of these practices. Even the modest (by modern standards) outfits of the early Olympics offered relatively exposed male and female bodies to an observing audience, and as early as the 1920s, reporters focused on the supposedly feminine characteristics of athletes as opposed to their strictly athletic qualities.[108] Male writers from antiquity offer a sexist paradigm: the sixth-century BCE poet Ibycus criticized Spartan women athletes as 'thigh-flashers' (*Poetae Melici Graeci* 339), while the first-century BCE poet Propertius used Spartan athletic women as erotic objects in his poetry (3.14). In both cases – ancient and modern – women are either chastised for donning the garb of athletics or sexualized with no regard for their athletic abilities.

Across antiquity and modernity, then, critiques of female athletics focus on the appearance of women, who *ought* to match a normative standard for feminine appearance,[109] while at the same time maintaining normative standards for feminine morality. These normative standards reveal a transhistorical obsession, within sport, of delineating and categorizing bodies. In the modern Olympics, 'gender verification' tests occurred as early as the 1930s, prompted by assumptions that some women weren't *really* women. While the IOC removed mandatory 'gender verification' prior to the 2000 Summer Games, it remains an option for women, when challenged, presumably, for appearing too 'masculine'.[110]

While gender verification was not an aspect of athletics in classical antiquity, there was, nonetheless, interest in monitoring and controlling the bodies that were given access to sports. In fact, women, by virtue of being prohibited from the site of Olympia during the Games, were said to have prompted some of these bodily inspections. When Pausanias relates the punishment doled out to women who breach these restrictions (5.6.7), he tells the story of Kallipateira (or Pherenike): because her husband had died before her, she disguised herself as a trainer to accompany her son, Peisirodos, to the Olympics. When he won, she leapt over a fence and 'showed herself' as a woman. Because of her family's athletic reputation (her father, Diagoras of Rhodes, was one of the most famous of all Olympians), she was not punished, but from then on, Pausanias says, trainers had to enter the arena naked so that their gender could be verified (5.6.8).

If gender, however, was not regularly inspected at the ancient Games, other aspects of the body were still measured and evaluated. At the ancient Olympics there were two age categories for competitors: *Andres* (men) and *paides* (boys). Without birth certificates to certify ages, nor a straightforward and universally accepted age for when a boy became an adult, bodily inspection seems to have been used. Ancient sources rarely report the precise ages of athletes, so we are not certain what the age ranges were. When he tells the story of Damiskos the 12-year-old boy who won in running at Olympia, Pausanias remarks that it is 'one of the most extraordinary things I have ever heard' (6.2.10). Presumably, then, boys of that age were unlikely competitors and especially unlikely victors.

Boys were inspected somehow to judge their age: Pausanias tells us of a particular statue of Zeus – 'Zeus of the Oaths' – in the *bouleuterion* at Olympia where 'the entry examiners of the boys and the colts swear to make their judgement rightly and without bribes, and to keep secret all information about passes and failures' (5.24.9–10).[111] Young people *and* young horses were inspected to see if they fit appropriately into an age category. Presumably, since the competitors were naked, physical development and indications of pubescence played a major role. At other venues, though not at Olympia, the *ageneioi* 'beardless youth' category existed, which seems to indicate that a beard was one mark, at least, that a participant belonged in the older category.

Anxieties about 'fairness', at least in part, drove these policies, since adult men who managed to be categorized in the boys' category were imagined to have an advantage, whereas boys who were promoted too early to the men's category were disadvantaged. The latter, especially, recurs. Epharmostos, the subject of Pindar's Ninth *Olympian* ode, is said to have been unfairly excluded from the 'beardless youths' category at an athletic festival in the Athenian village of Marathon, but he still won at wrestling despite this disadvantage and is all the more praiseworthy as a result (9.90–1). Winning despite this disadvantage was a particular cause for boasting. Pherias, who was disallowed from the boys' category by the Eleians, went on to win in the men's category and seems to have recorded it on his victory statue (Pausanias, 6.14.1–2). Obsession over gender and age verification exemplifies the problem with the assumption that the body can reveal or prove what are, in fact, socially constructed categories.

Monitoring continues in sports today, though focused less on age (now easily demonstrated through records) and more on the category of sex. There is little consensus about what constitutes sexual difference or where (or if) the dividing line between sexes ought to be.[112] The IOC has removed its mandatory 'verification' tests for sex,[113] but they remain an option. And, in any case, the rigid sex segregation of sports reinforces a gender and sex binary at a time when scientific and social consensus is moving in a different direction.

Transgender athletes, for example, are excluded from these binary understandings of sex and gender, and even when included, such as in the 'Stockholm Consensus' of 2004 that permitted transgender athletes into the Olympics, the policies assume only two sexes into which any person can be neatly fitted.[114] We have no evidence – so far as I know – for transgender athletes in classical antiquity but given the broad participation in athletics, it is likely they competed at some point. Much of the discourse today focuses on transgender women (there is little 'concern' with transgender male athletes), and, like that of ancient age verification, is focused on 'fairness'.[115] As with bodily development by age, bodily development across the sexes is hardly standard, and athletic and physical abilities are determined by a host of characteristics beyond sex,[116] not to mention individual and national wealth and social status. Other organizations and individuals are pushing for far-reaching changes that would challenge the division of athletes based on sex[117] and destabilize the perceived importance of gender identity to athletic participation. At the very least, the improving science behind determining what constitutes sex and gender demonstrates the imprecision of the categorization of human beings into 'male' and 'female',[118] especially for the sake of athletic participation, and points to the socially constructed value of masculinity and femininity in athletics. But, here, it seems, we can discern one of the main characteristics of sport – ancient and modern – beyond the question of inclusion of transgender or cisgender women (though women are, it is worth repeating, the focus of most modern restrictions): its focus on the measurement and categorization of bodies.

There are many more stories that could be told – ancient and modern – of resistance to the prescriptions of authorities about *what* makes an Olympic or other athlete.[119] Nonetheless, these accounts demonstrate that the drive for modernity in the modern Games, perhaps unintentionally, excluded some of the ancient features of sport that would be more universal. There exists, *in some of the ancient evidence*, examples of a universal and open sports competition that is focused on human excellence, much as the IOC imagines its own contests today. That these critics who championed sports as a political, cross-class and open to all sexes were derided and resisted emphasizes that the *modernity* of Olympic sport is, for the IOC, a modernity that rests on its monopoly on antiquity.

Other Olympics

The IOC's most important self-conception is their apparent monopoly on antiquity itself. They are famously cautious and exclusive about the rights to their symbols and trademarks. A 1995 law in the UK, for example, prevents unauthorized use of the IOC's symbols, but also the word 'Olympic'.[120] But, the IOC's Olympic Games are *not* the only modern Olympics, and 'Olympic' can and has been applied to many manifestations of the ancient Games that predate those of the IOC. As the story of other Olympic revivals makes clear, the antiquity of the Games is at the core of *all* Olympic revivals.

When Coubertin announced his idea for the re-establishment of the Olympic Games in 1892, and when those Games took place in Athens in 1896, they were styled the *Les Jeux olympiques* on posters and promotional material. Coubertin and the IOC represented these Games as the rebirth of the ancient ones, and opened by a Christian monarch, George I, in contradiction to their supposed prohibition by an ancient Christian monarch, Theodosius I in 393 CE. Absent from this description, however, is that Olympic revivals had been pushed for and been staged in Greece –and that a previous Greek monarch had already proclaimed open a revival of the ancient Games.

The story of modern Olympic revival begins decades before the IOC's first Games and is connected to the formation of the modern Greek state. Antiquity and modernization, their conflict or harmonization, were fundamental to the national project of independence and development after the Greeks won their war of independence in 1829.[121] Athletics, not necessarily for their own sake but because of their antique allure, could be imagined as part of nation-building.[122] In 1833, Panagiotis Soutsos (1806–68), a poet, journalist and novelist published 'Ruins of Ancient Sparta', where the shade of the Spartan King Leonidas rebukes the modern Greek state:

> And let the only contests that you have be those national games, the Olympics, to which the olive branch once summoned the sons of Greece in ancient times.
>
> Greece your future is brilliant![123]

Here, the Olympic Games are tied to the fortunes of the new country. Soutsos had similarly imagined Plato, who would not, he thought, recognize Greece without the Games, in 'Dialogue of the Dead', also published in 1833: 'if this is Greece, where are your Olympic Games?'[124]

Soutsos not only imagined the Games as intrinsic to modern Greece in lyric reflections, but he pushed for political action to make this dream a reality. In the early days of the modern Greek state, as Demetrios Vikelas observed decades later, 'politics was largely conducted through poetry', and Soutsos was expert in both spheres.[125] He joined the Ministry of the Interior in 1834 and petitioned the King to make 25 March a national holiday, and he suggested it be celebrated with Olympic Games that would imitate those of antiquity.[126] While this initial petition was unsuccessful, the Olympic idea was spreading, and Soutsos continued to petition the King (1842, 1845, 1851): he wanted a revival of antiquity to coincide with the revival of the Greek nation, and one predicated on a revived physical fitness and athletic ethos.[127] And Soustos was not alone:

the inhabitants of Letrinoi, a small village near the ancient site of Olympia, suggested staging the Olympics every four years in the nearby town of Pyrgos.[128] Soustos and others linked revival of the Games to international prestige and, as Coubertin also would, modified them to fit modern conditions: athletic competitions would go hand in hand with exhibitions of industrial and academic achievements.[129]

As Soutsos tried in vain to attract attention to an Olympic revival in Greece, another important Olympic revival was already in full swing in England. Dr William Penny Brookes, a local doctor in Much Wenlock initiated the Much Wenlock Agricultural and Reading Society in 1840; by 1850, he added physical fitness and inaugurated what he called the 'Wenlock Olympian Class'. The purpose of this society was to contribute to moral and physical and intellectual development through the encouragement of exercise and competition.[130] In their first iteration, the Wenlock Olympian Games featured an eclectic mix of sports: cricket, football, quoits, hopping on one leg for 50 yards, high jump, long jump; and three footraces with age groups for adults, boys to fourteen and boys over fourteen.[131] While the Games were not those that we would necessarily qualify as 'Olympic' sports today, they featured a parade of athletes at their opening, and connected pageantry, moral development and athletic competition in many of the same ways as the IOC's Games.

Brookes' Games continued to be staged yearly, and they intersect with the second great nineteenth-century Olympic revival, which began in Athens in 1859. While Soutsos had continued to appeal to the King and public through newspaper articles, one of his articles was read by Evangelis Zappas, a veteran of the Greek War of Independence and a businessman who had made his fortune in what is now Romania.[132] Zappas wrote to King Otto offering to fund the entire Olympic revival and, when the foreign minister, who opposed athletics as an anachronism, tried to curtail Zappas' interest by wildly exaggerating the cost, he agreed to pay as much as 1.2 million drachmas (much of which was supposed to excavate and restore the Panathenaic stadium). These Games did take place in the end, not at the stadium but in Plateia Loudovikou (today, Koumoundourou) with a combination of agro-industrial contests and athletics (200 metres, 400 metres, discus, javelin and long jump).[133] While not a complete success, these Games held great importance within Greece and in the Greek diaspora, by allowing for Greeks still under Ottoman rule to come to Athens, mingle with their compatriots and see a physical manifestation of ethnic and cultural unity.[134]

Despite the cultural, linguistic and geographical distances between the events, Dr Brookes heard of the Zappas Olympics and sent a prize to be awarded to the winner of the footraces; he also sent a programme of his Games as advice for the Greeks on how to organize Olympic events.[135] Perhaps inspired by the Greek revival, Brookes expanded his own Olympian Games and the 1859 edition introduced new Hellenic-style athletics like javelin alongside a poetry contest for poems inspired by the Games;[136] athletes were crowned with laurel and the winner of the new pentathlon event received a medal inscribed with a quotation, in ancient Greek, from Pindar.[137] The Much Wenlock Games continued with a plan to expand across Shropshire, and Brookes kept trying to build connections with the Greek organizers. Meanwhile, other British groups formed, though ideologies began to diverge almost immediately. The Liverpool Olympic Movement was founded, growing out of cricket clubs and German gymnastics clubs. Unlike the Much Wenlock Games, the Liverpool movement restricted participation in its Olympics to 'gentlemen athletes'.[138] In 1862, this group held Olympic Games, including a full track and field event, with footraces, triple jump, high jump, pole vault and the discus.

These Games continued for a couple more years and for a short while Liverpool was the home of the largest athletic festival in Britain and the best sporting facilities in Europe. Brookes took note. He teamed up with the organizers to found the National Olympian Association (NOA), which was charged to organize general meetings, encourage and reward athletic skill.[139] Competition between the National Olympian Association and the Amateur Athletic Club (AAC) threatened the stability and expansion of these Games in Britain. The AAC, in particular, were ardent 'amateurists', who refused to share dressing rooms or playing fields with working class men.[140] While the NOA carried on with Games in 1866, 1867 and 1868, the movement petered out, perhaps because of the conflicts of amateur status. In any case, Brookes' movement continued to hold Much Wenlock Olympian Games, and, with the death of Zappas (in 1865), whose fortune was left to the Athens Olympic Committee, it seemed like a permanent Greek Olympic revival was imminent.

Zappas' will specified that the Panathenaic Stadium be excavated and restored and that an exhibition hall be constructed nearby (the latter, the Zappeion, would be finished by 1888 and used for fencing competitions in the 1896 IOC Games). With Zappas' money in hand, some restoration of the stadium took place (wooden seating for spectators) and an 1870 Olympic Games was held with athletics and agro-industrial contests once again. The competitions were popular (over 30,000 spectators watched the athletics on 15 November 1870), and egalitarian: athletes were subsidized and cash prizes were given.[141] In true ancient style, athletes arrived weeks before the Games for supervised training; they swore oaths not to cheat; and they were crowned by King George I with an olive wreath.[142] Athletes were judged by *Hellanodikai* ('judges of the Greeks'), as in antiquity, and they wore leotards designed to resemble Caucasian skin and thus some of the nude athletes of antiquity.[143] These Games took place under royal patronage, in an excavated and partially refurbished stadium, with a combination of antiquity and modernity, before an audience larger than any previous – 'the first sports meeting worth of the name in the history of competition in modern Greece'.[144] While the Games prompted new ideas about physical education and citizenry,[145] complaints began almost immediately under the auspices of 'amateurism' since working men had won at the Games.[146] The next iteration, Olympiad III in 1875, permitted entrants from the upper classes only. The 1875 Games were a disaster: fewer competitors competed; fewer people watched.[147] The next Olympiad was immensely delayed while the committee misspent Zappas' money. By October 1888 when Olympiad IV was finally held, the athletic competitions were delayed, before being held in the following April.[148]

During these years of intermittent Greek revival, Brookes continued to offer the Wenlock Games. While the NOA had faltered, Brookes held his Games and worked for the introduction of physical education in schools. To emphasize this aspect of his society, he assembled prominent politicians and invited them to his Games and to membership in the Olympic Society. Most notably, he enrolled Thomas Hughes, the author of the famous *Tom Brown's Schooldays*.[149] With Hughes and other luminaries, he held the National Olympian Games in Wenlock in 1874. National competitions weren't enough for Brookes, who came up with the idea of an international Olympics and began to correspond with the Greek ambassador to England, John Gennadeius.[150] By the early 1880s, he was enthralled by the idea of an 'International Olympic Festival at Athens'.[151] Without a doubt, Brookes envisioned an Olympics much like that of the IOC, with the draw of antiquity and a 'classic land' combined with the thrill of international competition.

Despite Brookes' optimism, he was faced with roadblock after roadblock. The National Olympian Association faltered when faced, again, with derision from the amateurism movement of the now-reorganized Amateur Athletic Association.[152] They claimed suzerainty over British athletic events and, since they did not approve of the egalitarian National Olympian Games, they threatened that any athlete who participated in them would be barred from their events; attendance at Games then plummeted and the last staging in 1883 was a dismal failure. In Greece, politics and politicians changed as well, and Brookes found few sympathetic ears for his Olympic revival.[153]

Brookes, while ignored despite his constant letter-writing, continued to hold his Games and they attracted the attention of the young Pierre de Coubertin, who travelled to Much Wenlock in 1890. Coubertin had by this time already become interested in the cause of educational and sports reform, though Olympic revival had never occurred to him. When Coubertin and Brookes corresponded in 1890 prior to his visit, the words Olympic and Olympics never occur, and Coubertin's focus is on Brookes' work to promote physical education.

Coubertin's visit was, despite later obfuscation, crucial. Brookes staged a special edition of the Games for him and arranged a celebratory revel to greet him: there was a procession through town with banners welcoming Coubertin. The athletic events were held and Coubertin was made an honorary member of the Society. Brookes must have told Coubertin the history of his and the National Olympic movement, the Greek attempts and his own invitations to create an international festival. Coubertin observed his correspondence on Olympic matters as 'voluminous'. But, still, he was unimpressed by anything other than physical education reform. When he wrote about the Much Wenlock Games on his return, he remarked that the Olympic element was unnecessary, since their memory and the past were not necessary for the reform of education.[154] To say the least, a mere two years later, his opinion had completely changed, and Coubertin would invoke the past – Greece and Olympics in particular – as the salvation of physical education and the modern world more generally.

The role of Brookes, the Wenlock Games, the National Olympian Games and the Zappas Games, has, however, been effaced and obscured by the work of the IOC. Whereas Pausanias' Iphtios was thought to have remembered and re-established the older traditions, Coubertin and the IOC actively seemed to work to forget: Coubertin vociferously rebuked those who would see him as a 'wretched plagiarist of Evangelis Zappas',[155] and after his momentous announcement on 25 November 1892, he seems not to have even informed Brookes, whom he called his 'oldest friend'.[156] Coubertin borrowed the Romanticism and nostalgia of the Much Wenlock Games and Zappas Olympiads, though he attached the ideology of amateurism to them. Lost, in this way, and not recovered for decades, were the other Olympics, especially those tied to the true homeland of the Olympic Games, or those with strikingly different ideologies than those of the IOC.

*   *   *

When Michael Phelps won his thirteenth gold medal at the 2016 Summer Games, he supposedly prompted a connection between ancient and modern Games by 'breaking' a 2,168-year-old record, held by Leonidas of Rhodes, of most Olympic victories.[157] Despite the differences between ancient and modern athletes, Phelps' victories were taken to be in some kind of trans-historical competition with 'Olympic' athletes of all time. The idea that he could 'beat' Leonidas relies on the belief that the modern Olympics are a successor to those of antiquity; and, that sports accomplishments, despite differences, have an essential quality that makes comparison possible. Like the efforts of Philostratus to connect ancient and contemporary sports through the feats of athletes, the rhetoric surrounding Phelps' victory implies some degree of similarity between ancient and modern.

This chapter has endeavoured to undermine the very ideology underlying these comparisons, or at least to situate these arguments within the discourse of 'Olympic sport' in antiquity and today. Who is to say whether there *is* an essential 'Olympic' quality, or that the connection between ancient and modern is actually, rather than only ideally, meaningful? Or, more pointedly, that the IOC's Olympics are *the* successor Olympics beyond all others? Rather than actual connections, such Olympic continuities are, at best, nostalgic desires for a past that may never have existed – like the legendary Games of Pindar and Pausanias – that are driven by more present concerns with ideology, authority and control.

4

Beauty, Strength and Physical Culture

The reception and influence of ancient sport makes it seem as though competitive athletics and training were universally accepted in antiquity; far from it. While we have fragments of early critics of sports who focus on the unjust, in their opinion, prizes and status accorded to athletic victors (e.g. Xenophanes, *Iambi et Elegi Graeci* 2; Euripides, fr. 282 *Tragicorum Graecorum Fragmenta*), comprehensive critique comes to the fore in the discourse of training and medicine, that is, in a conflict over knowledge of the human body and its physical development and health.

As early as the Hippocratic corpus, a collection of mostly medical texts from the fifth- and fourth centuries BCE, athletes and especially athletic diets are criticized for overindulgence (Hippocrates, *Regimen in Health* 7).[1] A later, likely third century BCE text, a sort of summary of ancient medical opinion on the too-specialized bodies of ancient athletes, calls the 'condition of the athlete' 'not natural' (Hippocrates, *Nutriment* 34). Even at the highpoint of athletics in the second century CE, a figure like the medical writer and physician Galen castigated athletics and athletes, suggesting that the latter were unfit for any kind of intellectual work.[2] While athletics and physical health are often linked in contemporary medical discourse, in antiquity, too much physical development or too much emphasis on specific areas of the body could be considered unhealthy.[3]

This chapter considers the reception and adaptation of ancient Greek and Roman sport in the 'physical culture', fitness and health movements of the nineteenth and twentieth centuries, and picks up on questions surrounding physical development, health and the body as an indicator of moral and physical well-being. Reform and revival are constant themes throughout modern physical culture movements, which often cast themselves as responses to decline, or whose practitioners often imagine themselves as revisionists who turn back to the past to correct the evils of the present.

Before turning to modern physical culture and its indebtedness to classical antiquity, this chapter situates physical culture in the reality of ancient Greek body culture, especially how the body was read as indicative of physical and moral health. This chapter surveys concepts of the body, especially the male, and discusses how nudity and masculinity were intertwined in ancient Greek presentation and representation of nude men. From there, via the ancient Greek competitions of the *euandria* and *euexia*, the chapter traces the development of modern 'physical culture' regimes in nineteenth-century Europe before turning to Eugen Sandow and Bernarr Macfadden, who, more than any other figures in the Anglophone world, are responsible for the particular conceiving of health and physical fitness along what purport to be a rebirth of ancient Greek models.

Ancient Greek masculinity, nudity and beauty

Ancient Greek body culture was particularly male, and, given that nudity was part of athletics whether in the gymnasium or in competition, tied to eroticism as well. Particular types of bodies were thought to have meaning beyond the surface, and to express moral and physical attributes.

The relationship between the physical body and qualities like morality, health and virtue was present in ancient Greek culture from a very early point. Already, in Homer's *Iliad*, beautiful Greek and Trojan soldiers abound, with their beauty supposedly reflecting inner excellence. Beauty on the beaches at Troy could even be judged. Nireus, for example, is called the second most beautiful of all men at Troy, though he is also derided as 'feeble' (2.673–674); Ajax is given the same praise later in the poem (17.280). But appearance comes up negatively too: Thersites, a grumbling and complaining soldier who challenges Agamemnon is called 'the ugliest man to come to Troy' (2.211–264). Unlike the beautiful heroes, his faults are enumerated: he is disabled, hunchbacked, with a misshapen and balding head. As his appearance is derided by the narrator, so is his rhetorical ability (2.213). However, despite his degraded appearance and awful intellect, Thersites' speech comes close to that of the best speaker in the *Iliad*, Achilles, when he, too, attacked Agamemnon in the opening of the poem. So, while Thersites is mocked and then beaten for his insolence, nonetheless, beauty may not be a complete guide to intellectual, rhetorical, or moral qualities. This theme recurs in the *Odyssey*, especially in two instances when Odysseus is weary and mistaken for a lower-class man who doesn't know athletics (8.158–164), and when he takes on the guise of a beggar and thwarts any correlation between external beauty and internal value (18.1–107).

Perhaps most intriguing for any discussion that centres on actual and sculptural bodies and their influence and reception are two short lyric poems composed and performed in the centuries after Homer's epics. In a short and fragmentary poem, Simonides (*c.* 556–468 BCE) suggests the metaphor of the well-proportioned statue for the good man: 'it is difficult for a man to be truly good, four-sided and well made without flaw in hands and feet and mind' (542 *Poetae Melici Graeci*). The fragment, which is quoted in Plato's *Protagoras*, is not complete; the poem continues later in the dialogue but does not pick up from these lines. But, it seems that Simonides intends to evoke a statue, and in particular the rigid *kouros* statue of the archaic period. The *kouros*, a stylized and standing young male, nude except for occasional ornamental elements, was a dominant type of sculpture in the Archaic period. These statues were physical embodiments of the elite of archaic Greece, and here, Simonides suggests a correspondence of man and sculpture.

Simonides is not alone in using sculpture to delineate the possibilities of the human form and morality. An earlier poet, Archilochus (early seventh BCE), lauds a general in one poem: 'I have no liking for a general who is tall, walks with a swaggering gait, takes pride in his curls, and is partly shaven. Let mine be one who is short, has a bent look about the shins, stands firmly on his feet and is full of courage' (*Iambi et Elegi Graeci* 114). To some degree, Archilochus' preferred general approaches the description of Thersites (both are described as disabled in some way via the same vocabulary), and he reproaches the beautiful soldiers of Homer's *Iliad* and the well-coiffed *kouros* statues. Here, again, there is a discrepancy between appearance and reality, both in actual people and, presumably, in their sculptural counterparts. Beauty is not the only determinant of martial ability in Archilochus' view. That the meaning of the 'fit' or 'beautiful' body was debated and discussed in classical antiquity is important to remember when we turn to modern adaptations of the physical form and its supposedly moral content. Even in athletic praise poetry, such as that of Pindar, discrepancies between physical ability and physical beauty could be highlighted, for instance in the 'paltry' pankration victor Melissos (*Isthmian* 4.50). These concepts, thus, were neither simple nor obvious.

From the earliest periods, the nude male is a mainstay of ancient Greek art, and its representation is one of the most important influences of classical antiquity. Statuary was not the only place, however, that bodies could act as ciphers, both for individual and collective understandings of the importance of physicality to social and political existence. While athletics proper, and especially the civic celebration of athletic victors emphasizes their social and political importance, lesser-known competitions for beauty and physicality in ancient Greece are also components of ancient Greek body culture.

Among other nebulous competitions, the *euandria* and *euexia*, while unclear in many details, suggest something of the public and civic interest in beautiful bodies – and in judging them. A *euandria* was part of the Greater Panathenaia, a civic and athletic festival that took place at Athens every four years.[4] While many of the festival's competitions were open to all Greeks, certain contests, like the *euandria* and *euexia*, were only open to Athenian citizens and had special civic significance. The word *euandria* means something like a 'virility' or 'manliness' and is found in many instances as an abstract noun; it can even be a name. Two references tell us there were prizes for the victors in the *euandria*, as in any contest in Greek antiquity.[5] While the details are scarce, the competition *seems* to have been team-based, though individuals could also boast of having 'won' the *euandria* (Pseudo-Andocides, 4.42). As to what exactly was judged, regardless of all of the obscurity, it is clear that *beauty* was the key factor: one ancient writer tells us that in the *euandria*, 'they judge the most beautiful' (Athenaeus, 13.565). The *euandria* points to a belief in a set of criteria for beauty that may be observed, measured and judged; and, a belief that beauty might have a civic utility.

A second contest, the *euexia*, seems to refer to a slightly different set of criteria, although still based around general good health and its representation in physical development. *Euexia* derives from two words that combine to mean something like 'possessing wellness' or 'goodness'. The contest is attested in many cities across the ancient Greek world, though the details are even more obscure than those of the *euandria*. One source distinguishes between *euexia* and a 'beautiful body', and this distinction has been taken to indicate that unlike the *euandria*, beauty was not the only criterion (Lucian, *Anacharsis* 12.3). In his dialogue on athletics, Lucian defines *euexia* (the concept not the contest) as incorporating more than just strength or general good looks, but, especially by describing participants as '*symmetron* (proportional) in their lines' (25), something approaching the modern bodybuilding contest, where the visual representation is about definition and tone. *Symmetron* in ancient Greek is a key phrase, since the word carries figurative 'moderate', 'modest' and literal 'equal' meaning.

Symmetron connects us back to the world of ancient Greek art, though several generations after the *kouros* statues. The fifth-century BCE sculptor Polyclitus, the 'inventor' of the contrapposto stance and the style that came to be regarded as 'classical', explained his sculptural technique in a lost work (called the *Canon*) as embodying mathematical ratios that he called *symmetria*; or, as one commentator in antiquity described it, 'everything in proportion to everything' (Galen, *On the Doctrines of Hippocrates and Plato* 5.448).[6] *Symmetria* is found across ancient discussions of art: painters like Asklepiodoros were supposed to have written on the topic,[7] while Parrhasios was credited with introducing *symmetria* into painting.[8] Even temples are conceived with proportionality in mind: ancient writers on architecture as well as modern scholars of ancient Greek buildings have figured out the mathematical proportions behind some sacred buildings.[9]

These theoretical aspects of ancient art and, especially, their materialization in the 'male nude', pervade modern physical culture.[10] Ancient statues, divorced from the rich discourse of antiquity that questioned how to represent the body and how (or if) to find meaning in athletic bodies, have become simple models in their reception. Comparison with reality, one modern preoccupation with statuary, was not the only understanding of these sculpted bodies in antiquity. Ancient statues were not based on models, and, even in antiquity, their unreality was noticed: the Roman writer Quintilian observed that Polyclitus produced human forms that were beyond the real (12.10.8). As Michael Squire puts it, the legacy of Polyclitus is 'the *idea* of the ideal',[11] an influential concept from ancient art. The musculature of ancient statues, even naturalistic ones, is often impossible: while the iliac crest (the sides of the greater pelvis) may reach some definition with targeted exercise, the deep delineations of many statues is beyond the realm of possibility. This unreality is even implicitly acknowledged in the popular name of the iliac crest, 'Apollo's belt', since only a god – or more properly a sculpted representation of a godlike body – could hope to attain it.[12]

But, beyond the unreality of musculature, the very form of naturalistic sculpture itself needs to be questioned. While the influence of ancient Greek and Roman statuary on Western art has been such as to make naturalistic art unquestioned, the naturalization of 'realistic' as an 'objective' for art is not so simple.[13] The trajectory of ancient art from schematized and symbolic to naturalistic (and the imagined critical break between the two) is a story invented by early modern art historians in order to explain what they perceived as their own break from medieval art and their concurrent 're-discovery' of naturalism.[14] The 'assimilation' of ancient art to Renaissance art has been tightly bound up with the discipline of art history and the history of art.[15] When these narratives are imported into physical culture as explanatory tools of the human body itself, they need to be questioned carefully.

Naturalistic sculpture, of course, is imagined as *not* so naturalistic in one area: the stark white marble finish of sculpted classical bodies. The physical material of some sculpture, that is marble, and its preservation or lack thereof has been critical to how the ideal body has been imagined. While ancient Greek and Roman marble was coloured, to various degrees, with bright paints and decorative items, the decay of these paints combined with the 'cleaning' of excavated statues has made white marble *the* form of sculpture. In art history, too, colour has played a role in how beauty and sculpture are connected. Johann Joachim Winckelmann (1717–68) perceived the gleaming, stark white marble forms of (mostly) men as the physical manifestation of an ideal beauty,[16] though he also asserted that colour did not necessarily take away from beauty but rather enhanced it. He argues in the *History of the Art of Antiquity* that race – especially as formed by a 'moderate' environment – played a role in the ancient Greek appreciation of beauty[17] and that there is an ideal that corresponds to 'our own and the Greek concepts of beauty'.[18] Race plays a role for this extremely influential historian, not only inasmuch as the whiteness of marble enhances beauty, but also in the way that the environment and physical features of the ancient Greeks are taken as an ideal from which others – especially non-Caucasians – deviate. As we will see, the perceived normative whiteness of statues and their connection to a perceived racial superiority of ancient Greek and Roman civilization was reinforced by the statuesque displays of physical culture performers and the racial homogeneity of the performers and readers featured in popular magazines.

The physical culture revival

The question of 'revival' is central to how we conceive of the physical culture and sports cultures that rose to prominence in the late nineteenth century. Sports and physical fitness did not end with the end of the Roman Empire, and the medieval period in Europe had a diverse sports culture.[19] Despite these important historiographical revisions, it remains the case that for those innovators and reformers of the nineteenth century, revival was the mode in which they perceived they operated, or at least how they represented new physical culture and sporting regimes. The medieval period in particular became synonymous with a decline in the body, a decline further exacerbated by the industrialization and urbanization of the late eighteenth and nineteenth centuries. This rhetoric of decline and a return to the past – especially the ancient Greek and Roman past – was key to many of the nineteenth-century innovators of physical culture.

Nonetheless, 'renaissance' in the late nineteenth-century-movements is undermined by other physical culture movements. In both Germany and Britain, for example, physical culture regimes emerged that did *not* adapt specifically ancient attitudes towards health, nor did they imagine themselves as 'rediscovering' physical culture from antiquity. German gymnastics tied itself to, at first, revolutionary nationalist movements before becoming institutionalized in German education by the end of the nineteenth century.[20] 'Muscular Christianity', which developed in Britain around the same time as gymnastics began in Germany, focused on Charles Kingsley's call for a spiritual and physical development that would make for strong, healthy, virile Christian men.[21] This individual development was then connected to a vision of a patriarchal and imperial British Empire, served by stout and strong men, whose physical development was an indicator of their spiritual enlightenment.

While German gymnastics and 'Muscular Christianity' both understood physical activity as being able to contribute to individual development and character as well as national development and character – a focus that would have been understood by ancient Greek philosophers and athletes – neither explicitly modeled physical culture on antiquity. Without a doubt, the growing German interest in ancient Greece as a spiritual antecedent, especially after the formation of the German Empire in 1871, coloured gymnastics; and 'Muscular

Christianity"s reception would be framed by the British Imperial mission that understood itself as something of a latter-day Rome. Regardless, it was innovators from outside of the elite classes who produced the type of physical culture that has continued to influence the modern physical fitness, health and well-being industry, and one which was explicitly based around a return to antiquity.

Two larger-than-life figures helped to bring about the popularization of the most influential 'revivals' of physical fitness and health at the beginning of the twentieth century: Prussian-born strongman Eugen Sandow (1867–1925) and American entrepreneur-cum-fitness guru Bernarr Macfadden (1868–1955). While Sandow's poses, competitions and magazine started the movement – 'physical culture' – and firmly connected it with antiquity, Macfadden's extraordinarily popular magazine and exuberant ambition brought physical culture to the farthest reaches of the United States.[22]

Unlike the revivals of physical fitness and health in Britain and Germany in the early nineteenth century, from its beginning physical culture practitioners and popularizers connected it explicitly with antiquity. More to the point, physical cultural enthusiasts and theorists understood their movement in terms that were borrowed from the art historical tradition, though mapped onto human bodies instead of their artistic representation: mankind had declined, physically, after antiquity (or in some cases, in the Roman Imperial period); physical fitness and the body were supposedly rejected in the medieval period because of Christian focus on the soul; degeneration and decline continued into the immediate present because of industrialization, urbanization and the supposed ills that came along with them; the present period saw a return to antiquity inasmuch as the body was once again going to be central to the creation of a harmonious society. In the words of one early writer in *Physical Culture*: 'Times there have been when the physical ideals of man have degenerated, but ours is the era of the Physical Renaissance!'[23] A sketch in an early issue of *Physical Culture* makes clear the degeneration of today and the strange past-as-future that physical culture will create: a future race of Graeco-Roman type people wanders through a museum 'two thousand years hence' and sees thin and deformed statues representing 'Babus americanus', 'Manus americanus' and 'Girlus americanus' (see Figure 4.1).[24]

Physical culture was imagined to work in the same mode as Renaissance art: it found its inspiration and legitimacy in the revival of an imagined version of the past.

Decline, however, was not only inherited from the art historical tradition. Degeneration, for most contemporary critics in the 1890s, had been defined by Max Nordau's 1895 *Degeneration*. Some of this rhetoric was undoubtedly correct: The Industrial Revolution's transformation of European and American lives had contributed to a massive decline in health; workers' bodies were in terrible shape, their diets substandard, living conditions appalling and opportunities for leisure and recreation essentially non-existent.[25] Nordau connected urban growth, increased tobacco consumption and increased use of alcohol with degeneration: he specifically considered the exponential increase in urban population in the nineteenth century a causal factor in the growth of degeneration as a physiological disorder.[26] These concerns should be contextualized with the changes happening in nineteenth-century Europe where concerns about degeneration reflected, to some degree, elite reactions to great changes in the landscape, economy and politics.[27] Context matters, but physical fitness movements frequently position themselves against decline: the writings of Philostratus in the second century CE imagine his contemporaries as somehow weaker than the Greeks of the past (see the introduction to Chapter 3). In the 1950s, when a national physical fitness movement was suggested, observers claimed that the 'push-button gadget' culture of suburban living had made Americans, at least, physically worse than they were fifty years ago[28] – the same time period in which Sandow and Macfadden observed their contemporaries as degraded and weak.

While Sandow and Macfadden play a large role in my study, the former because he was in the vanguard of the new physical culture, the latter because of his longevity and proclivity, physical culture regimes of this style and influenced by the same worry about decay and the same

Figure 4.1 *Physical Culture*, August 1904. Image courtesy of the H.J. Lutcher Stark Center for Physical Culture and Sports at the University of Texas at Austin.

lackluster comparison of modernity with antiquity existed in other places. In France, for example, the discourse of decline was linked to France's defeat in the Franco-Prussian War in 1871, the same defeat that prompted Pierre de Coubertin's interest in physical education.[29] One magazine, *La Culture physique*, used photography and ancient sculpture to juxtapose ancient and modern men, and featured an editor, Edmond Desbonnet, like Sandow and Macfadden, who posed as a 'living statue'.[30] French photographs of classical and neoclassical statues in the Second Empire established the aesthetic that would be used, to great acclaim and influence, by Sandow and others: black background, exaggerated light and shade contrast to highlight musculature, camera positioned low to make the figure appear towering.[31] When we turn to Eugen Sandow and Bernarr Macfadden, they should be placed in a continuum of physical culture developers and innovators across Europe and North America, and in a discourse on art and the body – mediated through photography.

Eugen Sandow and Bernarr Macfadden

Sandow's and Macfadden's lives intersected at the World's Columbian Exposition of 1893 in Chicago. On 1 August, Florenz Ziegfeld Jr.'s *Trocadero* opened the most famous show in the club's history when Sandow, lit in front of a black velvet screen, posed in a variety of postures as a classical statue.[32] In the audience of one of these performances, 24-year-old Macfadden was entranced by Sandow – not only by his perfect physique, but by the mass market potential of the male body. From here, Sandow would capitalize on his burgeoning fame to launch an exercise, fitness and publishing empire, while Macfadden would toil to bring to birth his magazine and publishing business. For both, classical antiquity was part of their stylized biography and marketing.

Sandow was born on 2 April 1867 in Königsberg to a prosperous merchant (or greengrocer depending on the story) father and an unknown mother. He later related a childhood of physical decline and claimed not to have known 'what strength was' until he was ten years old.[33] This narrative, however, contradicts earlier stories of his youth as a healthy and happy child. As he became famous and authored his own biography, stories changed to fit his career and self-image. Sandow explained his turn to physical culture through an encounter with ancient art. As he later told it, he and his father went to Italy in 1877 and by means of an 'introduction to Greek and Roman statues' he was 'inspired . . . to strive beyond the weakness of his sickly youth'.[34] The trip is, to say the last, extremely convenient. Other points in his life narrative (e.g. an abbreviated education as a physician; a desire to run off and visit circuses and wrestling arenas) remain a mystery, and in any case by the time he was famous enough for his biography to be of consequence, his parents were dead and he was free to invent or embellish as he wished.[35]

The most consequential person in Sandow's transformation into a bodybuilding innovator and icon was Ludwig Durlacher, known as Professor Louis Attila, whom Sandow met in 1887.[36] With Attila's help, Sandow transformed his physique from the lean figure of an acrobat to the more physically developed figure that would cause a sensation.[37] Physical development was not the only key to Sandow's success, and previous strongmen had not attained his level of fame.[38] He was introduced to modeling and posed for sculptors and painters in the late 1880s.[39] His body became famous through the proliferation of these images, especially those set in legendary contexts: the Lapith in Gustave Crauck's sculpture *Le Combat du centaure* was based on him; he also modeled for a study of a gladiator in leopard skin by E. Aubrey Hunt.[40]

Sandow's pose as a gladiator is consequential, since for Sandow – and for Macfadden later – Roman models had the potential to act as physical culture paradigms. Of course, the gladiator, whose partially nude, physically alluring body had been an object of sexual desire in ancient Rome, was an obvious choice. In the portrait, Sandow stands as 'the character of a gladiator in the Coliseum [*sic*] at Rome', as he put it in a later book.[41] Gladiator here, however, simply seems to mean a partially clothed man in what appears to be a sand-filled arena: Sandow's leopard-skin costume and lack of weapons approximates no gladiatorial type from Roman antiquity. Rather, this portrait offers a reductive view of gladiators, who have become merely symbols of sex and strength.

Sandow's body existed in a physical form that could perform great feats of strength, but also as an art object that could be consumed by an interested public. The partial nudity of these photographs contributed to interest among the collecting public, whether male or female. In the 1890s, pornographic and athletic nudes were differentiated by the celebrity of the model, not by pose, posture or clothing.[42] British critics like Edmund Gosse[43] and John Addington Symonds eagerly pursued photographs of Sandow.[44] Strongman photographs, inasmuch as they offered a legitimate means for the circulation of images of barely clothed men, obtained at least part of their popularity through homoerotic desire and homosexual collectors.[45] Similar overlaps between physical fitness and gay magazines recur in the next fitness 'boom' of the 1950s: so-called 'beefcake' magazines and bodybuilding magazines often featured the same models.[46] The anxiety over male nudity and homoeroticism, a key distinction between ancient and modern physical cultures, serves to make displays of the male body both the epitome of a heterosexual masculinity and a suspicious act of potentially subservient and deviant sexual desire.

From an early point, Sandow's portraits depict him as a statue of the type seen in art galleries and museums, with a fig leaf for modesty and an inscribed podium to identify him (see Figure 4.2).[47] By 1893, when Ziegfeld Jr. was looking for acts for the *Trocadero*, Sandow was performing a small part – replacing an actor as a would-be statue – in the musical farce *Adonis* in New York City: reviewers of the play lavished praise on his body which had the 'beauty of a work of art' and was like 'the statue of Achilles, a Discobolus, or the Fighting Gladiator'.[48] Sandow's poses came full circle, with the man himself compared with the bodies of mythical figures – or statues of them – that inspired the earlier portraits and sculptures.

His time as a feature performer was key in transforming Sandow from the world's strongest man to the 'best-developed' man.[49] Sandow's

Figure 4.2 Eugen Sandow as the 'Dying Gaul' (Benjamin Falk, 1894). GL Archive, Alamy Stock Photo.

tableaux performances, before black curtains with his body caked with white powder, were one of many risqué displays of male and female bodies that imitated ancient Greek and Roman mythology. Sex and strength were combined in these performances, as Sandow was dressed in nothing more than silk briefs. One doctor in the audience declared him an 'Apollo, Hercules, and the ideal athlete.'[50] With the combination of his image in portrait, sculpture and photograph and in dramatic and physical development performances, Sandow was, as Kenneth Dutton puts it, 'one of the best known men in the world. Perhaps just as significantly, he was the possessor of the world's best known body'.[51] He had truly worldwide fame, and his name was a byword for strength.[52]

By 1897, Sandow began to take further control of his image and its possibilities by founding the Institute of Physical Culture in London,[53] and, in 1898, a magazine devoted to strength, health and development, *Physical Culture* (soon to be named *Sandow's Magazine of Physical Culture*).[54] Sandow had already ventured into publishing with 1894's *Sandow's System of Physical Training* (edited by G. M. Adam) and the 1897 *Strength and How to Obtain It*; the former a large-format book of exercises and Sandow images, the latter a more user-friendly and systematic body-building manual. The magazine, however, was a much bolder venture, since it intended a monthly schedule that would keep Sandow in the public eye, but that would also necessitate a staff, writers, etc.[55] It included a range of articles of varying quality and themes. But, from the start, it promoted bodybuilding competitions that would set the stage for ordinary people to participate in the physical culture movement.[56]

Sandow's success did not continue unabated. By 1905, attendance at his Institute was falling, and his magazine, though moving from strictly bodybuilding to more general health, ended its run in 1907. He continued to train individuals and publish through the 1910s, and new editions of *Strength and How to Obtain It* were issued until his untimely death, perhaps from a brain aneurysm, in 1925.[57] While the years after 1910 were difficult for Sandow, the decline of his businesses do not reflect a loss of public interest in physical culture more generally, nor its periodical form, if the fortunes of Bernarr Macfadden and *Physical Culture* are considered.

Macfadden was born as Bernard Adolphus McFadden in Missouri in 1868. After a difficult childhood, a short time at boarding school and a brief stint working in a Chicago hotel, he moved in with relatives who owned a small farm. Like Sandow, Macfadden's take on his biography prioritized classical sculpture and a perceived decline from antiquity. He said that when he saw classical statues in Chicago, he conceived of an ancient ideal from which contemporary Americans were degraded.[58] Undoubtedly more important, although he downplayed the encounter since they were publishing competitors, was Sandow's 'classical pose' performance. By 1898, he was in Britain, touring the country with a combination of fitness equipment demonstrations, physical development performances and lectures. While in Britain, Macfadden put together a pamphlet of his writings on physical fitness to distribute at lectures. When he returned to the United States, he rented office space in Manhattan and began the magazine that would be his life's work, *Physical Culture*.[59]

The classical world, or at least the recovered artwork of antiquity and more recent Neoclassical sculpture and painting, was central to *Physical Culture* from the start, as the first cover from 1899 – Bernarr Macfadden posing as Antonio Canova's *Damosseno* (*c.* 1800) – makes clear. But, from the outset, *Physical Culture*'s engagement with classical antiquity was not only focused on the male body or on bodybuilding and physical development. Classical art was, for example, used in the magazine's early and persistent campaign against the corset and prudishness. To Macfadden the corset twisted a woman's 'natural form',[60] while prudery was unnatural[61] and the inattention to sex and sexually transmitted diseases that it entailed was dangerous.[62] Macfadden's desire to show nude and semi-nude physical culturists and their classical inspirations even resulted in litigation against the magazine.[63]

In the March 1910 issue of *Physical Culture*, Sidney Cummings reported on the sensational appearance of Raymond Duncan, his wife Penelope and their son Menalkas on the streets of New York.[64] Raymond, the older brother of modern dance icon Isadora Duncan, had met Penelope, daughter of a modern Greek poet, while the family worked on building a 'temple' to dance in Athens.[65] On his arrival in Greece at thirty years of age, Raymond Duncan adopted sandals and a hand-woven tunic in what he regarded as the ancient Greek style; he would wear this dress continuously until his death in 1966.[66]

Duncan's appearance had caused a stir in New York, Cummings reports, but the garb of the child Menalkas, apparently covered only with loosely flowing garments in the December weather of the city, prompted a local Child Protection Society to argue that Duncan was mistreating his son.[67] While the dispute was soon resolved, the appearance of a report of it in *Physical Culture* is telling: the author contrasts prudish American custom to the apparently gentle reception of the Duncans in France, Britain and Germany.[68] For the author – and for Macfadden who wrote the editorial introduction – the Duncan case was exemplary of an alternative mode of 'natural' dress inspired by the ancients and a case-in-point for the magazine's hard-hitting advocacy.

The Grecian Costume in America

SOME DETAILS OF THE SENSATION CREATED BY THE DUNCAN FAMILY
IN VARIOUS EASTERN CITIES WHILE CLOTHED IN GRECIAN GARB

By Sidney Cummings

We have here an example of the pitiful ignorance of a few men who are invested with authority in America's greatest city. If parents do not choose to adopt conventional methods of caring for their children, there are so-called societies to take them off to jail. The experience of the Duncan family in New York City, where modern enlightenment in its highest degree is supposed to be in evidence, illustrates the sheeplike trend of modern civilization.—Bernarr Macfadden.

MANY readers of PHYSICAL CULTURE have perhaps noticed recent newspaper reports concerning the interference of the police of New York City with the personal liberty of Raymond Duncan, a physical culturist, and lecturer on ancient Greek music and dancing, and rhythmic exercise.

Though a Californian by birth, Mr. Duncan has lived abroad for about twelve years, spending most of this time in Greece. As a convert to the beauty of the ancient Greek art and customs, he is now on a lecturing tour around the world; planting the germ of his ideas in schools, clubs and the public mind generally.

Mr. Duncan expects to spend several months in America, after which he will sail to the Orient. He is lecturing at prominent universities, such as Columbia and Harvard, and before various clubs of artists and musicians. Mrs. Duncan is a singer and assists her hus-

band in his work. She is a native Greek. The Duncans both preach and practice simple living, and insist that those who do not hamper the body and mind with the chains of modern superstitions and conventions will develop normal physical and mental lives. They maintain that with proper balance of the mental and physical, work becomes as natural and easy as play, and no one needs any coercion in order to turn out such labor as is required for human livelihood.

Perhaps the most interesting personality in the Duncan family is Menalkas, the four-year-old son, who has never known the stunting restrictions of modern customs. Menalkas is as rosy and healthful a child as one could wish to see, and it was his midwinter appearance upon the streets of New York, dressed in Greek garb and without shoes and stockings that aroused the ire of the New York police and brought Mr. Duncan and

Raymond Duncan, garbed in the picturesque and common-sense costume which he wears even in the most inclement weather.

287

Figure 4.3 *Physical Culture*, March 1910. Image courtesy of the H.J. Lutcher Stark Center for Physical Culture and Sports at the University of Texas at Austin.

The magazine used history didactically, in an attempt to forestall inevitable decline, but also prescriptively, as a model to emulate. Greece and Rome did double duty as examples of magnificence and warnings against indulgence. For example, W. Crombie uses the cliché of indolence and luxurious living in ancient Rome to explain its fall from power, never mind historical accuracy.[69] In 'Civilization – Physical Culture', George Ruskin Phoebus similarly sketches a model of progress and decline onto which he can supposedly map ancient Greek history: youth, maturity, decay, destruction.[70]

One article by H. E. Jones entitled 'What Destroyed Rome' is prefaced with an introduction by Macfadden in which he declares that 'there is no more impressive object lesson on the relation that exists between the principles of physical culture and national greatness than furnished by the decline and fall of the Roman Empire'.[71] Beyond sport, the author brings in other tropes of *Physical Culture*: perceived Roman simplicity in food is contrasted with the 'indigestible atrocities' they inherit from the conquered ancient Greeks,[72] a supposed parallel to the magazine's belief in adulterated food and excessive consumption in contemporary society. In this article, Jones implicitly parrots the complaints of Roman elites from the early Empire, who similarly saw decline in the offing as Rome conquered the Greek world.

Across the magazine's first fifteen years, non-fiction from the world of ancient athletes and ancient Greek myth were used to illustrate the moral value of physical fitness, often with ancient personalities recast as contemporary physical culture practitioners. Alexander Marshall's 'Athletes in Story and History' is perhaps the most remarkable example. The nine-page article is illustrated throughout with images of classical or neoclassical statues. Heracles is portrayed as the prototypical physical culture adherent,[73] and even Atlas, who held the heavens on his shoulders in ancient Greek myth, is cast as an ardent devotee of physical culture.[74] Cover art frequently reproduced ancient or neoclassical artwork, or, in other cases, featured imaginary scenes from classical antiquity (see Figure 4.4).

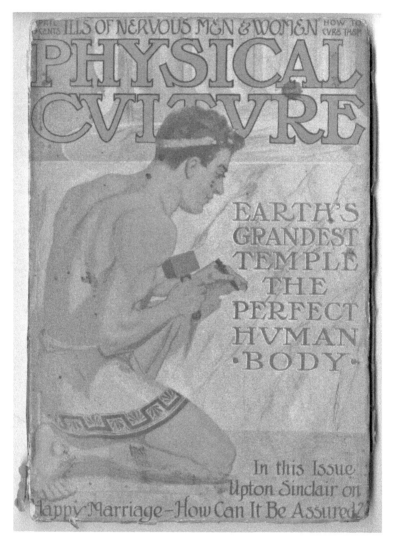

Figure 4.4 Cover, *Physical Culture*, April 1914. Image courtesy of the H.J. Lutcher Stark Center for Physical Culture and Sports at the University of Texas at Austin.

Given the fact that *Physical Culture* featured photographs of its readers and accounts of their physical fitness feats, readers could imagine themselves in the line of Heracles and Atlas – subjects for future stories or deification in the 'religion' of physical culture.[75] In the January 1902 issue, for example, Mr. A. Lovering of Harvard is featured (along with photographs) and the text regards him as 'very nearly to the proportions of the ideal Greek figure'.[76] In November 1900, an anonymous physical culture enthusiast was featured in a variety of poses, including that of the 'Dying Gaul'. Underneath these photos, the model, who is identified as 'Castor-Pollux', is regarded as 'a remarkable example of the results that can be acquired from physical training'.[77]

J. P. Wood's 'Is There Such a Thing as Abnormal Physical Development?' connects ancient and modern bodies through physical culture. While the text concludes that the ideal is ancient Greek and implores the reader to 'make yourself a Hercules',[78] images change from neoclassical statues to actual physical culturists and readers of the magazine. Outside of the magazine, Macfadden promoted the creation of heroic 'legend' around his physical culture enthusiasts through performance and competition. He staged these events frequently and used the magazine to search for the most 'perfectly developed man' and the 'most perfectly developed woman'. The first winner in the male category emblematizes the creation of modern-day legend; the winner was Angelo Siciliano, who would go on to become an American icon and fitness legend under the classically influenced name of 'Charles Atlas'.[79]

Those featured in *Physical Culture* were, invariably, white men and women, and Macfadden agreed with those who saw other races as possible 'contagions' of the 'English-speaking race'.[80] The magazine published articles advocating against intermarriage between races and published many early twentieth-century eugenicists.[81] Women's fitness was mostly absent in the first few issues, but it later became a mainstay (especially its eugenicist take on reproduction), and Macfadden launched *Women's Physical Development* in October 1900.[82] While women became prominent in the magazine and movement, non-white physical culturalists almost never appeared. Almost, because the magazine occasionally included 'anthropological' or 'ethnographic' articles about physical culture outside of the United States. Some of these concerned French, German and Swiss physical development (with appropriate competitive nationalism and derision incorporated), but others treated what the magazine's editors thought were more 'exotic' cultures.

Writers, both in articles and letters, ranged from across the world and mapped quite well onto those locales that Eugen Sandow had visited in his world tours in the first few years of the twentieth century:[83] Macfadden listed those 'agents' who could provide his magazine to readers in Melbourne, Sydney, Adelaide, Brisbane, Cape Town and Bombay.[84] While readers from these countries may have been of any ethnic background – and physical culture practitioners were diverse – writers invariably wrote from the perspective of 'Western civilization', a relatively new idea from the 1890s that aimed to establish continuity between the ancient Greeks and Romans and contemporary Europeans and Americans.[85] The magazine, by definition, participated in the ongoing imperial and colonial projects that linked colonies and settler-colonists to Europe and Europeans at the time as they dominated and assimilated the cultures – and bodies – of indigenous peoples.[86]

F. J. Hornibrook's 'The Fijians and Physical Culture', from the September 1907 issue of *Physical Culture*, is a good example.[87] It discusses the physical fitness and sports of Fijian Islanders through their 'encampment' in the New Zealand International Exhibition.[88] It begins with a short geographical description of Fiji before turning to an 'ethnographic' description of Fijians and a conclusion that Fiji is 'destined to become a popular health and pleasure resort of the South Pacific'. Hornibrook tells the story of Levi, an Islander at the Exhibition, who saw physical culture demonstrations at another booth and brought his compatriots, so that they could 'learn from the white man the secret of his hard arms'.[89] So curious are the Islanders, according to Hornibrook, that they concoct theories of the source of the muscles, such as stones in his arms, and Hornibrook opines condescendingly that they would have torn the man apart to find out.[90] Condescension and outright racism colour the whole piece, since for Hornibrook the Fijians' interest in physical development and their manner of learning reveals in contrast the intellectual and physical potentials of white men. The men are the source of amusement and wonder to the crowds, and a photograph is organized of the group. Hornibrook concludes by seeing the potential of a revived classical antiquity in other than white bodies (one Islander is posed as a 'Fijian Mercury'),[91] though this is mere foil for his conclusion, which asserts the simultaneous proximity and distance of the 'savage' and 'civilized' man. This is presented as a source of some sort of 'regret' for the author, though, in reality, the 'anthropological' narrative serves, as its core, to reinforce the mental *and* physical superiority of the white subjects and white readers of *Physical Culture*.

The supposed superiority of white subjects and readers was mapped back onto the supposed superiority of ancient Greeks and Romans, who were regarded as the progenitors of 'Western civilization' (and retroactively regarded as 'white'). Some writers conceived of a physical culture inspired by various ancient Greek cultures. These arguments, of course, integrated physical culture into classical antiquity and let it trade on the latter's lustre, as much as it reinforced the perceived racial and cultural continuity. For example, Macfadden heralded Spartans in an August 1901 editorial as the 'most perfect specimens of human physical life'.[92] An earlier article had applauded the Spartan practice of killing 'weak' children at birth as 'excessively human',[93] and another one would conceive of Lycurgus as a physical culture teacher like Macfadden.[94] In 1916, an extended story across several issues imagined Spartan physical culture as adventure and romance.[95] Macfadden and his readers were likely prepared to understand Sparta's connections to physical culture thanks to its prominence in American popular culture: by the 1920s, for example, Sparta became a popular name for high school and university sports teams (the Michigan State Spartans perhaps one of the earliest; they adopted the name in 1926).[96]

Alongside historical articles, fiction was important to the magazine from its inception and was engaged in the struggle to establish the new physical culture and to establish its connections with classical antiquity.[97] Through fiction, especially that set in the ancient world, Macfadden and his authors could match a compelling narrative and setting to their physical fitness teaching. If the amount of fiction in the magazine's first two decades is any indication, readers were demanding it.

Macfadden's novel, *The Athlete's Conquest*, was serialized in the first volume and set the standard for physical culture fiction: a weakling's frailty is solved through fitness, nutrition and a rejection of medical science; his newfound physique, confidence and morality give him romantic success as well. Macfadden revisited this plot with a classical veneer in 'The Gladiator's Romance', a story that was serialized in July and August 1900 and illustrated throughout with paintings like Jean-Leon Gerôme's 'Pollice verso' (captioned to fit the story and its characters). Clodius, who only entered the arena to avenge a wrong against his parents, continues to fight for glory even as he tires of the bloodlust of the crowd.[98] On one of his walks through a garden, he sees the beautiful and upper-class Helen,[99] and their illicit relationship begins.[100] Helen is likely drawn to Clodius' physical appearance – 'he was a gladiator. Strong, superb, lithe'[101] – as much as his intellectual abilities: Clodius, we are told, lived the life of a 'cultured gentleman' before he turned to the arena. As a result of this new betrothal, Clodius decides that his next fight in the arena will be his last; at the same time, he learns that Helen and her father loathe the gladiatorial combats.[102] During the festival, of course, while he defeats his opponents, Helen sees him and one of her companions recognizes him as a gladiator; needless to say, she retracts her prior affections.[103]

The story continues in the following issue and time has passed since the recognition scene at the festival. Helen has ceased coming to see Clodius and the latter, incensed and hurt, has returned to the arena. In the midst of practicing for a rematch, Helen comes to see him and apologizes for her behaviour. She has decided to love him regardless and implores him to give up the contest.[104] Clodius refuses, and he enters the arena with Helen watching from the stands. Helen faints in the middle of the battle and Clodius, distracted by her presence, is stabbed by his opponent. When he is spared by the reaction of the crowd and the emperor, he is enraged at the slight to his honour and, as Helen rushes into the arena to stay his hand, he plunges the sword into his chest in order to die a victor.[105]

The story is illustrative of the historical perspective of the magazine on civilizational decay. Naturally, the physically active aspect of gladiators was a possible model for *Physical Culture* and the ancient Romans were prior models to emulate. However, the story's depiction of gladiatorial combat demonstrates the perverse effect of spectatorship on the crowd, a key aspect of actual ancient Roman sports culture. In the climactic battle between Clodius and Saverno, Macfadden focuses simultaneously on their physical abilities and their bloodstained bodies.[106] For 'The Gladiator's Romance', the lesson is clear: physical fitness alone – that promised by myriad Macfadden competitors – is not enough, but the moral and physical advancement promised by Macfadden's *Physical Culture* magazine will stave off the inevitable decay of contemporary civilization.

Gladiators appear only rarely in the pages of *Physical Culture*, probably because their servile status and involvement in a blood sport did not sit well with most authors.[107] Henri Sandé-Stollnitz, for example, uses the gladiator (and modern boxer) as foil to the 'true athlete'. The former were 'slaves brought up and used to amuse the public', whereas the athlete, in Sandé-Stollnitz's view, is a 'benefactor' to mankind.[108] Other authors equated boxers and gladiators, both of whom were seen as a 'prize-fighters', though in Harold Stuart Eyre's short story, 'A Gladiator of To-Day', the prize is a bride and the boxer-cum-gladiator figure is rehabilitated.[109] And Eyre was not the only author to see the gladiator's potential. W. J. Crombie compared Greek athletes and Roman gladiators favourably, and he saw the later as an epitome of physical culture 'enshrined in her [Rome's] temples', even as too much of a good thing led to Roman decline.[110]

The premise of R. W. Walters' 'The Adventures of Trochilles' is the most provocative in combining past and present through an appeal to physical health, and a story that emphasizes the moral and physical renewal of physical culture. Morson, a professor of ancient Greek at Harvard, is forced to take a sabbatical because of his poor physical condition.[111] He decides to recuperate in Greece and spends time on the Acropolis, looking at the fictional statue of Trochilles, who was 'universally accepted as the perfect type of masculine beauty'. As he looks on the statue one moonlit night, bemoaning his own abject failure as a scholar and person, he falls asleep at the base of the statue.[112] When Morson awakens, he is shocked to find the statue of Trochilles stepping down from its pedestal to speak with him. When Morson tells Trochilles where (and when) he is, the statue leaps down from his pedestal and Morson sees his body in the moonlight, 'no longer marble but flesh and blood'. Trochilles informs him that he died at Marathon and he asks after the events of the Persian Wars, and Morson offers an impromptu course on classical and later history to the revived Athenian warrior.[113]

Trochilles accompanies Morson back to the USA, where Morson plans to install him as an assistant professor of ancient Greek at Harvard. While they sail, the two discuss physical culture: Trochilles observes that he had once been weak, but desire for a fit woman – as befits Macfadden's physical culture story arc – had made him practice sports.[114] Even his victories at the ancient Olympics, Trochilles claims, were only possible because he changed the course of his life, a change with which, he suggests, he can help the frail professor.[115]

The pair return, Morson now physically fit and Trochilles fluent in English, to Cambridge, Massachusetts, where the football coach begs Morson to let Trochilles enroll as a student so that he can play football. Trochilles' student credentials are easily confirmed (he takes ancient Greek!), and in his guise as the newly arrived foreigner Jonessy, Trochilles becomes the star of the Harvard football team and leads the team to a memorable season and a victory over Yale.[116] While the team celebrates, the ancient Athenian gives a speech to the crowd. In the course of the speech, he gives voice to the rhetoric of decline that characterizes *Physical Culture*: 'the doom of this nation will be sounded … when its young men neglect the culture of their bodies'. Trochilles goes on to eulogize the present age's technological advances, but to lament the 'pale-faced children' and 'money-mad men' that litter its streets: 'you have', he says, 'advanced in the science of trade, but you have retrograded in the science of living'.[117] With that, Trochilles' speech is finished and the next day he slips away to return to Greece and his pedestal, his mission to deliver the gospel of physical culture completed.

The Adventure of Trochilles' was a hit story (it won a short story contest in the magazine) and it is not difficult to see why. Even if a little hokey, the story deftly combines belief in the degeneration of contemporary life with the possibility of renewal, evangelized by a muscle-bound ideal specimen of humanity. Morson's transformation from the stereotypically weak and bespectacled professor to a healthy athlete mirrors Macfadden's life. Like Trochilles, Macfadden recognized the decline of contemporary bodies and the concomitant decline of civilization, but also their cure. If Trochilles was transformed from marble to flesh, Macfadden promised his readers the reverse alchemy: by following his dietary advice, moral lessons and, above all, his physical fitness regimes, readers could become the statues they had seen.

It is not just my reading of 'The Adventures of Trochilles' that demonstrates Macfaddden's belief in his own life as a model for society. In an authorized biography from 1929, Clement Wood takes Macfadden's life and body as emblematic of a new age for mankind. Wood inserts Macfadden into the Horatio Alger 'rags to riches' canon of American heroes: Rockefeller, Edison, Firestone, Ford and Macfadden.[118] But, he is not just a modern hero, or inasmuch as he literally embodies antiquity and modernity, he is the ultimate modern hero. When he moves, Wood writes, Macfadden becomes a classical sculpture and the anthropomorphized manifestation of an abstract – he is the physical Renaissance personified:

> There is utter symmetry, utter grace, in the powerful lines of the figure. . . . Powerful corded muscles in the legs, a torso like a sculptured Hellenic god, a magnificent chest expansion . . . he is physical fitness, if any man ever was.[119]

Both Sandow and Macfadden used a decline-and-rebirth narrative to describe their lives, methods and bodies. Consciously or unconsciously, these narratives borrowed from the deep-rooted art historical narrative of decline-and-rebirth that was, in fact, invented in the Renaissance. The classics, especially, played a role, not only in the use of classical bodies as apparently indicative of the physical and social health of classical antiquity, but by attaching itself to the classics, physical culture – a new and popular movement and series of magazines on the margins of mainstream sociological, educational and medical theory – added lustre to its message. If Heracles was a physical culturist, or the Spartans a physical culture society, how could anyone argue against the value of physical culture to contemporary America or the world?

*   *   *

The physically fit body, and its representation in many forms of art, is so naturalized in contemporary global society as to seem unhistorical, a given, a shape and form that has no history. Fit bodies have been interpreted as indicative of physical and mental health, a sort of mortal fortitude based around good diets and 'healthy living'. From antiquity to the present, however, the 'fit' body is a social and historical construct. What counts as 'fit' has changed across the centuries, and the moral quality of 'healthy' bodies depends on who is viewing – or writing about – bodies. Antiquity's sculpted male nudes have been made to play a major role in the development of contemporary physical culture and contemporary discourses on beauty. But, these reimagined and sometimes reanimated ancient Greeks and Romans, whose bodies we know, in fact, only through a complex representative art that only approximates the real, are themselves a construct, reflecting the social and cultural ideals not of classical antiquity, but of physical culture innovators of the late nineteenth century.

Arenas, Stadiums and Gyms

The Olympic Games of 2004 in Athens were a return to the literal and spiritual home of the modern Olympics in more than one way. While Athens constructed new Olympic facilities along its Aegean coast and farther afield, three venues for the 2004 Games hearkened back to 1896 and antiquity. Archery took place in the Panathenaic Stadium; the Zappeion Hall, the venue for fencing in 1896, was used as the press centre; and shot-put took place in ancient Olympia.

The Athens Olympics are not alone in playing with the connection between past and present that can be invested in sports venues. The 1960 Rome Olympics used the Baths of Caracalla and the Basilica of Maxentius as venues, and the Marathon ran through and by some of Rome's most famous ancient monuments. Even more incredible, perhaps, is the use of ancient structures for outdoor team sports: for example, in 2012, two hockey games took place on a rink constructed within the amphitheatre in Pula, Croatia.[1]

Venues have been fundamental to sports since their appearance in the ancient Mediterranean, and even today ancient Greek and Latin words for sport venues remain current in many modern languages and in many modern sports. Venues in antiquity were not static and, even at stubbornly conservative sites, they changed over time to accommodate innovations in architecture and change in sports and culture. This chapter begins by looking at some makeshift spaces for early sports before examining in two large sections the sports architecture of ancient Greece and Rome, respectively. It ends by turning to the sports venues of the modern world, whether those associated with the Olympic Games that claim a direct connection to the meaning of venues in antiquity, or the more thematic and diffuse connection of ancient and modern gymnasiums through the bodies and practices of their users.

Makeshift spaces

The earliest spaces set aside for sports were makeshift, neither permanently delineated for athletic activity nor monumentalized in any way. Even imaginary athletics in Homer reflects the absence of permanent spaces. In the Funeral Games of Patroclus in the *Iliad*, the athletic space is the battlefield in front of Troy, and items found on that site become part of the ad hoc venue (23.328–330). The same is true of the Phaeacian Games in the *Odyssey* (8.96–233), which seem to take place in a field or open space outside the palace. While there is an appropriate area for spectators, there is no indication that the site is specifically delineated as an athletic space.

In the historical period, long after stadiums were developed, other spaces continued to be used. For example, during their march out of Persia at the beginning of the fourth century BCE, the ten thousand Greek mercenaries of Xenophon's memoir *Anabasis* hold athletic competitions. They have no stadium or facility nearby, so like Homer's heroes they hold competitions on a mountainside (4.8.25). The *Anabasis* is not the only famous military campaign to include athletic competition. While marching east to conquer the Persian Empire in the 330s BCE, Alexander of Macedon held sixteen different sets of competitions. Purpose-built athletic facilities could not have existed in Memphis, Susa, at the Indus River and in other places far from Greece. Alexander, like Xenophon before him, and perhaps in imitation of the *Iliad*, used makeshift and informal spaces.[2]

Not only on campaign or far from Greece were there informal spaces for sports. At Sparta, for example, the main road was called *dromos* (track), which may indicate that it was used as a site of competition.[3] It is also worth noting that there is no indication that competitions for women at Sparta took place in a stadium. In Athens, the *agora* (a town centre and marketplace) was likely a place of competition during the Panathenaic Games well into the fourth century, at least until the completion of the Panathenaic Stadium in 330/329 BCE.[4] There is strong physical evidence that the road through the *agora* known as the *dromos*, also used for large-scale religious processions, was still being used regularly as a footrace venue into the late fifth century BCE.[5]

In Italy, Etruscan and Roman sport used improvised or at least non-monumentalized spaces for sports into the third century BCE. Etruscan sports were performed at funerals, and no evidence has appeared for any permanent sports facility. Tomb paintings show (presumably) temporary grandstands and landscape details like trees, which may indicate events took place in rural settings. Some tombs have 'theatres' that may have been designed with spectators in mind, perhaps for sports and for the other funerary rituals.[6]

The Romans were also late to move from makeshift spaces to something more formal. We will look at the development of the valley between the Aventine and Palatine Hills as a demarcated space for chariot racing (a 'circus') later in this chapter, but it is striking that this space was likely only outfitted with temporary stands and turning-posts for a long period. Gladiatorial combat, which started in Rome by at least 264 BCE, took place, originally, in the Forum Boarium and Forum Romanum and approximates Athenian and Spartan athletics that used central and open spaces in cities for sporting events.

Ancient Greek stadiums and hippodromes

By the late Archaic period, the stadium as an architectural form had emerged in Greece. Early stadiums were nothing more than spaces leveled and cleared for competition, with some sort of embankment, either natural or aided by earth-moving, for spectators. Even in this simple form, they point to a state or collective interest in athletics that prompted the setting aside of space for sports performances.

In general, stadiums were horseshoe or rectangular shaped areas, usually with one end open. The track constituted the bulk of the space of the stadium and was covered in fine sand, likely prepared each time an athletic festival took place. The stadium was the normal performance space for all athletic events, including the combat sports and the field events of the pentathlon. Presumably, boxing, wrestling and pankration, which occurred in the *skamma*, a turned-over area of dirt, took place near the closed end so that spectators could watch the event closely in theatre-like seating.

In ancient Greek, *stadion* refers to a unit of measurement, the footrace of that length, and the venue in which events happen. While the *stadion* as a unit of measurement was eventually standardized to 600 Roman feet (approximately 185 metres), individual stadiums in the ancient Greek world came only somewhat close to this distance: at Olympia the track was 192 metres long, at Delphi 177 metres, etc. Since athletic accomplishment focused on absolute victory on a single day, the difference was not considered important: if an athlete won at Delphi he won the *stadion* race as much as at Olympia, even though the latter was 15 metres longer. Width was also non-standardized, and stadiums range from 23.5 to 32.2 metres wide. Width would have affected the number of runners who could participate and narrower tracks may have required more heats if there were large numbers of competitors.

Stadiums appear in the ancient Greek world quite early, though the first monumentalized stadiums, those with stone seating or other architectural elements that make them more than just a level and roughly delineated rectangular space, date only to the middle of the fourth century BCE. Stone seats were first for judges and the priestess of Demeter at the stadium at Olympia.[7] In the stadium at Nemea, which otherwise shows evidence of the latest technological and architectural advances in stadium architecture, there were no stone seats on the hill sides.[8] At Epidaurus, stone seats were added to the long straight sides of the stadium near the end of the third century BCE, and after this time, many stadiums were constructed with stone seating or refurbished to include it.[9] From the Hellenistic period onwards, aside from the stadium at Olympia, stone seating became the norm for stadiums across ancient Greece (the reconstructed Panathenaic Stadium, Figure 5.1, shows many of the standard aspects of stadium construction after the classical period). Along with the installation of stone seating came stratification: status and rank, according to inscriptions, became, at times, an organizing principle for seating and the audience of a Hellenistic and later stadium could be seen, from the track, as a physically embodied social order.[10]

Other innovations occurred in the late classical and early Hellenistic period that became norms: Nemea has water channels along the sides of the stadium; there is good evidence too for posts in the *balbis,* or starting-line, that likely correspond to lane markings for short distance sprints like the *stadion* and *diaulos.* The starting mechanism, or *hysplex,* seems to have been in existence from at least the second half of the fifth century BCE.[11] That iteration, found in partial excavations of the stadium at Isthmia, was superseded by a more technologically sophisticated version that was in place as early as 330–270 BCE at Nemea. The device, a wooden frame with a sinew running at waist

Figure 5.1 Panathenaic Stadium, Athens. Photographer: Author.

level that could be dropped when an official yelled 'go', was intended to prevent false starts and to ensure fairness.[12]

Innovative technical developments went hand in hand with a realization that some aspects of stadium architecture in some places were best left in their 'archaic' state. Even with the addition, in the Hellenistic period (323–331 BCE), of a tunnel leading under the earthen embankments, the stadium at Olympia remained without complete stone seating. This absence cannot be explained by a lack of interest in the site or money from wealthy donors, since other infrastructure in ancient Olympia develops at a quick pace in the same period. Rather, we are likely seeing a kind of crystallization of the performance venue at Olympia to match the sanctuary's self-styled and widely recognized status as the most ancient of athletic sanctuaries and the Olympics as the greatest and oldest of athletic festivals.

Certainly, modern sports venues may obtain importance through technical innovation, age or maintaining old forms or technologies, even if they begin to impede their function as venues. The 'new' Yankee stadium that was built for the New York Yankees baseball team in 2009 approximates in many ways the design and decoration of the original, a baseball shrine popularly referred to as 'The House that Ruth Built' (referring to baseball legend Babe Ruth). Other baseball stadiums like the Red Sox Fenway Park, with its iconic and unusual 'Green Monster' wall that makes up for an otherwise absurdly short left field, were designed because of architectural necessity (in the case of Fenway Park, the size of the lot) but have now gained an iconic status that makes demolition almost impossible.[13] Both Fenway Park and the old Yankee Stadium date to the time of the first permanent steel and concrete baseball stadiums, and their connection with a presumed antiquity and 'golden age' of baseball compares well with the similar conception of ancient Olympia in antiquity. These modern baseball stadiums are a particularly good comparison, since stadiums in professional baseball have gone through periods of design and innovation that react or return to the architectural elements of earlier facilities. While Ebbet's Field (home of the Brooklyn Dodgers) and the Polo Grounds (home of the

New York Giants), for example, in Brooklyn and Manhattan, respectively, were derided in their day for poor sightlines, poor access and shoddy workmanship, by the time of their closure, they had gained a kind of nostalgic reprieve from criticism.[14]

Meanings were obtained in ways beyond innovative or conservative architecture, and stadiums became, along with theatres, market squares and fountains, defining characteristics of ancient Greek cities.[15] The involvement of civic authorities in the construction of stadiums speaks to their political importance, or at least the importance granted to them by those in positions of power. Cities, of course, did not finance and build all stadiums, and as with major civic infrastructure in the modern period, wealthy donors were sought out or volunteered to provide funds to cities or sanctuaries. Herodes Atticus, a wealthy philanthropist from the region around Athens, paid for a complete renovation of the stadium at Delphi in the second century CE. His contributions permitted the addition of stone seating, monumental entranceways for athletes and the reinforcing of a retaining wall. While Delphi and the Pythian Games obtained a renovated stadium, we cannot ignore the glory accrued by Herodes Atticus, who attached his name to a primary venue for athletic performance at one of the most important sites in ancient Greece. Many others, on more minor scales in their home cities or in smaller sanctuaries, likewise connected their names with building projects in athletic venues.

In the Roman period, the stadium form began to shift somewhat, influenced by architectural techniques and because stadiums were one of the main places in the ancient Greek world for gladiatorial shows or beast-hunts. Only three stadiums were ever constructed in the western, Latin-speaking part of the Roman Empire: one in each of Naples and Puteoli, and the Stadium of Domitian in Rome itself (today the Piazza Navona). Many stadiums in this period eschewed the natural valleys into which classical and Hellenistic stadiums had been built in favour of vaulted spectator stands on level ground.[16]

At Aphrodisias, for example, the vaulted stadium has two closed ends, perhaps influenced by Roman Circus architecture.[17] By the middle of the fourth century CE a semi-circular wall was built on one end to create a circular space walled on all sides in which gladiatorial combat and beast-hunts took place.[18] Epigraphical evidence suggests the Aphrodisias stadium was a multipurpose performance venue from its original construction,[19] and the large podium wall supports the notion that Roman-style Games were in mind during its construction.[20] Even at stadiums like the Panathenaic Stadium in Athens, by the second century CE, provisions were made for nets and other barriers suitable for beast-hunts and in later antiquity, one end had been turned into a permanent amphitheatre.[21] Given the reduction in track length, it's unclear whether this indicates that athletics proper ceased in these spaces, or whether the various footraces continued, just over shorter distances. In any case, the appropriation of the stadium for gladiatorial or beast-hunt Games is a shift in its architectural history and just as jarring, though without the historical discontinuity, as the use of an amphitheatre for ice hockey, or the Panathenaic stadium for Olympic archery.

While footraces, combat sports and the field events of the pentathlon took place in the stadium, equestrian events had their own venue, the hippodrome. The hippodrome is, to some extent, not an architectural form at all, since, with few exceptions, no monumental hippodromes existed and the structure itself was so ephemeral that almost no physical evidence remains.[22] Despite the fact that Roman-style circuses (still called hippodromes) were built in Greece during the first centuries of the Common Era, there is no evidence for a monumental Circus having been built from the remains or structure of a classical hippodrome.[23] Thus, we must surmise that hippodromes of the Greek type provided little in the way of structures that could serve as foundations for Roman-style circuses.

Among a paucity of archaeological evidence, the hippodrome from the sanctuary of Zeus on Mount Lykaon stands out and provides good evidence for the size and shape of a hippodrome in the classical period. This sanctuary, situated on the slopes of a mountain in Arkadia, held athletic Games known as the Lykaia as part of a yearly festival in honour of Zeus. An ongoing survey and archaeological excavation of the sanctuary site has uncovered some of the athletic facilities, which were located on a plateau below the sacred site of Zeus and the large ash altar.[24] The hippodrome likely dates to sometime in the fourth century BCE as inscriptions that attest to equestrian victors from that period were found on site.[25] Remarkably, the large retaining wall of the eastern side of the hippodrome has been revealed, and from this some estimates of the size of the entire structure have been made: the length along a north–south axis was likely 250 metres; the width along the east–west axis was 50 metres.[26] Spectators could have sat on the natural hills on the north, east and west sides; to the south and lower on another terrace was the sanctuary's stadium, exactly as Pausanias reported, 'in front of the hippodrome' (8.35.5).[27] Mount Lykaon was not exactly unique, but it was unusual in having a relatively large hippodrome structure and one which has left evidence to the present day.

Another piece of evidence for ancient Greek hippodromes comes from Pausanias.[28] When he visited the sanctuary of Olympia, he saw the hippodrome and wrote an extensive description of its starting gates. Though neither the hippodrome nor these gates have been excavated (if anything remains of them, it is buried under several metres of dirt and below olive trees south of the stadium), Pausanias' description gives us a good sense of the gates, which were almost certainly influential on the idea for gates, if not the design, of the early Circus Maximus in Rome.[29]

The gates were shaped like the prow of a ship facing the race-course of the hippodrome (Pausanias, 6.20.10). The scale was spectacular: Pausanias says that each side angling down from the point of the 'prow' was 400 Greek feet long (approximately 123 metres) and starting stalls lined each side. A rope, stretched in front of the stalls, held back the horses, and when it was dropped by the official, a device shot an eagle into the air and a dolphin flew down to signal the beginning of the race (6.20.13). As the horses from the farthest back stalls emerged, they pulled down the rope of the next stall and so on until, when even with the 'prow', all the competitors were racing. In this way, a staggered start was ensured so that no horse rider or chariot team had an advantage from their randomly assigned starting stall (6.20.14).

Roman circuses and arenas

Until the early Imperial period, the main performance venue for almost all sports and spectacles at Rome was the Circus Maximus (see Figure 5.2).

The Circus was the primary place for sports in part because it was the oldest, and, until the construction of permanent amphitheatres and then the Stadium of Domitian, the only permanent sports venue. The Circus form, while superficially similar to the stadium and hippodrome, was idiosyncratically Roman.[30] It began as nothing more than a marshy depression between two hills, but by the second century CE it was one of the most massive and important buildings in the Roman Empire. In the Imperial period, there were other circuses at Rome, though they seem to have been used only intermittently, and the Circus Maximus was the main performance venue for chariot racing for most of Roman history.

Figure 5.2 Detail of Plastico di Roma Imperiale showing Circus Maximus and Colosseum, Museum of Roman Civilization. D-DAI-Rome 73.1080.

A circus is essentially two long sides with two ends, one of which is semi-circular, enclosing a flat space. The performance space was sand: the ground of the Circus is called *harena* in the Latin sources, the same word used to describe the sands of the amphitheatre and the source of the English word 'arena'. By the Imperial period, other architectural elements had become standard: a central barrier (a *euripus*), a series of starting gates (*carcares*), and a monumental entrance way. These elements, while standard across the Empire by the second century CE, only slowly developed, and for much of its history, the Circus Maximus was little more than a level and cleared space.

The early history of the Circus is hard to reconstruct, and was likely so for ancient historians as well. It is probable that regularly occurring races took place in the valley from the end of the sixth century BCE, though even minor improvements such as special seats or wooden starting gates cannot be placed earlier than 494 and 329 BCE, respectively.[31] For a long time the Circus was more conceptual than physical: turning-posts were erected for competitions, the floor levelled and smoothed, but otherwise left unadorned. One exception was drainage. The Circus was prone to flooding for centuries and some hydrological work must have been necessary before it could even host Games. This may be part of the work of the Etruscan kings to whom later tradition assigned the role of building the early Circus. The regulation of the various streams in the valley and their channeling must have been one of the first public works associated with chariot racing at Rome.[32]

Most of the work to make the Circus into a permanent structure likely dates to after Rome's defeat of the Carthaginians in the second Punic War (218–201 BCE). Livy reports that various public works projects took place, including, importantly, the construction of a road leading to the Circus. Seating also became hierarchical, with senators separated from plebeians, while the earliest evidence for a central barrier area decorated with statues, a mainstay of the later Circus, comes from 182 BCE.[33] In the middle of the first century BCE, Julius Caesar undertook major work on the building: he reinforced the now standard shape of the Circus and added two water channels along the sides near the stands. These channels were 3 metres wide and reflect the use of the Circus as a venue for beast hunts, i.e. they protected audience members from errant wild animals. Caesar's circus was a proper building, 650 metres long and 125 metres wide with wooden seating on all sides providing a capacity of around 150,000 people.[34] Augustus largely left the structure in this form, though he made one crucial addition: the *pulvinar*, a small temple-like structure in the seating of the Circus in which the images of the gods that were processed into the Circus prior to the Games were seated. From Augustus' time on, with few exceptions, emperors also watched the Games from the *pulvinar*.[35] This solidified their reputations as 'men of the people' but simultaneously implied connections with divinity.

While further changes occurred in the early Empire, the Circus Maximus as it survives today – and as it is represented on so many ancient depictions – is largely the work of the emperor Trajan (98–117 CE). Trajan's Circus was a massive reconstruction and was largely completed by 103 CE.[36] He had the entire Circus refitted in brick-faced concrete and made all of the seats in stone. The third row stood upon large vaults that formed shops on the outside walls so that the area around the Circus, especially on race days, became a giant entertainment and sports plaza. The design of this version of the Circus influenced circuses across the empire and was memorialized in its artistic representation across many media, from relief sculpture to coins: marble *carcares,* well-decorated *euripus* down the centre, stone seating around all sides and the *pulvinar,* now shifted to the back of the seating rows, looming over the audience (see Figure 5.3, a lamp that depicts, in a circle, the starting gates at the top right; the decorated *euripus* at the bottom; the crowd at the top left; and the chariots themselves in the centre).

Perhaps the most impressive element of the Circus Maximus was the central barrier. The *euripus* grew slowly, but by the time of Trajan's Circus it was a monumental barrier that served the practical function of preventing head-on collisions and the ideological function of

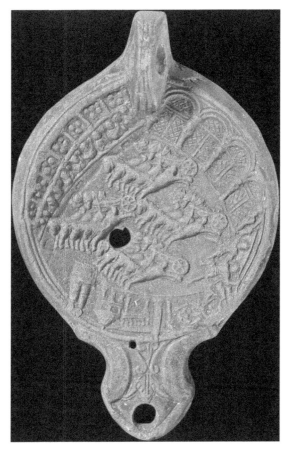

Figure 5.3 Pottery lamp (*c.* 175–225 CE). 1814,0704.106. British Museum.

demonstrating Roman Imperial dominion. The *euripus* was at its base a continuous water-channel along the middle of the Circus. Its waters were interrupted by many monuments, but they also served as a water source for the *sparsores*, race attendants whose job was to throw water on horses.

At either end of the *euripus* were the *metae*, turning-posts, likely the oldest feature of the barrier (see Figure 2.1 where the *metae* are visible at the far right; or Figure 5.3 where the *metae* are upside down on the bottom left). By the time of their first representation on a late first-century

BCE cup from Pompeii they are already in their canonical form: three vertical cones on a high platform with straight sides and topped with objects that resemble eggs. The shape may be connected to that of Roman surveyors' markers, so that the *metae* approximate, in form, the markers used to make the valley a racecourse in the first place.[37] From as early as 174 BCE, we hear of the eggs on the *metae*, which operated as lap-counting devices. The eggs were raised or lowered by an attendant on a ladder to indicate either the number of laps completed or those remaining. It seems that the eggs, however, were not enough, or they caused some confusion, since by 33 BCE, sculpted dolphins were installed as another lap-counting device. These were also placed on top of the *metae*, though exactly how they worked remains something of a mystery: some representations show a ladder near them, which suggests that they were moved in some fashion by hand to indicate completed or remaining laps.[38]

Beyond the functional elements of the *metae* on either end and the water channel running along the central barrier, the *euripus* also acted as a stage for the display of imperial trophies, sacred elements and statuary: there were towers and pavilions, statues on columns and various other monuments.[39] Perhaps the most prominent and important monument on the *euripus* was the Obelisk taken from Heliopolis in Egypt by Augustus after his defeat of Antony and Cleopatra at the Battle of Actium in 31 BCE.[40] Augustus inscribed the north and south sides (facing spectators) with a message alluding to the new place of Egypt within the Roman Empire, and the Obelisk itself connected well with the long-standing importance of the Roman god of the sun – Sol – in the Circus Maximus. This inscription referenced his political and military role and the fact that the Obelisk, prominently in the Circus Maximus, represented the subjugation of Egypt to Roman rule.

The connection between imperial or martial conquest and sports venues, implicit in the presence of martial monuments in the Circus Maximus, was integral to the development of Rome's primary venue for gladiatorial combat, the Flavian Amphitheatre, also often called the Colosseum. While the history of the Circus Maximus can only be tentatively reconstructed from material, literary and documentary evidence, that of the amphitheatre as an architectural form is even more tenuous. There was no permanent stone amphitheatre at Rome until the venue built by Tiberius Statilius Taurus in 30 BCE.[41] Even the history of the form has not been settled, with some scholars seeing it as part of a general movement of gladiatorial combat from the south of Italy to Rome and others seeing it in the opposite way: that temporary amphitheatres in the Forum Romanum were the models for the first permanent amphitheatres in southern Italy.

Katherine Welch's bold theory for the amphitheatre connects the development of stone venues in southern Italy to the regular erection of temporary, wooden amphitheatre-like structures in the Forum Romanum from at least 216 BCE. Gladiatorial combat was wildly popular and increasingly frequent through the years of the Middle Republic (264–133 BCE).[42] Welch observes that the Forum Romanum would permit the erection of an oval shaped series of stands – called *maenia* in Latin – that would be positioned against or above the buildings surrounding the central open space.[43] The shape of the Forum Romanum and the necessity to fit stands into the area surrounding the open space mandated the oval shape of the amphitheatre.

The culmination of amphitheatre development was the Flavian Amphitheatre, the largest in the world and one of the largest buildings constructed in antiquity. It is usually called the *amphitheatrum* or *amphitheatrum Caesarum* (the imperial amphitheatre) in the ancient sources. The name 'Colosseum' is attested first in the eighth century CE and is derived from either the colossal statue of Nero that stood beside it or the building's incredible size.[44] Modern scholars call it the 'Flavian' amphitheatre after the Flavian dynasty (Vespasian, Titus and Domitian, 69–96 CE) who conceived it and completed its construction. The Flavian Amphitheatre was not only important for its size, but its location in the centre of Rome, its transformation of the Emperor Nero's 'Golden House' into a venue for public spectacle and its self-conscious presentation as a dedication of the spoils of war.

All permanent amphitheatres prior to the Colosseum were located on the outskirts of towns, either integrated into their walls or just outside of them. One of the main innovations of the Flavian Amphitheatre is its location in the centre of the city. This area, prior to the construction of the amphitheatre, was home to the Emperor Nero's *domus aurea*, or 'Golden House'. The large villa-like development was built after the Great Fire of Rome in 64 CE, when two-thirds of the city was devastated. The exact nature of the Golden House has proven contentious: ancient sources describe it as a 'pleasure-palace' and characterize Nero's construction as theft of land in the confusion following the fire (Suetonius, *Life of Nero* 31). Some modern scholars, however, have argued that the Golden House was more like a typical Roman elite's home, though on a large-scale: that is, much of the house and gardens would have been regularly open to the public without regard for social status. Ancient sources may be critical of the Golden House for this exact reason: Nero expropriated the property of wealthy elites in central Rome and built an extravagant palace that was open to Romans of all social statuses.[45] In this context, then, the construction of the Flavian Amphitheatre takes on new meaning. Ancient writers suggest that the Emperor Vespasian and his son Titus, on the opening of the amphitheatre, had 'returned' these grounds to the Roman people. They celebrate the transformation of supposedly private space into public space, an amphitheatre where one may find all of Rome (Martial, *On the Spectacles* 2). The construction of the Flavian Amphitheatre, however, transformed a radically reimagined space into a much more traditional public space in Rome: the rigidly stratified seating of the Flavian Amphitheatre contrasts sharply with a vision of gardens in the *domus aurea* that were open to all Romans.

We may compare the location and situation of stadiums today, which reflect broad movements in society and can incorporate similar political and social motivations. As Americans moved into the suburbs and came to rely on cars in the years after the Second World War, baseball stadiums and other sports facilities moved with them, with access by car considered the most important characteristic of a modern stadium.[46] Yet, these suburban colosseums – the New York Mets' Shea Stadium (1964) was explicitly intended to resemble the Flavian Amphitheatre[47]

– became, in turn, outdated. Stadiums moved back to the downtown cores of cities across North America, mirroring the gentrification of many urban centres in the 1990s.[48] While constructed in radically different time periods and under radically different social conditions, the Flavian Amphitheatre and the archetype for the return of the 'downtown' stadium, Baltimore's Oriole Park at Camden Yards (1992), suggest similar possibilities for sporting space. The particular situating of a sports venue sends messages about the proper use of space in various parts of the city, and it reflects or helps to generate new conceptions of that space.

The Flavian Amphitheatre is unambiguous in its self-presentation as a gift to the Roman people from the spoils of war. The dedicatory inscription, only published in 1995, seems to read, 'The emperor Titus Caesar Augustus commanded that a new amphitheatre be made from the spoils of war.'[49] The inscription demonstrates that the only other permanent amphitheatre at Rome, that of Statilius Taurus, remained important in public memory even after its destruction in the fire of 64 CE, and that the Flavian Amphitheatre was seen as a replacement. 'Spoils of war', Latin *manubia*, connects the building project to a long tradition of wealth redistribution through public projects. *Manubia* specifies that the amphitheatre is a present to the Roman people that comes directly from the work of imperial conquest: by subduing the Jewish Revolt and sacking Jerusalem in 70 CE, Titus was able to procure the funds necessary to produce the amphitheatre. In contrast to Nero, who never led an army on campaign,[50] Titus' martial success permitted the transformation of the Golden House into a new gift to the Roman people. In this way, in its very presence in Rome, the Flavian Amphitheatre is a monument to empire and emperor.

Beyond its symbolic and ideological meaning in the landscape and in its historical context, the Flavian Amphitheatre is a remarkable building: stratified seating, service entrances, audience accommodations and wayfinding systems approximate those of modern stadiums. The amphitheatre's focus on audience, above all, demonstrates the Roman approach to sport and spectacle and makes the building similar to those of today. Modern stadiums also focus on audience comfort, spectator safety and their imposing and well-decorated interiors and exteriors shape their reception among modern sports fans.

The scale of the Colosseum is incredible: in antiquity it was four complete levels, 52 metres high with a major axis of the ellipse (roughly east–west) of 188 metres and the minor axis (roughly north–south) of 156 metres.[51] The seating area, broken into five different sections and permitting an audience of 50,000, reached almost to the top of the building, so that those seated in the highest seats, beneath a colonnaded portico, had wonderful views of the Roman 'skyline', but perhaps less so of the arena itself.[52] Directly above their heads would have been the operators of the *velarium,* massive sails supported by a wooden frame that was attached to the exterior of the upper wall of the amphitheatre that provided shade to audience members.[53] Those who have sat in the 'cheap seats' of a multipurpose stadium, especially a roofed one where it seems like your seat is part of the infrastructure, would probably feel right at home.

With so many seats and tiers and with fire or other emergencies in mind, the wayfaring system for entrance and exit into the amphitheatre was critical. What emerges from a study of this system is that the amphitheatre was designed so that the stratified seating would be paralleled by segregated entrances – at almost no point would those of one class be elbow-to-elbow with those of another class whether in their seat or in the process of getting there.[54] Aside from four special entrances (the four on the north, east, south and west axes), all 76 arches were labeled by a number and each corresponded to five different systems of entrance. Individual tickets, much like those of modern stadiums today, would indicate the appropriate entrance way to take along with the specific row in the tier of seating.[55] Some arches, like arch 10 for example, led directly to staircases and landings that took audience members up to the highest tiers of seating. Others, like arch 28, took members of the senatorial class out to the prime seating on the lowest level.

Aside from audience members, as befits an entertainment complex – and that's what it is was: the entire area around the amphitheatre was a giant plaza, blocked off from traffic by means of boundary markers and chains[56] – there were myriad entrances for the emperor and his retinue, performers and service personnel. From the west axis, the *pompa* entered directly onto the arena floor. The east axis acted as an exit point for gladiators, dead or alive, and was connected by an underground chamber to the nearby *Ludus Magnus*.[57] Below the wooden, sand-covered arena floor, in the *hypogeum* or underground, there were fifteen different chambers, some of which incorporated lifts or elevators that could move performers or animals up to the arena floor. The entire *hypogeum* sat on top of the amphitheatre's massive 13-metre-deep concrete foundation and it was surrounded by a thick retaining wall.[58] The underground construction, support, drainage and sewer facilities (the latter two to support fountains and lavatories on seating tiers) are as impressive as the above-ground edifice.[59]

Making stadiums modern

By the end of the fifth century CE, the main forms of sports architecture in antiquity, with the exception of the Circus, had become obsolete, so much so that even the vaunted Flavian Amphitheatre was left to fall into ruin and eventually become a quarry.[60] Even the Hippodrome of Constantinople, by the thirteenth century CE, was largely abandoned as chariot races finally fell out of favour. There is a distinct architectural discontinuity in the history of stadiums, hippodromes, circuses and amphitheatres – for hundreds of years, forms that had dominated the ancient Mediterranean were forgotten and the buildings themselves demolished or left to fall further into disrepair.

If their athletic or spectacular function had been forgotten, the great sports venues of the ancient world were still used for something. The Colosseum – as it then became known – was at times a residence for lower-class artisans in Rome who worked the stone of the building in the middle of the old arena.[61] Even later, when its original purpose as a performance venue was rediscovered, it was venerated mainly as a site of martyrdom for Christians; Pope Benedict XIV (1740–58) even declared the Colosseum a public church and members of his order performed the stations of the cross inside the amphitheatre.[62] The Panathenaic stadium was also largely left to fall into ruin, and the remains of kilns are evidence that the processing of marble into lime took place on site.[63] Other facilities, in less prominent locations, were destroyed by natural causes – earthquakes, lightning strikes and fires – and without anyone to repair them, they tumbled to the ground to be covered, in many cases, by metres of dirt or sand.

The return of athletics, supposedly in the ancient Greek tradition, was coincident with the return of these venues. The early Olympic revival in Athens was tied, though unsuccessfully, to the restoration of the Panathenaic Stadium, and other revivals in Britain and France, even without access to ancient facilities, adopted the names of the ancient forms for their new sports venues. By the middle of the nineteenth century in Britain, the word 'stadium', previously used to refer to the ancient form or length, could be used to refer to any area designated for sports, since an analogy was drawn between the place for the sports practice the ancient Greeks loved and the place for athletic performances appropriate to modern England. In modern sports venues, the words 'colosseum' (e.g. the Los Angeles Memorial Coliseum, which hosted Olympic Games in 1932 and 1984), 'arena' (now a generic term for ice-hockey facilities) and 'stadium' (countless examples) are used mostly interchangeably, and other words like 'forum' even pop up (e.g. the old Montreal Forum hockey arena), inadvertently resurrecting the Forum Romanum's ancient connection with spectacle and sport. In many aspects, with their focus on audience comforts, modern sports venues resonate with the spirit of the Flavian Amphitheatre rather than the more performer-focused ancient Greek stadium.

The Circus Maximus compares well with modern, entertainment-oriented professional sports facilities. Like the Colosseum and like many modern stadiums, it was surrounded by pedestrian friendly sidewalks and porticos that helped handle the crowds that waited, sometimes overnight, for entrance. The neighbourhood, as with so many modern, downtown stadiums and facilities, was part of the experience of attending an event. A 12-metre-wide road ran around the Circus which aided in the procession that began the Games, but also helped crowds gain access to the facility.[64] Seating size at the Circus Maximus compares with that at modern stadiums, though Roman spectators were expected to sit closer to their compatriots and were afforded less space; nonetheless, the ancient seat depth of 60–70 cm is not far removed from the modern standard of 70 cm.[65]

Beyond physical comparison, Amanda Devitt makes clear that the experience of attending a chariot race can be usefully compared with that of a modern sports event. Fans came to chariot-racing events for reasons similar to those of modern sports fans: to get pleasure from entertainment, to feel the stress and adrenaline of the unknown outcomes of sports, etc.[66] But, perhaps most striking is the evidence for group affiliation in the stands of sporting events. Fans in the Circus Maximus would have heard other people cheering on their own favourites, and since seating was open and largely unrestricted (as in general admission stadiums today), friends would have sat together, groups could have formed and communities could have begun in the stands.[67] The supporters' sections well known in football stadiums are an organized version of the same phenomenon.[68] Fans did not, as in many ancient and modern moralizing narratives, lose their own identity in a mob, but rather found new communal identities that complemented or reinforced their existing individual and collective selves.[69] Still, these identities are constrained in a way that those found in protests, strikes and riots are not. It is telling that twentieth-century totalitarian regimes – and other less obviously authoritarian states – love stadiums.

The strong emotional reactions that ancient and modern sport provoke and their connection to specific locales is a complex and potent combination. Ancient and modern sports venues are places of sporting action but also places of sporting memory. Like other spaces that house important events for communal and individual identities, sports facilities gain meaning over time. Meaning, memory and place come together in Olympic ceremony, a centerpiece of the modern Games. The opening ceremonies themselves have become, over time, an entertainment extravaganza that usually takes places in and inaugurates the use of the Olympic stadium. Like the processions of gladiatorial games and circus games in ancient Rome, the opening ceremonies are a ritualistic event that opens the Games and incorporates its traditions, but they are also a spectacle in and of themselves that demonstrates the power and wealth of the hosts. Pageantry and pomp, for Pierre de Coubertin, was necessary for the modern Games, the rituals and traditions of which have become part of the narrative of the Games' importance to contemporary global society.

Maybe the most suggestive of these ceremonies comes before the Games themselves in the stadium of ancient Olympia. Not only was this space the most ancient athletic site in antiquity, but its modern history looks back to ancient times even as it stands as the home of the revival of the Olympics. In 1927, for instance, a marble pillar in honour of the refoundation of the Games was unveiled at the site. Even the stadium's excavation was prompted by the Berlin Olympics of 1936, and after Coubterin's death in 1937, his heart was buried under a pillar just north of it. But, it is the torch relay, devised for the 1936 Games, that relies most heavily on Olympia's perceived role as a place of athletic memory. Since its first iteration in 1936, the torch relay has begun at Olympia with a lighting ceremony, often near the Temple of Hera. While Berlin Games organizer Carl Diem is credited with the idea for the torch relay, the lighting ceremony was devised by Alexander Philadelphus, a Greek archaeologist.[70] Actresses and locals, dressed as 'priestesses' of the Games, use mirrors and lenses to focus the light of the sun into a brazier that is then used as the source of the 'sacred flame' of the relay.[71] While torch-relay races existed in antiquity (e.g. the *lampedophoros* 'torch-bearing race' of the Panathenaic Games), there is no connection in the ancient world between Olympia and torch-lighting or relays.[72] Flames were part of ancient sacrifice, and Olympia's ash-altar symbolized the continuity of ritual into the distant past; its guardians, however, were male priests of Zeus. The relay, and especially the ceremony, point to the modern Olympics' mythologizing tendencies, but also to the ways in which sporting spaces, as places of memory, are potentially ready to be reactivated.

From the outset, modern Olympic venues have engaged with their ancient predecessors and worked to reactivate or generate sporting memory. Since 1908, a stadium has been a centerpiece of the modern Games and one of the main civic benefits thought to accompany the awarding of the Games. Olympic stadiums, perhaps because they partake of the imagined connection with antiquity and because they are often purpose-built for one event, are special places for the production and maintenance of sports memories. Many remain intact today, and complicated arguments surround their modernization as sports facilities or their preservation as historical monuments.[73]

Sports facilities at the 1900 Paris Olympics were makeshift: athletes ran over bumpy, uneven ground at the Croix-Catalan Stadium of the Racing Club,[74] a founding member of the Union Sportive that Coubertin cobbled together prior to forming the IOC.[75] Coubertin attempted to convince the organizers of the Games of something more grandiose, a near-exact replica of the ancient Olympic sanctuary for what he imagined, prior to the decision to hold the 1896 Games in Athens, would be the first modern Olympics.[76] In the end, the complex and difficult negotiations with the authorities involved in the World's Fair caused the facilities for sport to be widely dispersed across Paris, and no true 'Olympic stadium' was part of the Games.

The first Olympics with a purpose-built facility, and one which became a model for future stadiums, were those of London 1908. The 'White City Stadium', built on the grounds of the Franco-British Exhibition of 1908 on farmland west of London, incorporated a 536-metre track, and on the infield were platforms for swimming and gymnastics along with a 100-metre pool for swimming, diving and water polo.[77] Purpose-built stadiums became the norm from then on:

the 1912 Stockholm Olympics featured a stadium with gothic inspiration in its architecture, vaulted arcades and a tunnel for athlete access to the infield; it is still in use today and was used for the equestrian competitions of the 1956 Games. One of the most beloved and famous stadiums of the early Olympics, the Amsterdam Olympic Stadium, housed the first – and then standard – 400-metre running track. Entrance and exit procedures were given close attention: the stadium was said to be able to be evacuated in 12 minutes. Today, it has been in continuous use as a sports facility for almost 100 years.[78]

Modern Olympic stadiums diverge significantly from their ancient antecedents since they are, with some exceptions, purpose-built facilities. Of course, this is in keeping with the international and mobile character of the modern Games. It is noteworthy, however, that several stadiums have been reused when the Games return to a previous host city. In this way, we approach the same type of reverence for space, landscape and venue that characterizes ancient sport facilities. The Los Angeles Memorial Coliseum hosted the Olympics in 1932 and 1984, and will host athletics for a third time in the 2028 Olympics. The *Stade de Colombes* (the stadium of the 1924 Paris Games), while in an advanced state of disrepair at present, will host field hockey in the 2024 Olympic Games. This move to old facilities is at odds with the future-facing ideology of the modern Olympic movement, tied as it is to the construction of new facilities and new urban infrastructure. One of the supposed benefits of hosting the modern Games is the infrastructure improvements. Until recently, in fact, new and permanent facilities were virtually mandated by the IOC, and only environmental and economic concerns have pushed back against this tradition.[79] In turn, however, the IOC's self-conscious mythologizing of its own antiquity, combined with the ancient and modern reverence of sports venues, suggests the reuse of prior stadiums. By turning back to the venues – and cities – of the first decades of the twentieth century, the IOC's Olympics emphasize their tradition at the very moment their cost and scope have come under question.

Ancient and modern gyms

While they were not normally competitive spaces for athletics in classical antiquity, and while the physical form of the ancient gymnasium-*palaestra* complex has not influenced the formal development of modern gymnasiums, the concept of the 'gym', a specially demarcated place or purpose-built facility dedicated to athletic training, is still an influential idea from ancient Greece. The ancient gymnasium and its modern counterpart, essential components of their respective cityscapes, resonate: they represent a prioritizing of physical fitness and a particular type of 'fit' body in classical antiquity and today.

Athens provides the earliest evidence for the architecture of the gymnasium and its support by the state. By the classical period, there were three major gymnasiums in Athens, all outside of the city proper: the Lykeion, Academy and Kynosarges.[80] All three were, like those places where competitive athletics took place, sanctuaries devoted to gods or heroes (Demosthenes, 24.114). Initially, gymnasiums were simply groves or other outdoor spaces with rudimentary and likely ephemeral running tracks and other athletic facilities, but by the classical period, Athenian statesmen began to devote private and then public funds to their upkeep and development.

The classical gymnasium took its standard form by the end of the fourth century BCE.[81] The *palaestra*, a square or rectangular colonnade surrounding an open courtyard, was used for practicing the combat sports and in its various recesses, it contained baths, *apodyteria* (undressing rooms) and other rooms suitable for conversation or informal teaching. The gymnasium was much larger, with two sides at least one *stadion* in length so that a covered (*xystos*) and uncovered (*peridromis*) practice track existed for footraces.[82] The central area of the gymnasium was used as a practice space for the field sports of the pentathlon. The gymnasium-*palaestra* complex was always more than a venue for athletic training and included space for social and intellectual pursuits.

From these beginnings to the end of antiquity, the gymnasium was a key part of public infrastructure in the ancient Greek world. Evidence of gymnasiums has been found wherever the ancient Greeks went, and the gymnasium (along with a few other important buildings) was a necessary component of the *polis* itself (Pausanias, 10.4.1). By the fifth century CE, along with the collapse of large-scale trade and the logistical support of the athletic circuit and spectacular Games came the end of the gymnasium and *palaestra* as central elements of public life in the Mediterranean. While these institutions would be recalled in literary circles, especially because of their prominent place in ancient Greek philosophy, the physical sites and buildings were looted for their marble or left to decay from disrepair. Throughout the medieval period, while sports were more prominent than some narratives suggest, no purpose-built athletic training facility along the lines of a gymnasium-*palestra* appeared. Only by the early nineteenth century, in Europe, did spaces along the lines of athletic training facilities slowly begin to appear again.

While earlier groups developed what could be conceived of as gymnasiums, especially the *Turner* or German gymnastics movement created by Friedrich Jahn in the 1810s,[83] French strongman and entrepreneur Hippolyte Triat opened one of the first modern gymnasiums in Paris in 1850: it was a large indoor space, with areas devoted to Triat's system of training that included dumbbells, Indian clubs and barbells.[84] Men participated in group fitness classes in uniforms, and in perhaps his most prescient innovation, Triat offered memberships at different rates depending on how often you wished to visit.[85] This innovation shifts from the publicly supported gymnasium of classical antiquity and earlier modern state-supported efforts. Whereas the gymnasium-*palaestra* had been a necessary part of city life in antiquity and supported by the state or its wealthy citizens for all (or at least, for the use of free-born males), the modern gymnasium of Triat reveals a modern ideology: individual improvement was an individual pursuit, and one to be paid for by the individual.

Triat's gymnasium eventually closed and he died impoverished, but a later contemporary and successor, Eugen Sandow (see Chapter 4),

built on his example with his own Institutes of Physical Health, the first
of which opened in 1897. Sandow's club was part health and fitness
facility and part gentlemen's club, and in fact the decor was modelled on
the private clubs with which many members would be familiar.[86]
Sandow's fortunes waxed and waned. Athletic facilities were and are
expensive to maintain and operate, though their fortunes are not only
tied to economic booms. Early American fitness impresario Charles
Atlas observed that the unemployed were in fact a great pool of potential
customers, since physical power, he thought, could help in the pursuit of
employment.[87] Nonetheless, the fitness-club boom sparked by Sandow
and aided by publishers like Bernarr Macfadden faded as the Depression
and then the Second World War deprived businessmen of their potential
customers.[88] By the end of the war, the fitness club was known as a dank,
male-only place,[89] associated with the city and the working class.[90]

The modern gym that will be familiar to readers of this book
is largely a development of the post-war economic boom and
suburbanization. In *Getting Physical: The Rise of Fitness Culture in
America*, Shelley McKenzie deftly narrates the various changes that
suburbanization brought to American bodies and their potential access
to fitness.[91] She reflects on the burgeoning 'health clubs' of the 1950s,
especially those of Vic Tanny, which boasted 500,000 members by 1959:
these were 'glitzy' facilities that were reimagined as middle-class and
largely white spaces.[92] Their bright lights and friendly atmosphere were
aimed at attracting women and men, a major departure from most
earlier fitness facilities. Social aspects became more and more important,
and health clubs added spas and juice bars and supported members'
activities like outings and clubs. The gym became a 'third place' between
work and home, a public/private location that nurtured relationships
based on collaboration and competition.[93] This was especially important
for the populations who had been marginalized from many public
spaces in the twentieth century: health clubs thus became a 'linchpin of
social life' for the gay community.[94]

By the early twenty-first century, the 'gym' is once again a mainstay
of the cityscape, a necessary element of a desirable city, just as it was in

classical antiquity. The form of today's gym is startlingly different from that of antiquity: located in various urban and suburban centres, glowing bright and full of glimmering equipment, vibrant and encouraging music, television screens and – above all – mirrors for the observation of one's self and others. Still, even in the highly commercial gym of today some of the ethos of the gymnasium-*palaestra* of antiquity remains. Both are rarities in history: highly numerous, well-maintained, long-lasting facilities dedicated to training. Both connect physical fitness with social and intellectual activities, with bonds of friendship formed through mutual struggle or competition. In the gym, in fact, even in the highly commercialized version of the twenty-first century, more than in the stadiums and arenas of professional sports, something like the sports ethos of ancient Greece remains: a focus on personal development and training, with perceived benefits for the community.

* * *

Sports is intimately connected with space. From the makeshift spaces that characterized early sport through the Flavian Amphitheatre and to modern urban stadiums and gymnasiums, sports were shaped by the spaces in which they took place. Space has shifted the expectations of the audience, complemented or challenged the ideologies associated with sport and made sports have meaning beyond the results on the stadium track, sands of the arena or dirt of the baseball diamond. The modern spaces associated with sport often take their inspiration, and sometimes their names, from ancient spaces, and the visceral and material connection of body, sports practice and venue, make space a potent way to connect past and present. Still, as with most reimaginings of the past in the present, these apparently essential connections are tenuous, and the places and spaces of modern sports, perhaps when they most claim a connection with those of classical antiquity, are anything but simple manifestations of historical and athletic continuity.

Olympic Art and Cinema

From the nudity of the athlete, to the symmetry of bodies sculpted into marble, to the representations of the abject and admired bodies of gladiators and charioteers in Roman art, sport and art were intricately connected in antiquity. When Pausanias visited Olympia, he not only lauded the athletic accomplishments that victory statues made manifest, but he praised artistic accomplishments; he named artists and suggested that the appreciation of an athletic body was also the appreciation of a work of art.

When the Olympics returned to Greece in 2004, the opening ceremonies unabashedly evoked antiquity. Artwork, brought to life by costumed and painted people, cycled through the eons: from the fresco of boy boxers at Thera, to athletic figures of the classical period and even black-and-white figures who re-enacted the IOC's 1896 Games. While the Olympics is a festival of sports, in this return to its actual modern birthplace and its figurative homeland, Athens used an artistic display to evoke the ideal of the timelessness of the Olympics and its continuity with the past.

Although there are many visions of ancient sport to be found in cinema and art today, especially Roman sport (*Ben-Hur* in 1959 and *Gladiator* in 2000, among others), this chapter focuses on two artistic representations of modern sports: the posters and official films of the Olympic Games. These works act as a capstone to this entire book, since the modern Olympic movement's representation of and engagement with antiquity is the most complex and intricate of any ancient sports revival. By tracing the imagining of antiquity in Olympic art, this chapter demonstrates the merger of past and present that is central to the ancient and modern Olympics – and to the modern sports and physical cultures that similarly imagine their origins in classical antiquity.

Olympic posters

Since 1912, official posters have been essential, not only to the promotion of the Olympic Games, but for the creation of the symbols and rituals of the Olympic Movement.[1] Symbolism was key to the modern Olympics since their inception. For Pierre de Coubertin, the Olympics were not simply an international sporting competition, but an aesthetically and culturally significant event.[2] Posters participated in the creation of a specifically Olympic artistic vocabulary along with their more prosaic function as advertisements.

From the beginning of the official poster tradition to 1956, with some exceptions, Olympic posters prominently feature nude male figures, whether actual athletes or representations of statuary. In blurring the lines between athlete and statue, Olympic posters, like ancient victory monuments, highlight that athletics transforms the male form into an aesthetic and eternal object rather than what it is: an ephemeral and mortal human body. Only when the Olympic Games move to Melbourne (1956) and Tokyo (1964) does the symbolism of antiquity and masculinity vanish. These two concepts, especially through actual depictions of statuary or representations of male bodies imagined as statues, are deeply connected in early Olympic art.

The first official poster, for the Games of the Vth Olympiad (Stockholm 1912), demonstrates this core iconographic programme: Olle Hjortzberg's design represents the community of nations, embodied in a male nude, whose colouring makes it unclear whether this is a statue or a human being (Figure 6.1). The Swedish Olympic Committee chose Hjortzberg's design over two competitors' designs: one featured the entrance of a marathon runner into the stadium, the other a javelin thrower with the stadium in the background.[3] Hjortzberg's poster instead eschews images of competition for a figure, like those of ancient Greek victory statues, who shows virtually no emotion.[4]

The poster was produced in three sizes and in over 110,000 copies. It also set the stage for future Olympic advertising by being produced in multiple languages (16 different languages in the large format).[5] Like

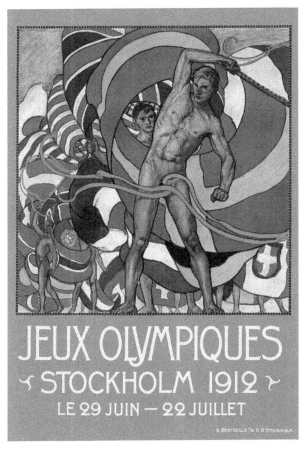

Figure 6.1 Poster of the Games of the V Olympiad (Stockholm, 1912). International Olympic Committee.

most early Olympic posters, it prominently features the phrase 'Olympic Games' along with the place and date. Given the use of these posters as advertising and promotion for the Games and for Swedish tourism, especially in railway stations, basic information was critical, and Olympic posters traded on the extant design tradition of railway posters that advertised holiday destinations.

Despite this appeal to classical ethics and ancient victors' statues, the poster was not uncontroversial. Even the idea of a poster that did not feature sports was an issue.[6] The Olympic Committee's report recalls that despite universal acclaim for its artistic merits, its motif was debated.[7] Furthermore, Hjortzberg's initial design, a completely nude athlete, was too risqué.[8] Even after the ribbons were added, it was still not distributed in some countries. In the Netherlands, for example, it was removed from a railway station because it was 'in the highest degree immoral', while it was banned altogether in China 'as being "offensive to Chinese ideas of decency"'.[9]

The flags of the nations also prompted discussion, especially from 'diplomatic quarters' as to the order of precedence. Hjortzberg's design arranged the flags for 'coloristic, and not political, reasons',[10] but complaints were raised, or possible complaints were imagined. In some countries, though the Official Report omits their names, the poster was not displayed because of the order of flags. The poster's very design worked against, to some degree, its effectiveness at advertising.

Despite these complaints, when the Games resumed after the First World War and were assigned to Antwerp only 16 months prior to the opening ceremonies,[11] the Organizing Committee still commissioned a poster to advertise the event, a design that was very similar to that of the 1912 Stockholm Games (Figure 6.2).

An almost nude male figure is again central and flags of participating nations are again displayed, this time in a continuous banner. Instead of a generic victor-athlete (or statue?) as in the Stockholm poster, this poster focuses on an explicitly classical figure: a nude discus thrower. He looks left towards the discus that is clasped in his hands, and the bronze colour makes clear that this is a creative interpretation of Belgian sculptor Matthias Kessels' 1828 statue *Diskobolos Preparing to Throw* rather than a representation of a living athlete.[12] The design, by husband-and-wife duo Walter Van der Ven and Martha Van Kuyck,[13] had been used already in Antwerp's 1914 brochure, *Will We have the 7th Olympiad in Antwerp?* and it was a simple (and economical) choice to use it again.[14] The poster was printed in multiple languages and in two sizes with 130,000 printed over all.[15]

Figure 6.2 Poster of the Games of the VII Olympiad (Antwerp, 1920). International Olympic Committee.

To the left of the nude male statue is a banner made up of the flags of the world, an image that may have been especially striking in the aftermath of the First World War, and one that further connects this poster with that of Stockholm. Behind the statue is the cityscape of Antwerp, and the coat of arms of the city stands prominently in the upper-right corner. The origin of the design in a brochure aimed at highlighting Antwerp likely contributed to the focus on the city, but the emphasis on civic symbolism, an emphasis borne from the constantly changing venue and internationalism of the modern Olympic Games, would become a major iconographic element in subsequent posters.

The following two Olympic Games – 1924 in Paris and 1928 in Amsterdam – continued the trend of combining classical iconography with national or civic imagery, alongside the emerging symbols of the modern Games. Moreover, they both give prominence, as those of 1912 and 1920, to male figures, whether nude or clothed.

For the 1924 Paris Olympics, two designs were eventually selected as official posters: both were produced in 120 x 80 cm size and 10,000 copies of each were printed.[16] They were distributed in a variety of contexts: to National Olympic Committees, but also to banks, credit agencies, schools and universities, theatres, cafes and French embassies in foreign countries.[17] A series of stamps were also produced with the words 'Paris – 1924' and '8th Olympiade' alongside depictions of semi-nude (and this time, explicitly human, male and white) athletes giving the 'Roman' or 'Olympic' salute or in athletic poses. One stamp shows – presumably – a Greek goddess figure with a victory posed on her hand in front of cityscape of Paris in miniature.[18]

The two posters, while focused on male athletes, reflect different Olympic ideologies. Jean Droit's design showed the end of a parade of nearly nude athletes with their right arms raised (see Figure 6.3). Behind the parade is a flowing French flag, while below the athletes are laurel wreaths and the coat-of-arms of Paris. In contrast, the other design by graphic artist Orsi depicts a moment of competition – the javelin toss – superimposed over a globe and the landmarks of Paris. Droit's poster, while borrowing the symbolism of the nude male (again, with a content expression), emphasizes a particularly modern Olympic ideal, collective effort and unity,[19] concepts that were anathema to ancient Greek athletics. One detail makes this clear: the central athlete, while looking right with his right arm raised has placed his left hand on the shoulder of the athlete next to him. In this unreal depiction of the parade of nations, Droit has placed a tender moment of camaraderie, the sort of gesture of goodwill and friendship that is central to modern Olympic values.

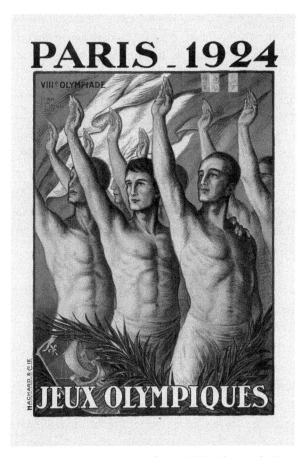

Figure 6.3 Poster of the Games of the VIII Olympiad (Paris, 1924). International Olympic Committee.

Despite the numerous 'firsts' for Olympic rituals at the next Olympics in Amsterdam in 1928 – the flame, the flag, the now canonical order of Greece first, host last for the parade of nations – the poster for these Games mostly eschewed any reference to ancient Greece or classical antiquity more broadly, a choice that was derided by critics.[20] The central figure is still male, but instead of a nude or near-nude athlete or statue, it is clearly a modern runner, dressed in singlet and shorts, surrounded by the new stadium and the new symbols of the modern Olympic movement (the interlocking rings, approved as the IOC's symbol in 1914, are here on a poster for the first time). The Amsterdam poster does show some continuity with the poster for the 1924 Paris Games since modern athletes, of identifiable race and gender, take centre stage.

In the next three Olympic Games, classical imagery proper returned to prominence. In 1932, for example, the poster for the Los Angeles Games was a technically novel imitation of classical relief sculpture. The design was modeled in clay, photographed, coloured and reproduced by colour lithography, to give it a three-dimensional feel.[21] The *Official Report* claims that the poster was inspired by the ancient Greek custom of sending a young man out to announce the Games.[22] This misinterpretation of ancient tradition has resulted in a poster that focuses on a clothed young man who is depicted shouting aloud as he holds a garland; to the right of his feet is the message, a 'Call to the Games of the Xth Olympiad'.

The poster for the 1936 Berlin Olympics returned to the merger of antiquity, modernity and city. An initial design competition produced an 'unsatisfactory' result. Still, the first prize was given to German designer Willy Petzhold, whose poster featured a wreathed bronze head. He had, however, not met the parameters of the competition, to indicate 'the importance of the Olympic Games' and 'Berlin as the host city' and to publicize the Games in an effective and easily understood manner.[23]

A committee instead commissioned artists and settled on Franz Würbel's design: a victor wearing a wreath, with the Olympic rings behind him; in the foreground is an image of the *quadriga* of Berlin's famous Brandenburg Gate (see Figure 6.4). The composition merged the Olympics (ancient and modern) with the city of Berlin.[24] The athlete, whose body is golden, is not clearly a representation of a person or statue. In either case, the 'heroic realism' style officially endorsed by the Nazi regime is on full display here.[25] More than that, the poster makes clear Nazi claims to classical antiquity and their self-representation as the inheritors of ancient Greece.[26] Like the cinematic record of the Berlin Games, the poster demonstrates the modern Olympics' intertwining of ancient and modern, combined with civic and national symbolism, for the glorification of the National Socialist state and its ideology.

Figure 6.4 Poster of the Games of the XI Olympiad (Berlin, 1936). International Olympic Committee.

The poster for the Games of London 1948, delayed by twelve years because of the Second World War, was in direct dialogue with the visual images of its predecessor. The London Games were organized quickly and with tight budget constraints. As a result, with no time for a competition,[27] the organizing committee chose a design by Walter Herz, chief artist of Heros Publicity Studio. He superimposed a picture based on the *Townley Discobolus* (in the British Museum) on top of the Olympic rings and the Houses of Parliament (see Figure 6.5).

Figure 6.5 Poster of the Games of the XIV Olympiad (London, 1948). International Olympic Committee.

The London poster – and the London Games – respond to that of Berlin: the *Discobolus*, central to the iconography of the Berlin 1936 Olympics, is repurposed here as the icon of the 1948 Games. The Nazi regime had purchased the Lancellotti *Discobolus* from the family in Rome in 1938 and installed it in the Glyptothek, the home of the German collection of ancient Greek and Roman antiquities. After the War, even though the statue was not one of the many works of art plundered by the Nazi regime, it was returned to Italy just after the 1948

Olympics.[28] The Lancellotti statue was literally removed from Germany (and the Germans, for a time, removed from the Olympics) while the British version – the British Museum's *Townley Discobolus* – became the new emblem of the Olympic movement. Art, sport and antiquity, here, therefore, more than in any other poster, come together in the supposedly non-political arena of the modern Olympics.

The next two Olympic Games take wildly divergent paths in their poster design: Helsinki 1952 hearkens back to the Amsterdam Games of 1924 with a poster that eschews antiquity for modern sports. It features a bronze statue of running legend Paavo Nurmi in front of a globe with Finland outlined in red. The 1956 Melbourne Games, the second modern Olympics to take place outside of Europe, are harbingers of things to come. The poster is unequivocally modern: its central motif of a folding invitation contains the Olympic rings and the coat of arms of Melbourne while the blue might evoke the South Pacific Ocean.[29] The Organizing Committee explicitly acknowledged its departure from the traditional motifs of Olympic posters.[30] In stark contrast is the poster for the equestrian competitions of 1956, which were held in Stockholm because of Australia's strict quarantine laws. The poster, like that of the 1932 Los Angeles Games, imitates a relief sculpture, this one very similar to riders on the Parthenon frieze.[31] Below an egg-and-dart moulding are the particulars of the equestrian competitions, the words for which surround the Olympic rings.

Despite the bold, new design of the Melbourne 1956 Games, the official poster for the 1960 Rome Games returned to the traditional mode of antiquity, modernity and civic ideology. Of course, civic identity in Rome is tied to its ancient past.

The design was a result of a contest between artists of Italian descent, though the organizing committee did not like any of the 249 entries. In a second competition, Armando Testa's design was chosen and met the brief of the Organizing Committee that it contain the following: '(a) the idea of Olympic sport; (b) the five Olympic rings; (c) the wording "Games of the XVII Olympiad-Rome-MCMLX".'[32] The poster, unapologetically ancient and Roman, is a modern version of the

Belvedere capital (from one of the monumental columns at the Baths of Caracalla) (see Figure 6.6). It features the Capitoline wolf on top of a column capital, and the remainder of the capital depicts a victor, who holds a palm, crowning himself with stylized individuals – possibly wearing togas – surrounding him.

The Rome 1960 Games' poster serves as a useful endpoint for this survey of Olympic posters and their use, adaptation and interpretation of classical antiquity. The Tokyo 1964 poster returned to the stark

Figure 6.6 Poster of the Games of the XVII Olympiad (Rome, 1960). International Olympic Committee.

modernity of Melbourne's poster, and abstract designs became the stock-in-trade of Olympic posters through the 1960s, 1970s and 1980s.[33] Only with the centennial Games in Atlanta in 1996 did a human shape return to the poster, this time a stylized – and without explicitly represented gender or race – person against a backdrop of the Olympic colours.[34] And then, with Athens 2004, antiquity returned, though now perhaps as part of the civic symbolism of Athens rather than as a core iconographic principle for the Modern Olympics (Figure 6.7).

Figure 6.7 Poster of the Games of the XXVIII Olympiad (Athens, 2004). International Olympic Committee.

Rome's poster, therefore, marks the endpoint in one style of the modern Olympic movement that characterized its early years: the centrality of mostly nude, exclusively male and mostly white athletes alongside the slow development of specifically modern Olympic symbols that overtake and replace allusions to and imagery borrowed from classical antiquity.[35]

Olympic films

The modern Olympics are almost as old as film.[36] Many early films are of sports or about them: the first 'feature-film', *Corbett-Fitzsimmons Fight* (Enoch J. Rector, 1897) is of a boxing match, a sport that continues to have a special connection to cinema.[37] Olympic films in particular are an old category of sports film. They are part 'time capsule' and documentary since they preserve old outfits and practices in a specific context that may be compared across time and place.[38]

The earliest footage comes from Stockholm in 1912. While not intended as a 'feature film' – rather it was footage recorded for newsreels – it was edited and released as a feature version in 1915, in time for the third anniversary of the Games; it was edited again in 1962 for a fiftieth anniversary screening.[39] The footage was shot by the Swedish company A. B. Svensk-Amerikanska Filmkompaniet, who worked with Pathé to edit the footage and produce the newsreel clips.[40] Some clips were shown almost immediately after filming, and the organizers conceived of film as a way to broaden the audience of the Games and collect the events, held at disparate venues, into one place in the cinema.[41] Even at this early point, the film focuses on some of the inchoate 'rituals' of the modern Games: the parade of nations before the King of Sweden and the presentation of prizes.

When the Olympics returned to Paris in 1924, the first feature-length Olympic film was produced (*The Olympic Games in Paris*, directed by Jean de Rovera). The silent film runs 174 minutes and contains some iconic Olympic moments: for example, the 100 metres and 400 metres sprints of Harold Abrahams and Eric Liddell, later immortalized in *Chariots of Fire* (1981). Ritual is prioritized in the film: the opening speech by the President of the French Republic; the release of carrier pigeons 'to proclaim the Games to the home countries of the athletes'; the athletes' oath; and the parade of nations. Immediately after the scenes of the opening ceremonies and the parade of athletes, title cards create a narrative and derive meaning from the athletic footage – an introductory card reads: 'these athletes, the flower of their race, showed the finest exemples [*sic*] of courage'. This card is followed by an athlete who falls and recovers to run up a hill in the cross-country race, while a pole-vaulter makes it over the bar and a title appears reading 'Agility'. The hammer throw is shown with a title reading 'Strength', and a Swedish gymnastics workout is teamed with a card reading 'discipline to the greater glory of sport', followed by a final card that reads 'and to the honour of their respective countries'. The five rings of the IOC are in the background of these title cards, and the whole sequence, coming directly after the opening ceremonies but before the sequential coverage of the events (which begins immediately with the title card 'Wrestling'), puts the emphasis on the meaning of sport – especially the Olympics – that is embodied in the Olympic motto (*citius, altius, fortius* – 'Faster, Higher, Stronger' – itself, in fact, introduced at the 1924 Games). The supposedly essential meaning of sports, implicitly tied to the rituals of the opening ceremonies, is brought into focus in these short clips.[42]

After 1924, Olympic films became part of the International Olympic Committee's expectations for host cities. There exist more or less official films from the Amsterdam Games of 1928 to the present day, with the exception of the 1932 Games in Los Angeles. While the Olympic film always has a component of reportage or a documentary element, they frequently use the medium of film to reiterate a connection with classical antiquity, to introduce and emphasize Modern Olympic rituals or to create and transmit other messages. Even in the relatively straightforward account of the 1928 Amsterdam Games, the focus on rituals stresses the 'traditions' of the Games; the 'sacred flame' atop the stadium tower, featured in many shots, was an important addition in this Olympiad. While much of the content remains focused on the record of events, some 1928 camera work stresses a connection between antiquity and modernity: for example, immediately prior to the commencement of the shot-put, a shot is situated with the camera behind a silhouetted statue of a shot-putter, with the stadium, and prominently the Marathon Tower with the 'sacred flame', in the background. This relatively primitive attempt to communicate the similarity of statue and athlete, amid the sporting landscape of the Olympics, would be expanded dramatically with the innovations of Leni Riefenstahl in *Olympia* (1938, directed by Leni Riefenstahl).

Riefenstahl's *Olympia* changed the genre of the sports film and Olympic documentary. Indeed, *Olympia* is the most important sports film ever produced and one of the most influential films of all; there is, as a result, a veritable library of criticism and commentary on it. The limited account here therefore focuses on aspects of the film's evocation of classical antiquity, a characteristic of the Olympics that Riefenstahl brought into focus beyond any of her predecessors.

Riefenstahl's access to an enormous budget and the increasing technical sophistication of film-making made more dramatic representations of events possible.[43] For example, cameras move beside athletes in running events, and the camera follows divers from the top of the board under the water. Riefenstahl's film also exposes, if only implicitly, the technical limitations that restrict film-making from capturing some events: for example, the pole vault competition that lasted long into the night could not be captured on film because the IOC refused to allow the arc-lighting necessary to illuminate the scene. Rather than lose the chance to show the climatic final, Riefenstahl simply restaged it the following day, with the final competitors re-enacting their last few jumps.[44] In this restaging of some events, Riefenstahl's film is exposed as not a documentary of the specific events of the Olympics of 1936, but as a study of the human body,[45] and, most importantly, as a vehicle for the perceived connection of modern athletics – and Fascist ideology – with the athletic and aesthetic practices of Greek antiquity.

Riefenstahl made antiquity central to her cinematic representation of the Games, and her emphasis on antiquity has been seen as part of a Fascist aesthetic program,[46] Other iterations of the Games had already stressed the connection with the past, most notably in the rituals that were imagined to have ancient antecedents and the primacy given to supposedly ancient Greek disciplines (like Graeco-Roman wrestling and discus) and to the modern nation of Greece itself (marching first in the parade since 1928). Riefenstahl's film expands on these connections considerably and engages more substantially with the perceived connection between antiquity and modernity.[47]

These connections appear from the moment her film begins: the opening titles and credits are represented as if they are inscriptions surrounded by relief sculpture (depicting ancient Greek sport). As the opening titles fade to clouds, the camera bursts through and descends to the Acropolis of Athens. The camera moves slowly around and through the ruins of the Acropolis, which are rendered in soft focus with mournful music. Modern Athens is captured in the out-of-focus background of shots, but otherwise, the ruins stand alone, as if out of time, and certainly without modern inhabitants or any utility, beyond the Romantic and the monumental.[48] Here, Riefenstahl's film, despite its modern aesthetic, adapts and accords with the ideologies behind classicism, in which the modern Greeks and modern Greece are, at best, a unfortunate addition.[49] From the ruins of the Acropolis, the scene changes to an interior populated by classical sculpture. As the camera moves from sculpture to sculpture, it lingers on Myron's *Discobolus*, which comes to life, a moment later, through the body of German decathlete Erwin Huber.[50]

When the film leaves the ruins of the Acropolis, the scene remains out of time and space. We see a variety of athletes, starting with the discus throwers, who are increasingly shown in silhouette as the scene proceeds. Athletes wielding the javelin and shot-put appear as the camera pans around their bodies. The camera is positioned to foreground the athletes in front of clouds. At no time are these athletes placed definitively in time or space; are they ancient statues of athletes come alive? Are they manifestations of abstracts like 'athleticism'? Are they anthropomorphic representations of athletic disciplines?

As the camera focuses on a shot-putter who tosses a shot from one hand to another, the scene fades from his nearly naked arms and body to the silhouetted arms of a nude woman. As the motion of the shot-putter was not athletic (or in fact ancient), but rather a rhythmic movement abstracted from the practice of athletics, it serves as the transition to the rhythmic movement of dancers, who toss a ball, jump with hoops and then dance in unison. Whereas the men had been nearly naked and placed in front of the sky, the women are completely naked and staged in front of flowing grass, shimmering water and a cloudless sky or sun. David Hinton connects this scene – in which Leni Riefenstahl herself supposedly performed – with the torch lighting and relay that follows by suggesting that these dancers represent 'the ancient Greek temple dancers, the keepers of the sacred flame'.[51] Michael McKenzie in contrast argues that Riefenstahl's own background in anti-modernist German dance contributed to this scene, and the ethos that is central to *Olympia*, which was to remove sport from capitalist democracies and imbue it with an 'anticapitalist, antimodern, romantic cultural discourse'.[52] His suggestion is more convincing than vague assertions of temple dancers and sacred flames in antiquity (neither of which has much to do with the ancient Olympics). While *Olympia* throughout demonstrates little interest in the record-keeping and quantification that define modern sports (and connect them with modernity and capitalism), this is not immediately surprising since the Olympic project itself is an attempt to solve the paradox of antiquity within modernity. The IOC's vision of the Olympics and Olympism at once embodies modernity (through international competition predicated on the state) and antiquity (through notions of athletic aestheticism, rituals and tradition). *Olympia*, certainly more than any earlier film and on a grander scale, stages this paradox and its apparent resolution within the Olympic Movement.

As the nude dancers fade into a superimposed image of fire, the scene changes to the lighting of the Olympic torch and the beginning of the torch relay. The torch-lighting was restaged by Riefenstahl, who missed the actual ceremony, and in any case, wanted a specific type of person and scene to connect with her vision of the torch relay's imagined antiquity.[53] Modern Greece was effaced; events were staged to suit aesthetic concerns over reality. Her film features one of the later torchbearers as the one who lights the flame; the lighting ceremony was restaged at Delphi instead of ancient Olympia.[54] The motive behind the torch relay was to encourage a connection between the origin of the Olympics and its incarnation in Berlin.[55] In *Olympia*, this motive overrides documentary film-making, but Riefenstahl goes further in ensuring that the cinematic representation of the torch lighting conforms to her idea of Olympia and the Olympics. By placing the torch lighting in a completely ahistorical landscape, the torch relay is not only the transfer of the 'Olympic spirit' from ancient Olympia to Berlin, but a representation of a merged modernity and antiquity. Even the bodies of torch-runners demonstrate this merger, since 'as they journey from past to the present', they wear modern clothing (gym shorts) and their hair changes from 'classical curly locks' to 'rigidly parted' German.[56] Riefenstahl's emphasis on Greece's empty, ruined and Romantic landscape will be central to cinematic representations of this ceremony in future Olympic films.

Olympia finally reaches Berlin and the Games themselves. The opening ceremonies focus on the symbols of the Games, whether the rings hanging in the Olympic stadium or the Olympic and other flags circling its top level. The camera moves between audience – almost invariably, in these opening shots, giving the *sieg Heil* salute – and flags, symbols or the parade of nations. After Hitler opens the Games, the torchbearer enters and lights the Olympic flame, and a chorus begins singing a hymn entitled 'Olympia'. The impressive rendition of the song intermingled with shots of Olympic symbols leaves the impression that the opening ceremonies are, as they in fact are in the course of the film, the culmination of the entire prologue: from the Acropolis, to athletes, nude dancers and the lighting of the flame – from vision of the past to its realization in modern Berlin.

After the opening ceremonies, Riefenstahl's film fits more securely with earlier Olympic documentaries, though the technical quality and breadth of coverage is more impressive. Nonetheless, alterations are made here and there to reinforce the connection with antiquity. One seemingly minor change occurs as the Games proper begin. Radio announcers from around the world (in six languages) report on the opening contests, and 'the first event of the day' is the discus throw. The implication of Riefenstahl's film is that the men's discus competition followed directly from the opening ceremonies, a parallel to *Olympia*'s move from ritual and aesthetics in the Acropolis scene in the opening to discus thrower come to life in the *Discobolus* scene. However, the first athletic event of the Games was in fact the shot-put competition on 2 August (the first day of athletics competition); the discus competition was not held until 5 August.

Although ten years separates the film of the 1948 Olympics in London – entitled *The Glory of Sport* (directed by Castleton Knight) – from that of the Berlin Games, Riefenstahl's *Olympia* still resonates. The film focuses on the Olympics as a force for peace: early on in two sequences enormous 'V for Victory' symbols are shown (one formed by people in the Swiss Alps, the other by hedges on a British hillside), but the narrator explains, 'victory not in war, not in wealth, not in tyranny, but in sportsmanship and in peace'. Peace and reconciliation may be a focus, but these Games excluded Germany and Japan, banished for their role as aggressors in the Second World War.

The opening scene, set in Delphi (it begins with a shot of the *tholos* temple in the sanctuary of Athena), turns almost immediately to a statue of a discus thrower. It is not Myron's *Discobolus*, which was so memorably used in the prologue of *Olympia*, but the camera nonetheless spins around the statue in way that is reminiscent of *Olympia*'s cinematography. The statue, however, does not come to life, and the role of antiquity as 'blueprint' for a new super-race in 1936 is replaced with a 'frozen athlete from the distant past', who can still inspire greatness in sport.[57] The opening of the film lingers in a non-historic and Romantic landscape of ruins: shots of Delphi are intermingled with those of the

Acropolis of Athens without explanation or labels – in all the scenes, people, and modern Greece, are absent. Like Riefenstahl's *Olympia*, the landscape of ruins is the stage for the torch-lighting ceremony (here represented as taking place on the Acropolis of Athens; in actuality the torch was lit at Olympia). A male narrator remarks on the antiquity of the Games as women dressed in 'classical garb' light the 'sacred flame'. The narrator connects the 'sacred flame' with antiquity, and mystifies even the modern torch relay: 'it is this flame which nowadays is carried by the relay of torchbearers to wherever the games are being held'. 'Nowadays,' of course, obfuscates the origin of the torch relay, which had only been held once, twelve years earlier in Berlin. By obscuring its very recent – and politically inopportune – origins, the narration and 'ceremony' imagine the relay back into antiquity so as to avoid any taint from its actual beginnings in Nazi Germany. The 'Torch Relay' chapter of the *Official Report of the London Games* repeats this myth: 'the lighting of the Sacred Fire should be carried out by a Torch kindled in the traditional manner at Olympia in Greece, and carried by relays of runners across Europe to London'.[58] The torch had only been lit *one time* at Olympia and was not 'traditional' in any sense of the word.

The landscape of ruins seemingly for the sake of ruins continues as the torch relay begins. The runner runs inexplicably through the colonnade of the Parthenon, then through the Sanctuary of Eleusis (some 20 km away), before running down the south slope of the Acropolis through the Theatre of Dionysus. Needless to say, this 'route' represents aesthetic impulses, not reality. In fact, unrest in Greece meant that the torch route was altered significantly and went from Olympia to the coast at Katakolon and by ship to Corfu; the scenes of torch runners in Delphi, Athens and Eleusis, are a fantasy of ruins and antiquity, not a representation of the actual relay.

Romanticism continues to drive the representation of the relay after these scenes amid classical ruins. After the interlude of the Winter Games in St. Moritz, the scene is of the beaches of Dover (where in fact a British warship did deliver the flame from Calais; the torch had passed through Italy, Switzerland, Luxembourg and Belgium), where a semi-nude runner passes the torch over to a British runner clad in the Olympic jersey of the British team. The scene jumps from the hillside 'V for Victory' to the ethos of the modern Games, Pierre de Coubertin's Olympic credo ('the important thing in life is not the triumph, but the fight; the essential thing is not to have won, but to have fought well'), emblazoned on a billboard at Wembley Stadium. The narration of the opening ceremonies begins, with the climactic moment of the entry of the torch described as the true connection between the past and present in the Olympic movement: '[the torch bearer is] the last link in the long chain of runners between ancient Olympia and Great Britain … an athlete spanning the centuries'. The centuries, perhaps, but ancient Olympia itself is strikingly absent, in a representation that trades on obfuscation and staging to imply a new – though actually influenced by *Olympia* and the 1936 Berlin Games – Olympic fusion of past and present.

The fusion of past and present continues to drive Olympic films after 1948. The official films of 1956 and 1960 make a striking contrast. *Melbourne Rendezvous*, a 106-minute-long film directed by French film-maker René Lucot focuses on the modernity of Australian 'civilization' and the novelty of travel to distant Melbourne. The opening depicts modern industry while the narrator contrasts the complexity of machines and the 'simple movements' of the human form. The shot then changes to a semi-nude runner carrying a torch, as the film explains its purpose: 'let us turn to where the flames of ancient Greek civilization have been rekindled'. Throughout, Melbourne's 'newness' and the antiquity of the Olympics are compared: near the opening of the film the narrator claims that 'the world's youngest city is hosting the world's oldest celebration'. The apparent discord between the novelty of (white) settlement in Australia and the antiquity of the Olympics continues in the coverage of the rituals and traditions of the opening ceremonies. When Greece enters first in the parade of nations, the narrator opines that Greece is given pride of place because 'for two weeks under the Melbourne sky, the entire world will rediscover the glory of ancient Greece'. The new stadium in Melbourne is contrasted with the 'ruins' of ancient stadiums, but *Melbourne Rendezvous*, unlike the films of 1936 and 1948, does not contain images of the Greek landscape.

Even without views of ancient Greek ruins, ancient Greece is evoked in the form of Pindar, whom the narrators wonder about in the aftermath of Bobby Morrow's 100 metres victory: 'what would Pindar say? He himself scoffed at scores and times. Perhaps "a handsome man, graceful in action". Despite this nod to ancient Greek praise poetry and the agonism of ancient athletics, Melbourne's Games are portrayed, like the 1948 London Games, as Games of peace and friendship. The film's emphasis on the struggle even to get to Melbourne makes the entire film a modified meditation on the Olympic credo: simply arriving in Melbourne – having 'Olympic memories' – is as important as having won.

The Grand Olympics (the official film of the 1960 Olympic Games in Rome, directed by Romolo Marcellini) returns to the theme of antiquity reborn. An opening flyover focuses on the ancient sites of the city, and in the opening lines of the film, the narrator explains that athletes have come from all over the world to honour the Olympic truce: 'Pindar said 2500 years ago, "Let toil and battle pause, so that young men may face each other in the peaceful contest of the Games."' The parade of nations begins, but the appearance of Greece prompts a movement back to Greece and the lighting of the Olympic flame; ancient and modern Greece are linked by their connection to the rituals of the Olympic Movement. The torch-lighting ceremony is represented as it actually occurs, i.e. with women dressed as 'priestesses' lighting a torch with the rays of the sun near the Temple of Hera at ancient Olympia. This is the first Olympic film to show the torch-lighting ceremony taking place in the correct place in Greece! Unfortunately, the narration is an absurd error: not only does it say the ceremony takes place in the Temple to Jupiter, but it says it happens 'on Mount Olympus', some 500 km north of ancient Olympia.

But it is not only Greek antiquity that is on display in the Games and the film. Ancient Roman sites are leveraged for their (rather slim) connection with the ancient sports that inspire the modern Olympics: gymnastics is staged at the Baths of Caracalla; wrestling at the Basilica of Maxentius. In the opening shot of the latter, the supposed connection of Basilica and sport is made explicit: 'The Roman Olympiad has reopened among the ruins of the Palatine, the old home of wrestling.' The wrestlers are described through allusion to classical literature and art: 'living sculptures, modern representations of Homeric tales'. However, ancient Rome's connection to ancient Greek sport is tenuous at best. Perhaps in the 1960 Olympics at Rome, more than anywhere else, is the modern Olympic ideology of internationalism versus the ancient Greek belief in the connection with the landscape of Olympia and the Olympics made clear. If in earlier films a hazy and unreal Romantic ruined landscape stood in for ancient Greece, *The Grand Olympics* demonstrates that *any* classical ruin is good enough. The perceived antiquity of the modern Games is indebted more to a retrospective categorization of ancient Greek and Roman civilization as a continuity, even if ancient Greek sports, and the Olympics, are one aspect of antiquity that distinguishes ancient Greek from Roman culture.

The trajectory of Olympic films from 1912–60 demonstrates a decoupling from an actual classical antiquity (i.e. the place and time of the ancient Olympics) and a merging of imagined 'antiquity' (represented in either non-specific or Romanticized 'ruins') with modern Olympic traditions. While the presence or absence of ancient Greece varies, Olympic films give preeminence to Olympic rituals, and in several cinematic representations, antiquity serves to buttress the 'traditional' qualities of otherwise modern Olympic ceremonies like the 'sacred flame' or torch relay; or expressly modern Olympic ideologies like those encapsulated in the Olympic Credo.

*   *   *

By the time of the Tokyo Olympics, in their visual art and in the cinematic masterpiece *Tokyo Olympiad* (1965, directed by Kon

Ichikawa), the modern aspects of the Olympics prevailed: Greek antiquity has been reduced to a veneer over a modern festival with traditional pretensions that claims to embody world peace and human aspiration. *Tokyo Olympiad* and the Games of the XVIII Olympiad herald a new era for the Olympic Games. Not only were they the first Games not to be held in Europe or one of its settler-colonies, but their representation disconnects the Games from their perceived connection with Greek antiquity. Greece and the ancient heritage, of course, remain central to the IOC's claims for the exceptionalism of the Olympics, but the new traditions and ideologies of the modern Games became key parts of Olympic identity. Olympic films and posters chronicled these rituals and traditions and imbued them with apparent connections with antiquity. By setting new and old Olympic ideologies side by side, and by connecting, via symbolism and text, cuts, special effects and narration, they effectively juxtapose the apparent antiquity of IOC's Games and their actual modernity.

Further Reading

Introduction

For readers interested in a general history of sport with copious suggestions for further reading from one of the greatest sports historians, see A. Guttmann, *Sports: The First Five Millennia* (University of Massachusetts Press, 2004). Several collections of essays cover many aspects of ancient sport and are good places to start for interested readers: D. G. Kyle and P. Christesen (eds), *A Companion to Sport and Spectacle in Greek and Roman Antiquity* (Wiley-Blackwell, 2014); and P. Christesen and C. Stockings (eds), *A Cultural History of Sport in Antiquity* (Bloomsbury, 2020). A. Futrell and T. F. Scanlon (eds), *The Oxford Handbook of Sport and Spectacle in the Ancient World* (Oxford University Press, 2021) appeared too recently for me to incorporate it fully into this book.

Chapter 1

There are many overviews of ancient Greek sport. For example, two strong books often assigned in classes on ancient sport are: D. G. Kyle, *Sport and Spectacle in the Ancient World*, 2nd edn (Wiley-Blackwell, 2014); and S. G. Miller, *Ancient Greek Athletics* (Yale University Press, 2004).

For those with specific interest in the cultural importance of sport in ancient Greece, see M. Golden, *Sport and Society in Ancient Greece* (Cambridge University Press, 1998). For those seeking more information on athletes, two recent books address these figures: R. Bertolín Cebrián, *The Athlete in the Ancient Greek World* (University of Oklahoma Press, 2020); and Z. Papakonstantinou, *Sport and Identity in Ancient Greece* (Routledge, 2019).

On Pindar, epinician poetry and dedications, among a very large and specialist bibliography, see: A. Ford, *The Origins of Criticism* (Princeton University Press, 2002); and N. Nicholson, *Aristocracy and Athletics in Archaic and Classical Greece* (Cambridge University Press, 2005).

Chapter 2

There are many overviews of Roman sport. In addition to Christesen and Stocking and Kyle and Christesen (both mentioned above and with chapters on ancient Rome), the following represent a diverse range of perspectives on the meaning of Roman sport, especially but not only gladiators: C. Barton, *The Sorrows of the Ancient Romans: The Gladiator and the Monster* (Princeton University Press, 1995); G. Fagan, *The Lure of the Arena: Social Psychology and the Crowd at the Roman Games* (Cambridge University Press, 2011); A. Futrell, *Blood in the Arena: The Spectacle of Roman Power* (University of Texas Press, 2001); and D. G. Kyle, *Spectacles of Death in Ancient Rome* (Routledge, 2001).

Chapter 3

Many volumes exist on Olympic history. For the end of the Games in antiquity, see S. Remijsen, *The End of Greek Athletics in Late Antiquity* (Cambridge University Press, 2015). For the interconnections between the birth of modern Germany and excavations at Olympia, see S. Marchand, *Down from Olympus: Archaeology and Philhellenism in German, 1750–1970* (Princeton University Press, 2003).

The classic account of the birth of the modern Olympics is D. C. Young, *The Modern Olympics: A Struggle for Revival* (Johns Hopkins University Press, 1996). But some of the best treatments of the first Olympics and their connections to ancient and modern Greece are more recent. See K. Georgiadis, *Olympic Revival: The Revival of the Olympic Games in Modern Times* (Ekdotike Athenon S.A., 2003); and A.

Kitroeff, *Wrestling with the Ancients: Modern Greek Identity and the Olympics* (Greekworks.com, 2004).

Chapter 4

For an overview of physical fitness, health and bodybuilding, see J. Fair, *Mr. America: The Tragic History of a Bodybuilding Icon* (University of Texas Press, 2015); and S. McKenzie, *Getting Physical: The Rise of Fitness Culture in America* (University Press of Kansas, 2013).

Eugen Sandow and Bernarr Macfadden are the subject of many books, the best of which are: D. L. Chapman, *Sandow the Magnificent: Eugen Sandow and the Beginnings of Bodybuilding* (University of Illinois Press, 2006); and R. Ernst, *Weakness is a Crime: The Life of Bernarr Macfadden* (Syracuse University Press, 1991).

Chapter 5

There does not exist a good overview of ancient Greek stadiums, though see relevant chapters in D. G. Kyle and P. Christesen, *A Companion to Sport and Spectacle in Greek and Roman Antiquity* (Wiley-Blackwell, 2015). For the hippodrome, interested readers may consult a very recent collection that deals with the most up-to-date evidence: C. Moretti and P. Valavanis (eds), *Les Hippodromes et les concours hippiques dans la Grèce antique* (Ecole française d'Athènes, 2019).

Readers who are interested in Roman circus and amphitheatres are served well by the following: J. H. Humphrey, *Roman Circuses: Arenas for Chariot Racing* (B. T. Batsford, 1986); and K. Welch, *The Roman Amphitheatre: From Its Origins to the Colosseum* (Cambridge University Press, 2007).

Perhaps the only book on modern Olympic stadiums is the beautifully illustrated and recent G. John and D. Parker, *Olympic Stadia: Theatres of Dreams* (Routledge, 2020).

Chapter 6

There are no overviews of the connections between antiquity and Olympic posters and films. Those interested in the posters are best served by a book that accompanied an exhibit of Olympic posters at the Victoria and Albert Museum (V&A): M. Timmers, *A Century of Olympic Posters* (V&A Publishing, 2008). For sports films in general, see B. Babington, *The Sports Film: Games People Play* (Wallflower Press, 2014). Leni Riefenstahl's *Olympia* (Olympi-Film, 1938), which she directed, has generated a huge bibliography over the years, but a good introduction is T. Downing, *Olympia* (BFI Publishing, 1993).

Notes

Introduction

1 S. Connor, *A Philosophy of Sport* (Reaktion Books, 2011), 15.
2 A. Guttmann, *Sports: The First Five Millennia* (University of Massachusetts Press, 2004), 1–3.
3 On the 'jubilee run', see W. Decker, trans. A. Guttman, *Sports and Games of Ancient Egypt* (American University in Cairo Press, 1987), 24–9; on archery, see ibid., 36–43.
4 Ibid., 70–88.
5 See J. Rutter, 'Sport in the Aegean Bronze Age', in P. Christesen and D. G. Kyle (eds), *A Companion to Sport and Spectacle in Greek and Roman Antiquity* (Wiley-Blackwell, 2014), 37–43.
6 S. G. Miller, *Ancient Greek Athletics* (Yale University Press, 2004), 159.

1 Sport in Greek Antiquity

1 J. Rutter, 'Sport in the Aegean Bronze Age', in P. Christesen and D. Kyle (eds), *A Companion to Sport in Greek and Roman Antiquity* (Wiley-Blackwell, 2014), 48 n. 8.
2 The archery contest and armed combat are exceptions: Achilles delineates the rules (23.855–8, 805–6), although the decision in archery, in the end, actually ignores them.
3 T. Scanlon, 'Homer, the Olympics, and the Heroic Ethos', *Classics@*, 13 (2015).
4 M. Golden, *Sport and Society in Ancient Greece* (Cambridge University Press, 1998), 23–8.
5 T. Scanlon, 'The Vocabulary of Competition', *Arete*, 1 (1983): 154–6. Even if *aethlos* does not derive from a root indicating fatigue, competition is at the core of its meaning; see R. Beekes, *Etymological Dictionary of Greek* (Brill, 2009).
6 'Vocabulary of Competition', 151–4.

7 The name derives from *periodos*, 'circuit', another name for the Panhellenic Games. It is attested no earlier than the Roman Imperial period (e.g. *Inscriptiones Graecae* 5.1.105.4); *periodos*, to mean the four Panhellenic Games, is attested in an inscription that dates to before 229 BCE (*Inscriptiones Graecae* 9.1.694.30).

8 The Isthmian crown was changed from pine to dry celery at some point in antiquity (Plutarch, *Moralia* 675D–676F). The location of the Nemean Games changed as cities contested control over it.

9 For brief versions of the foundation tales of each sanctuary, see S. G. Miller, *Ancient Greek Athletics* (Yale University Press, 2004), 87–112.

10 At Nemea, a fourth race called the *hippios* was staged; it was likely four lengths of the stadium. The Marathon was introduced in the 1896 Olympics and its now standard 42.195 km was introduced in the 1908 Olympics in London.

11 On scoring and winning in the pentathlon and the type of jump performed, see J. Mouratidis, *On the Jump of the Ancient Pentathlon* (Hildesheim, 2012).

12 T. Scanlon, *Eros and Greek Athletics* (Oxford University Press, 2002), 208–10.

13 Translation by author.

14 L. Bonfante, 'Nudity as a Costume in Classical Art', *American Journal of Archaeology*, 93, 4 (1989): 543–70.

15 D. Sansone, *Greek Athletics and the Genesis of Sport* (University of California Press, 1988); *Sport and Society*, 17–19; *Eros and Greek Athletics*, 64–72.

16 C. Mann, 'Products, Training, and Technology', in P. Christesen and C. H. Stocking (eds), *A Cultural History of Sport in Antiquity* (Bloomsbury, 2021), 69–94.

17 *Sport and Society*, 119–20.

18 J. Neils, *Goddess and Polis: The Panathenaic Festival in Ancient Athens* (Princeton University Press, 1992), 20.

19 *Sport and Society*, 104–12.

20 On determining who fit into which category, see Chapter 3.

21 On class and status, see P. J. Miller, 'Segregation, Inclusion, and Exclusion', in Christesen and Stocking, 141–58; and Z. Papakonstantiou, 'Conflict and Accommodation', in Christesen and Stocking, 121–40.

22 S. G. Miller, *Nemea: A Guide to the Site and Museum* (Archaeological Receipts Fund, 2004), 34–5. The story is known from fragmentary sources dating to the fifth century BCE.

23 On athletes as heroes, see *Ancient Greek Athletics*, 160–5.

24 *Nemea*, 122.

25 Ibid., 113.

26 See ibid., 169–70 for details on this restoration project.

27 S. G. Miller, *Excavations at Nemea II: The Early Hellenistic Stadium* (University of California Press, 2001), 12.

28 Ibid., 25–9.

29 Ibid., 18.

30 *Nemea*, 199.

31 *Excavations at Nemea*, 62–83.

32 *Nemea*, 195.

33 Ibid., 197–8.

34 At Nemea today, every four years, the Society for the Revival of the Nemean Games stages athletics competitions using the tunnel and stadium, so that the sanctuary is once again alive with the sights and sounds of athletics.

35 T. H. Nielsen, *Two Studies in the History of Ancient Greek Athletics* (Royal Danish Academy of Sciences and Letters, 2018), 106.

36 D. G. Kyle, *Sport and Spectacle in the Ancient World*, 2nd edn (Wiley-Blackwell, 2014), 258–75.

37 On the Dionysiades, see *Eros and Greek Athletics*, 104–5, 133–5, 287–90.

38 R. Bertolín Cebrián, *The Athlete in the Ancient Greek World* (University of Oklahoma Press, 2020), 2.

39 O. Van Nijf, 'Global Players: Athletes and Performers in the Hellenistic and Roman World', *Hephaistos*, 24 (2006), 226–7.

40 R. R. R. Smith, 'Pindar, Athletes, and the Early Greek Statue Habit', in S. Hornblower and C. Morgan (eds), *Pindar's Poetry, Patrons and Festivals* (Oxford University Press, 2007), 84.

41 H. Hermann, 'Die Siegerstatuen von Olympia. Schriftliche Überlieferung und archäologischer Befund', *Nikephoros* 1 (1988), 123–4.

42 D. T. Steiner, *Images in Mind: Statues in Archaic and Classical Greek Literature and Thought* (Princeton University Press, 2001), 17–18. Statues today may often be white marble, but in antiquity detail could be added to marble statues with paint (for an accessible overview of polychromy, that

is, paint and Greek statuary, see M. Talbot, 'The Myth of Whiteness in Classical Sculpture', *New Yorker*, 29 October 2018, available online: https://www.newyorker.com/magazine/2018/10/29/the-myth-of-whiteness-in-classical-sculpture (accessed 26 May 2022).

43 *Images in Mind*, 19.

44 On the origins of epinician song, see: R. Thomas, 'Fame, Memorial, and Choral Poetry: The Origins of Epinikian Song-an Historical Study', in S. Hornblower and C. Morgan (eds), *Pindar's Poetry, Patrons, and Festivals: From Archaic Greece to the Roman Empire* (Oxford University Press, 2007), 141–66; R. Rawles, 'Early Epinician: Ibycus and Simonides', in P. Agócs, C. Carey and R. Rawles (eds), *Reading the Victory Ode* (Cambridge University Press, 2012), 3–27.

45 Translation by author.

46 On these issues in epinician song, see L. Kurke, *The Traffic in Praise: Pindar and the Poetics of Social Economy* (Cornell University Press, 1991).

47 *The Athlete*, 127.

48 W. Petermandl, 'Growing Up with Greek Sport: Education and Athletics', in Christesen and Kyle, 239.

49 *The Athlete*, 168–76.

50 'Growing Up', 240.

51 D. Hawhee, *Bodily Arts: Rhetoric and Athletics in Ancient Greece* (University of Texas Press, 2004), 110.

52 Ibid., 38.

53 On Greek pederasty and athletics, see *Eros and Greek Athletics*, 64–97. On pederasty and homoeroticism in Greek culture more generally, see J. Davidson, *The Greeks and Greek Love: A Radical Reappraisal of Homosexuality in Ancient Greece* (Wiedenfeld & Nicolson, 2007).

54 N. Nicholson, 'The truth of pederasty', *Intertexts*, 2, 1 (1998): 26–44.

55 On the 'Spartan Mirage', the ancient and modern reception of Sparta that obscures historical reality, see, among others, A. Powell and S. Hodkinson, *Sparta: Beyond the Mirage* (Classical Press of Wales, 2002); and, for modern reception in particular, see S. Hodkinson and I. M. Morris, *Sparta in Modern Thought: Politics, History and Culture* (Classical Press of Wales, 2012).

56 See *Eros and Greek Athletics*, 77–83; and P. Christesen, 'Sport and Society in Sparta', in Christesen and Kyle, 146–58.

57 'Sport and Society in Sparta', 151.

58 N. M. Kennell, 'Spartan Cultural Memory in the Roman Period', in A. Powell (ed.), *A Companion to Sparta* (Wiley-Blackwell, 2018), 646.

59 On the challenges of Olympic revival in this vein, see Chapter 3.

60 'Spartan Cultural Memory', 648.

61 On these issues, see L. S. Fotheringham, 'The Positive Portrayal of Sparta in Late-Twentieth Century Fiction', in Hodkinson and Morris, 393–428; V. Losemann, 'The Spartan Tradition in Germany, 1870–1945', in Hodkinson and Morris, 253–314; H. Roche, *Sparta's German Children: The Ideal of Ancient Sparta in the Royal Prussian Cadet Corps, 1818–1920, and in the National Socialist Elite Schools (the Napolas), 1933–1945* (Classical Press of Wales, 2013). On Sparta and sports teams in the twentieth and twenty-first centuries, see S. R. Jensen, 'Reception of Sparta in North America: Eighteenth to Twenty-First Centuries', in A. Powell (ed.), *A Companion to Sparta, Volume II* (Wiley-Blackwell, 2018), 712–22.

62 *Sport and Spectacle*, 263–4.

63 *Eros and Greek Athletics*, 139–74.

64 S. McKenzie, *Getting Physical: The Rise of Fitness Culture in America* (University Press of Kansas, 2013), 10–11.

65 *Getting Physical*, 24.

66 Ibid., 66–81.

67 Ibid., 119–25.

68 Ibid., 145.

69 E. Chaline, *The Temple of Perfection: A History of the Gym* (Reaktion Books, 2015), 205.

2 Sport in Roman Antiquity

1 On whether gladiatorial games are properly termed sport (as this book argues), see P. Christesen and R. Maclean, 'The Purpose of Sport', in P. Christesen and C. H. Stocking (eds), *A Cultural History of Sport in Antiquity* (Bloomsbury, 2021), 37–9.

2 See D. G. Kyle, *Sport and Spectacle in the Ancient World*, 2nd edn (Wiley-Blackwell, 2014), 15–17.

3 On an attempt to contextualize the Ovid with respect to modern 'pick-up' artists, see the brilliant chapter in D. Zuckerberg, *Not All Dead White Men:*

Classics and Misogyny in the Digital Age (Harvard University Press, 2018), 89–142.

4 Plutarch cites Fabius Pictor (*c.* 3rd century BCE) as his source for the story (*Life of Romulus* 14).

5 A. Futrell, 'Sex in the Arena', in A. Futrell and T. F. Scanlon (eds), *The Oxford Handbook of Sport and Spectacle in the Ancient World* (Oxford University Press, 2021), 677.

6 F. Meijer, *Chariot Racing in the Roman Empire* (Johns Hopkins University Press, 2010), 29.

7 The first Roman historian, Fabius Pictor, wrote near the end of the third century BCE.

8 G. Bevagna, 'Etruscan Sport', in P. Christesen and D. G. Kyle (eds), *A Companion to Sport and Spectacle in Greek and Roman Antiquity* (Wiley-Blackwell, 2014), 397.

9 Rear wall of the Tomb of the Chariots at Tarquinia; see 'Etruscan Sport', 400 for images.

10 S. Bell, 'Roman Chariot Racing: Charioteers, Factions, Spectators', in Christesen and Kyle, 496.

11 P. Christesen and C. H. Stocking, 'Introduction', in Christesen and Stocking, 25.

12 S. Bell, 'Horse Racing in Imperial Rome: Athletic Competition, Equine Performance, and Urban Spectacle', *International Journal of the History of Sport*, 37 (2020): 12; *Chariot Racing*, 67–8.

13 *Chariot Racing*, 81.

14 Ibid., 67–8.

15 R. Maclean, 'People on the Margins of Roman Spectacle', in Christesen and Kyle, 582.

16 *Chariot Racing*, 76.

17 A. Futrell, *The Roman Games: Historical Sources in Translation* (Wiley-Blackwell, 2006), 197.

18 The toilet is a marble latrine in the form of a chariot now located in the British Museum (1806, 0703, 224).

19 This list comes from a cursory glance at the official shop of the NHL's Winnipeg Jets.

20 'Roman Chariot Racing', 495–6.

21 The best collection is G. Horsmann, *Die Wagenlenker der römischen Kaiserzeit Untersuchungen zu ihrer sozialen Stellung* (Franz Steiner Verlag, 1998).

22 'Horse Racing in Imperial Rome', 19.

23 Translation by A. Mahoney, *Roman Sports and Spectacles: A Sourcebook* (Focus, 2001).

24 A distinction, of course, is that Hank Aaron's plaque is located in a specialty building for baseball, so the audience can be assumed to have specialized knowledge. Funerary inscriptions for charioteers were, in contrast, located in public places.

25 'Horse Racing in Imperial Rome', 19.

26 *Chariot Racing*, 85–6.

27 Ibid., 92–3.

28 Ibid., 89.

29 'Horse Racing in Imperial Rome', 17–18.

30 J. Zaleski, 'Religion and Roman Spectacle', in Christesen and Kyle, 598–9.

31 *Chariot Racing*, 102.

32 Ibid., 101.

33 D. A. Parnell, 'Spectacle and Sport in Constantinople in the Sixth Century CE', in Christesen and Kyle, 633.

34 'Spectacle and Sport', 638.

35 Ibid., 642.

36 The so-called PHERSU image in the Tomb of the Augurs has prompted some to see gladiatorial combat in Etruria, but the image almost certainly shows funerary customs or beast-hunt-like events; see J.-P. Thuiller, *Les Jeux athlétiques dans la civilisation étrusque* (Ecole française de Rome, 1985), 339.

37 G. Ville, *La Gladiature en Occident des origines à la mort de Domitien* (École française de Rome, 1981), 1.

38 T. Wiedemann, *Emperors and Gladiators* (Routledge, 1993), 31.

39 Ibid., 32.

40 K. E. Welch, *The Roman Amphitheatre: From Its Origins to the Colosseum* (Cambridge University Press 2009), 18–21.

41 *Sport and Spectacle*, 286.

42 *Emperors*, 8.

43 Ibid., 8.

44 E. Köhne, C. Ewigleben and R. Jackson (eds), *Gladiators and Caesars: The Power of Spectacle in Ancient Rome* (University of California Press, 2000), 132.

45 Being sentenced to a gladiatorial school was, in fact, a lesser penalty, since it was not necessarily a capital punishment. During the reign of Hadrian (117–38 CE), gladiators were freed after a period of servitude (*The Roman Games*, 123–4).

46 *Auctoratus* comes from the verb *auctoro*, 'to bind or pledge'.

47 D. G. Kyle, *Spectacles of Death in Ancient Rome* (Routledge, 2001), 87.

48 G. Fagan, *The Lure of the Arena: Social Psychology and the Crowd at the Roman Games* (Cambridge University Press, 2011), 212–13.

49 *Gladiators and Caesars*, 37.

50 Even emperors did so, most notoriously Commodus (Cassius Dio, 73.16–17).

51 M. J. Carter, 'Romanization through Spectacle in the Greek East', in Christesen and Kyle, 627.

52 *La Gladiature*, 318–21.

53 'People on the Margins', 580–1.

54 *Spectacles of Death*, 83–4.

55 There was, for example, a guard post at the door to the *ludus* in Pompeii, but similar guard posts are found in large houses as well; see G. G. Fagan, 'Training Gladiators: Life in the *Ludus*', in L. L. Brice and D. Slootes (eds), *Aspects of Ancient Institutions and Geography: Studies in Honor of Richard J.A. Talbert* (Brill, 2014), 125.

56 'Training', 123.

57 Ibid., 125.

58 The best modern treatment, with images including re-creations, is in *Gladiators and Caesars*, 46–64. As they point out, there are other categories, although they are far less frequent in the extant evidence.

59 'Training', 130.

60 Ibid., 136–7.

61 Ibid., 130.

62 *Lure*, 219.

63 Ibid., 137 n. 35.

64 S. Brunet, 'Women with Swords: Female Gladiators in the Roman World', in Christesen and Kyle, 479.

65 British Museum 1847, 0424.19.

66 *The Roman Games*, 86–7.

67 'Romanization through Spectacle', 627.

68 Translation from A. Mahoney, *Roman Sports and Spectacles: A Sourcebook* (Focus Publishing, 2001), 23.
69 '*Missio* standing' may refer to a sort of draw.
70 C. Barton, *The Sorrows of the Ancient Romans: The Gladiator and the Monster* (Princeton University Press, 1995), 15.
71 *Spectacles of Death*, 48.
72 *The Roman Amphitheatre*, 27–8.
73 K. Hopkins, *Death and Renewal* (Cambridge University Press, 1983), 1–30.
74 *The Roman Amphitheatre*, 5–7.
75 E. Rawson, '*Discrimina Ordinum*: The *Lex Julia Theatralis*', in F. Millar (ed.), *Roman Culture and Society* (Oxford University Press, 1991), 512.
76 On this topic, see C. Williams, *Roman Homosexuality*, 2nd edn (Oxford University Press, 2010).
77 'Sex and the Arena', 680.
78 Ibid., 679.
79 *Sport and Spectacle*, 331.
80 On the ineffectiveness of such edicts, see ibid., 336.
81 M. Golden, *Greek Sport and Social Status* (University of Texas Press, 2008), 70.
82 See Chapter 5 for modifications to ancient Greek stadiums to permit Roman sports.
83 L. Robert, *Les Gladiateurs dans l'orient grec* (Adolf M. Hakkert, 1971). The Games of Antiochus in 166 BCE are an exception, though scholars debate whether the *monomachoi* there were actual gladiators and whether they were imported from Italy; see C. Mann, 'Gladiators in the Greek East: A Cast Study in Romanization', in Z. Papakonstantinou (ed.), *Sport in the Cultures of the Ancient World* (Routledge, 2010), 128.
84 'Romanization through Spectacle', 620–1.
85 M. J. Carter, 'Gladiators and Monomachoi: Greek Attitudes to a Roman "Cultural Performance"', in Papkonstantinou, 166.
86 *Greek Sport and Social Status*, 73.
87 S. W. Pope, 'Imperialism', in S. W. Pope and J. Nauright (eds), *Routledge Companion to Sports History* (Routledge, 2010), 232–6 on Britain, 236–9 on the United States.
88 Ibid., 233.
89 Ibid., 234–5.
90 'Gladiators in the Greek East', 132.

91 Ibid., 134.
92 *Greek Sport and Social Status*, 77.
93 'Gladiators and Monomachoi', 160.
94 *Les Gladiateurs*, 208.
95 Ibid., 227.

3 The Ancient and Modern Olympics

1 J. König, *Athletics and Literature in the Roman Empire* (Cambridge University Press, 2005), 27–8.
2 On Philostratus more generally, see G. Miles, 'Philostratus', in D. S. Richter and W. A. Johnson (eds), *The Oxford Handbook of the Second Sophistic* (Oxford University Press, 2017), 273–90 with bibliography.
3 J. Rusten and J. König, *Philostratus: Heroicus, Gymnasticus, Discourses 1 and 2* (Harvard University Press, 2014), 358.
4 Ibid., 359.
5 J. König, 'Greek Athletics in the Severan Period', in S. Harrison, J. Elsner, S. Swain (eds), *Severan Culture*, (Cambridge University Press, 2007), 145. Athletes were also likely aware of their lineage: see S. Brunet, 'Living in the Shadow of the Past: Greek Athletes during the Roman Empire', in B. Goff and M. Simpson (eds), *Thinking the Olympics: The Classical Tradition and the Modern Games* (Bristol Classical Press, 2011), 90–108.
6 On the 'nostalgic-didactic perspective', see C. Stocking, 'Age of Athletes: Generational Decline in Philostratus' *Gymnasticus* and Archaic Greek Poetry', *Classics@*, 13 (2015).
7 For another perspective on what constitutes 'Olympic' sport, see H. L. Reid, *Olympic Philosophy: The Ideas and Ideals behind the Ancient and Modern Olympic Games* (Parnassos Press, 2020).
8 There are exceptions. Pausanias admits that there was 'no ancient record' of boys' contests (5.8.8); the race-in-armour was not ancient and implemented, so he thinks, 'for the sake of military training' (5.8.10). It is from this point that Pausanias talks about the 'unbroken' series of Olympiads.
9 G. Nagy, 'Athletic Contests in the Contexts of Epic and Other Related Archaic Texts', *Classics@*, 13 (2015).

10 See also H. Spelman, *Pindar and the Poetics of Permanence* (Oxford University Press, 2018), 196–203.

11 The site has been progressively restored and reconstructed over the last 150 years. The stadium was excavated and restored in 1936 (in association with the 1936 Olympic Games). A column of the Temple of Zeus was restored prior to the 2004 Olympic Games. The Phillipeion was restored in 2005. On these restorations, see H. Kyrieleis, *Olympia: Archäologie eines Heiligtums* (Verlag Philipp von Zabern, 2011), 26–8.

12 M. Scott, *Delphi and Olympia: The Spatial Politics of Panhellenism in the Archaic and Classical Periods* (Cambridge University Press, 2010), 169–78.

13 Today, an access road on the north side of Olympia disturbs this geographical continuity.

14 H. M. Lee, 'A "Fifty-Month" Olympiad in Bacchylides *Odes* 7.2', *Klio*, 73 (1991): 47. The *ekechieiria* is *not* a cessation of all hostilities, as often represented; see M. Golden, 'The Ancient Olympics and the Modern: Mirror and Mirage', in H. J. Lenskyj and S. Wagg (eds), *The Palgrave Handbook of Olympic Studies* (Palgrave, 2012), 20.

15 S. Remijsen, *The End of Greek Athletics in Late Antiquity* (Cambridge University Press, 2015), 40.

16 T. Stevenson, 'The Fate of the Statue of Zeus at Olympia', in J. McWilliam, S. Puttock, T. Stevenson and R. Taraporewalla (eds), *The Statue of Zeus at Olympia: New Approaches* (Cambridge Scholars Publishing, 2011), 155–6.

17 *End of Greek Athletics*, 43.

18 Ibid., 44–7.

19 Ibid., 343–4.

20 Ibid., 47.

21 On the origins of the four-year period in antiquity and its modifications in the modern period, see J. F. L. Ross, 'Tracing the Olympiad's Chronological Arc', *International Journal of the History of Sport*, 28, 13 (2011): 1810–30.

22 See H. M. Lee, 'Politics, Society, and Greek Athletics: Views from the Twenty-First Century', *Journal of Sport History*, 30, 2 (2003): 167–71.

23 K. Georgiadis, *Olympic Revival: The Revival of the Olympic Games in Modern Times* (Ekdotike Athenon S.A., 2003), 23–6.

24 M. R. Zebrowksi, 'Gilbert West's *Dissertation on the Olympick Games* (1749): "Established upon Great Political Views"', *Journal for Eighteenth-Century Studies*, 35, 2 (2012): 239–47. H. M. Lee, 'Gilbert West and the

English Contribution to the Revival of the Olympic Games', in Goff and Simpson.

25 R. Chandler, *Travels in Greece: or An Account of a Tour Made at the Expense of the Society of Dilettanti* (Clarendon Press, 1776), 325–32.

26 A. Blouet and A. Ravoisié (eds), *Expédition scientifique de Moree: Ordonnée par le Gouvernement Français; Architecture, Sculptures, Inscriptions et Vues du Péloponnèse, des Cyclades et de l'Attique* (Didot 1833), 56–8.

27 S. L. Marchand, *Down from Olympus: Archaeology and Philhellenism in Germany, 1750–1970* (Princeton University Press, 2003), 81.

28 *Down from Olympus*, 114. On this definition of positivist history, see D. Schaps, *Handbook for Classical Reception* (Routledge, 2011), 34.

29 *Down from Olympus*, 86, 92.

30 Ibid., 87.

31 J. J. Winckelmann, *History of the Art of Antiquity* (Getty Research Institute, 2006), 186.

32 *History of the Art of Antiquity*, 208.

33 K. Baedeker, *Greece: Handbook for Travellers* (Karl Baedeker, 1889), 321.

34 *Greece: Handbook for Travellers*, 325.

35 *Down from Olympus*, 91.

36 P. de Coubertin, *Souvenirs d'Amérique et de Grèce* (Hachette, 1897), 105.

37 N. Müller (ed.), *Olympism: Selected Writings*, (International Olympic Committee, 2000), 254.

38 *Olympism*, 325.

39 Ibid., 511.

40 Ibid., 511.

41 Ibid., 563–4

42 Ibid., 564–6.

43 Ibid., 569.

44 Ibid., 576.

45 J. J. MacAloon, *This Great Symbol: Pierre de Coubertin and the Origins of the Modern Olympic Games* (University of Chicago Press, 1981), 83–112.

46 *Olympism*, 221.

47 Ibid., 309.

48 Ibid., 309.

49 Ibid., 313–14.

50 This chapter is not a comprehensive account of the foundation of the modern Olympics. See Further Reading.

51 *Olympism*, 295. On the background of this Congress, see *This Great Symbol*, 164–79.

52 *Olympism*, 297.

53 On the productive failures of Coubertin's Olympics, see B. Goff, 'Introduction: Game Plan', in Goff and Simpson, 4–8.

54 *Olympism*, 314.

55 Ibid., 297.

56 On Vikelas, see *Olympic Revival*, 70–2; on Vikelas in Athens in 1895–6, see ibid., 105–69.

57 On Averoff, see ibid., 121–3 and 151–2.

58 Ibid., 196–8.

59 D. C. Young, *The Modern Olympics: A Struggle for Revival* (Johns Hopkins University Press, 1996), 125.

60 *Olympic Revival*, 158.

61 Ibid., 90.

62 *Olympism*, 336.

63 Ibid., 202.

64 Ibid., 335.

65 Ibid., 512.

66 Ibid., 335.

67 A. Kitroeff, *Wrestling with the Ancients: Modern Greek Identity and the Olympics* (Greekworks.com, 2004), 39.

68 *Olympism*, 332; *Wrestling*, 50–2.

69 *Olympic Revival*, 200–1.

70 On the intercalated Games, see *Wrestling*, 53–76.

71 *Olympism*, 129.

72 *Wrestling*, 86.

73 *Olympism*, 336.

74 Ibid., 350.

75 M. O'Mahony, 'In the Shadow of Myron: The Impact of the *Discobolus* on Representations of Olympic Sport from Victorian Britain to Contemporary China', *International Journal of the History of Sport* 30, 7 (2013): 11–12.

76 *Olympism*, 352.

77 Ibid., 544.

78 Ibid., 265.

79 Ibid., 548,. 558, 695, etc.

80　T. Nielsen, 'Panhellenic Athletics at Olympia', in P. Christesen and D. Kyle
　　(eds), *A Companion to Sport and Spectacle in Greek and Roman Antiquity*
　　(Wiley-Blackwell, 2014), 136; S. Remijsen, 'Only Greeks at the Olympics?
　　Reconsidering the Rule against non-Greeks at "Panhellenic" Games',
　　Classica et Medievalia, 67 (2019): 1–61.

81　B. Kidd, '"Another World is Possible": Recapturing Alternative Olympic
　　Histories, Imagining Different Games', in K. Young and K. B. Wamsley
　　(eds), *Global Olympics: Historical and Sociological Studies of the Modern
　　Games* (Elsevier, 2005), 143–58.

82　D. C. Young, *The Olympic Myth of Greek Amateur Athletics* (Ares
　　Publishers, 1984).

83　D. C. Young, 'Greece and the Origins of the Modern Olympic Games', in
　　W. Coulson and H. Kyrielies (eds), *Proceedings of an International
　　Symposium on the Olympic Games, 5–9 September 1988* (Deutsches
　　Archäologisches Athen, 1992), 65–6.

84　M. Golden, *Greek Sport and Social Status* (University of Texas Press, 2008),
　　40–67.

85　*Olympic Charter* (2020), Principle 6.

86　D. C. Large, 'The Nazi Olympics: Berlin 1936', in Lenskyj and Wagg, 62.

87　*Olympic Charter*.

88　On Hooper, see C. O. Bonsawin, 'From Black Power to Indigenous
　　Activism: The Olympic Movement and the Marginalization of
　　Oppressed Peoples (1968–2012)', *Journal of Sports History*, 42, 2 (2015):
　　200–19.

89　*Olympism*, 403. See G. R. Matthews, *America's First Olympics: The St. Louis
　　Games of 1904* (University of Missouri Press), 206.

90　K. B. Wamsley and G. Pfister, 'Olympic Men and Women: The Politics of
　　Gender in the Modern Games', in *Global Olympics*, 106–12.

91　'Olympic Men and Women', 112.

92　*Olympism*, 711–13.

93　Pausanias contradicts himself at 6.20.8–9 when he says 'maidens' could
　　watch the Games.

94　D. G. Kyle, *Sport and Spectacle in the Ancient World*, 2nd edn (Wiley-
　　Blackwell, 2014), 266–7.

95　K. Mantas, 'Women and Athletics in the Roman East', *Nikephoros*, 8 (1995):
　　132–3.

96 On other female equestrian victors, see 'Women and Athletics', 128–9; and C. Willekes, 'Feminizing the Hippodrome: Finding the Female in a Male World', in A. Roja and T. Dawson (eds), *Historical Practices in Horsemanship and Equestrian Sports* (Trivent: forthcoming).

97 A passage that inspired Victorian reformist Charles Kingsley to advocate for women's physical fitness. See D. Challis, 'The Race for a Healthy Body: The Ancient Greek Physical Ideal in Victorian London', in Goff and Simpson, 149–52.

98 Z. Papakonstantinou, *Sport and Identity in Ancient Greece* (Routledge, 2019), 168–75.

99 '"Another World"', 148.

100 'Olympic Men and Women', 110, 112.

101 Ibid., 110.

102 I. Buchanan and B. Mallon, *Historical Dictionary of the Olympic Movement* (Rowman & Littlefield, 2001), 270–1.

103 '"Another World"', 148.

104 'Olympic Men and Women', 113.

105 '"Another World"', 148.

106 Ibid., 149.

107 See J. Krieger, M. Krech and L. Parks Pieper, '"Our Sport": The Fight for Control of Women's International Athletics', *International Journal of the History of Sport*, 37, 5–6 (2020): 451–72.

108 'Olympic Men and Women', 116.

109 V. Heggie, 'Subjective Sex: Science, Medicine and Sex Tests in Sports', in J. Hargreaves and E. Anderson (eds), *Routledge Handbook of Sport, Gender, and Sexuality* (Routledge, 2016), 346.

110 L. A. Wackwitz, 'Verifying the Myth: Olympic Sex Testing and the Category "Woman"', *Women's Studies International Forum*, 26, 6 (2003): 553–4; and P. Mitra, 'Male/Female or Other: The Untold Stories of Female Athletes with Intersex Variations in India', in Hargreaves and Anderson, 38–94.

111 W. Petermandl, 'Growing Up with Greek Sport: Education and Athletics', in Christesen and Kyle, 242.

112 'Subjective Sex', 345–6.

113 Ibid., 343–4.

114 A. Love, 'Transgender Exclusion and Inclusion in Sport', in Hargreaves and Anderson, 378–9.

115 As I finished this manuscript, the first four openly transgender athletes – Quinn, Alana Smith, Chelsea Wolfe and Laurel Hubbard – competed at the Games of the XXXII Olympiad (Tokyo, 23 July–8 August 2021).

116 H. J. Carroll, 'Joining the Team: The Inclusion of Transgender Students in United States School-Based Athletics', in Hargreaves and Anderson, 370–1.

117 'Transgender Exclusion', 381–2.

118 A. Travers, 'The Sport Nexus and Gender Injustice', *Studies in Social Justice*, 2, 1 (2008): 82–3.

119 Another story is that of the Gay Games and the continued discrimination against lesbian and gay athletes. See C. Symons, *The Gay Games* (Routledge, 2010).

120 J. Horne and G. Whannel, *Understanding the Olympics* (Routledge, 2016), 100.

121 *Olympic Revival*, 27.

122 *Wrestling*, 5.

123 Translation in *Struggle*, 3.

124 Ibid.

125 *Olympic Revival*, 31.

126 *Struggle*, 4; *Wrestling*, 9.

127 *Olympic Revival*, 29.

128 *Wrestling*, 10.

129 *Olympic Revival*, 34.

130 *Struggle,* 8.

131 Ibid., 8–10.

132 Ibid., 14.

133 Ibid., 22 records the results.

134 *Olympic Revival,* 36.

135 *Struggle*, 18–20.

136 Ibid., 26.

137 *Olympic Revival*, 56.

138 *Struggle*, 31.

139 Ibid., 33.

140 Ibid., 35.

141 Ibid., 43.

142 Ibid., 43–4.

143 *Wrestling*, 17.

144 *Olympic Revival*, 38.

145 Ibid., 41.

146 *Struggle,* 45–6.

147 Ibid., 46–8.

148 *Olympic Revival*, 47.

149 *Struggle*, 55.

150 Ibid., 59. See also, *Olympic Revival*, 53–6.

151 *Struggle*, 60.

152 Ibid., 61.

153 Ibid., 62.

154 *Olympism*, 286.

155 Quoted in *Olympic Revival*, 204.

156 *Olympic Revival*, 63.

157 S. Dova, 'On Olympic Victors, Ancient and Modern', *Mouseion*, 16, 3 (2019): 494.

4 Beauty, Strength and Physical Culture

1 Z. Papakonstantinou, 'Ancient Critics of Greek Sport',' in P. Christesen and D. G. Kyle (eds), *A Companion to Sport and Spectacle in Greek and Roman Antiquity* (Wiley-Blackwell, 2014), 325.

2 'Ancient Critics', 327.

3 There were vigorous nineteenth- and early-twentieth-century debates on the merits of exercise for health. See, J. C. Whorton, '"Athlete's Heart": The Medical Debate over Athleticism, 1870–1920', *Journal of Sport History*, 9, 1 (1982): 30–52.

4 On other *euandria* competitions, see N. G. Crowther, *Athletika* (Hildesheim, 2004), 335.

5 D. G. Kyle, *Sport and Spectacle in the Ancient World*, 2nd edn (Routledge, 2014), 161–5.

6 M. Squire, *The Art of the Body: Antiquity and Its Legacy* (I.B. Tauris, 2011), 8.

7 J. J. Pollitt, *The Art of Rome: c. 753 B.C.–A.D. 337: Sources and Documents* (Cambridge University Press, 1990), 173.

8 Ibid., 153.

9 Ibid., 233.

10 On the critical importance of the 'Greek ideal' to early bodybuilding, see J. D. Fair, *Mr. America: The Tragic History of a Bodybuilding Icon* (University of Texas Press, 2015), 41–6. The symmetrical body faded in importance as the size of muscles and the drugs to attain them dominated bodybuilding in the 1960s, see ibid., 195–265.

11 *Art of the Body*, 9, emphasis in original.

12 Ibid., 60–1.

13 Ibid., 32–68.

14 Ibid., 47.

15 Ibid., 24–6.

16 J. J. Winckelmann, *History of the Art of Antiquity* (Getty Publications, 2006), 195.

17 Ibid., 186–7.

18 Ibid., 194.

19 J. McClelland, *Body and Mind: Sport in Europe from the Roman Empire to the Renaissance* (Routledge, 2007), 8–9.

20 M. Krüger, 'Body Culture and Nation Building: The History of Gymnastics in Germany in the Period of Its Foundation as a Nation-State', *International Journal of the History of Sport*, 13, 3 (1996): 414.

21 B. Haley, *The Healthy Body and Victorian Culture* (Harvard University Press, 1978), 107–19.

22 My history here is abridged, focuses on two individuals and about twenty years, and emphasizes classical influences. The most comprehensive history of bodybuilding is Fair's *Mr. America*. On physical fitness, see S. McKenzie, *Getting Physical: The Rise of Fitness Culture in America* (University Press of Kansas, 2015).

23 A. Marshall, 'Are Man's Physical Ideals Degenerating?' *Physical Culture* (May 1916): 20.

24 'Two Thousand Years Hence', *Physical Culture* (August 1904): 134.

25 M. Budd, *The Sculpture Machine: Physical Culture and Body Politics in the Age of Empire* (Palgrave Macmillan, 1997), 9.

26 M. Nordau, *Degeneration* (University of Nebraska Press, 1993), 35–6.

27 R. A. Nye, 'Sociology and Degeneration: The Irony of Progress', in J. E. Chamberlin and S. L. Gilman (eds), *Degeneration: The Dark Side of Progress* (Columbia University Press, 1985), 51.

28 *Getting Physical*, 16–17.

29 T. Garb, *Bodies of Modernity: Figure and Flesh in Fin-de-Siècle France* (Thames & Hudson, 1998), 55.

30 *Bodies*, 61.

31 Ibid., 70–1.

32 D. L. Chapman, *Sandow the Magnificent: Eugen Sandow and the Beginnings of Bodybuilding* (University of Illinois Press, 2006), 60.

33 *Sandow*, 4.

34 B. Burns, 'Classicizing Bodies in the Male Photographic Tradition', in L. Hardwick and C. Stray (eds), *A Companion to Classical Receptions* (Wiley-Blackwell, 2011), 444.

35 *Sandow*, 6.

36 On Professor Attila, see K. Beckwith and J. Todd, 'Requiem for a Strongman: Reassessing the Career of Professor Louis Attila', *Iron Game History*, 7, 2–3 (2002): 42–55.

37 *Sandow*, 9.

38 On previous strongmen, who also used Greek and Roman antiquity for its allure, see M. Wyke, 'Herculean Muscle! The Classicizing Rhetoric of Bodybuilding', *Arion*, 4, 3 (1997): 53–4.

39 *Sandow*, 11.

40 K. R. Dutton, *The Perfectible Body: The Western Ideal of Physical Development* (Cassell, 1995), 119.

41 *Sandow*, 18.

42 'Classicizing Bodies', 442.

43 *Sandow*, 34.

44 'Classicizing Bodies', 443.

45 *Sculpture Machine*, 48; on later connections between homoeroticism and bodybuilding, see 'Herculean Muscle!', 59–63.

46 *Getting Physical*, 159–60.

47 'Classicizing Bodies', 442.

48 Quoted in *Perfectible*, 121.

49 Ibid., 121.

50 J. Buck, 'Sandow: No Folly with Ziegfeld's First Glorification', *Iron Game History*, 5, 1 (1998): 32.

51 *Perfectible*, 124.

52 'Sandow', *Oxford English Dictionary*.

53 *Sandow*, 101.

54 On Sandow's self-marketing and 'branding', see D. G. Morais, 'Branding Iron: Eugen Sandow's "Modern" Marketing Strategies, 1887–1925', *Journal of Sports History*, 40, 2 (2013): 192–214.

55 *Sandow*, 109.

56 Ibid., 129.

57 Ibid., 180–4.

58 W. R. Hunt, *Body Love: The Amazing Career of Bernarr Macfadden* (Bowling Green State University Popular Press, 1989), 10. On the 'White City', classics and white supremacy, see R. F. Kennedy, 'Otis T. Mason and Hippocratic Environmental Theory at the Smithsonian Institution in the Nineteenth and Early Twentieth Centuries', in E. Varto (ed.), *Brill's Companion to Classics and Early Anthropology* (Brill, 2017), 154–82.

59 R. Ernst, *Weakness is a Crime: The Life of Bernarr Macfadden* (Syracuse University Press, 1991), 21.

60 B. Macfadden, 'New Corsets and Their Victims', *Physical Culture* (May 1901): 73; and ibid., 'The Corset and the Weak Woman', *Physical Culture* (August 1901): 204–5.

61 C. E. Page, 'All about Sun and Air Baths: Their Potent Influence toward the Prevention and Cure of Disease', *Physical Culture* (November 1900): 61; F. Ostwald, 'The Genesis of Prudery', *Physical Culture* (April 1901): 17–18.

62 J. Coryell, 'Prurient Prudes', *Physical Culture* (September 1902), 326.

63 B. Macfadden 'Details of the Prosecution of the Editor', *Physical Culture* (February 1910): 132; see *Body Love*, 42–4.

64 S. Cummings, 'The Grecian Costume in America', *Physical Culture* (March 1910): 287–9.

65 M. Martinelli, '"Would Live Like the Ancient Greeks": The Art and Life of Raymond Duncan' (MA diss., University of Rhode Island, 2013), 12.

66 A. Palmer, '"At Once Classical and Modern": Raymond Duncan Dress and Textiles at the Royal Ontario Museum', *Dress History: New Directions in Theory and Practice* (Bloomsbury, 2015), 132–3.

67 'The Grecian', 288.

68 Ibid., 289.

69 W. Crombie, 'Inactivity Means Death', *Physical Culture* (November 1900): 80.

70 G. Ruskin Phoebus, 'Civilization—Physical Culture', *Physical Culture* (April 1900): 21.

71 H. E. Jones, 'What Destroyed Rome', *Physical Culture* (January 1906): 605.

72 Ibid., 607.

73 A. Marshall, 'Athletes in Story and History', *Physical Culture* (November 1915): 57.

74 Ibid., 57.

75 On photographs and *Physical Culture*, *Mr. America*, 31–2.

76 'Mr. A. Lovering of Harvard', *Physical Culture* (January 1902): 164.

77 Untitled, *Physical Culture* (November, 1900): 56.

78 J. P. Wood, 'Is there such a Thing as Abnormal Physical Development?', *Physical Culture* (June, 1902): 137.

79 *Body Love*, 31. On these early competitions, see *Mr. America*, 32–5.

80 Quoted in S. Fitzpatrick, '*Physical Culture*'s World of Bodies: Transnational Participatory Pastiche and the Body Politics of America's Globalized Mass Culture', in E. S. Rosenberg and S. Fitzpatrick (eds), *Body and Nation: The Global Realm of U.S. Body Politics in the Twentieth Century* (Duke University Press, 2014), 94.

81 'World of Bodies', 96; *Mr. America*, 27.

82 J. Todd, 'Bernarr Macfadden: Reformer of Feminine Form', *Journal of Sports History*, 14, 1 (1987): 71–2.

83 C. A. Watt, 'Cultural Exchange, Appropriation and Physical Culture: Strongman Eugen Sandow in Colonial India, 1904–1905', *International Journal of the History of Sport*, 33, 16 (2016): 1921–42.

84 'World of Bodies', 88.

85 K. A. Appiah, 'There is No Such Thing as Western Civilisation', *The Guardian* (9 November 2016).

86 Ibid., 97.

87 Among others, see H. H. Byrne, 'The Aborigines of Australia', *Physical Culture* (October 1903): 301–4; W. Smithson, 'Samoa – The Isles of Eternal Summer', *Physical Culture* (December 1903), 479–82.

88 See also 'World of Bodies', 98–9, on this article, especially her discussion of photographic angles.

89 F. A. Hornibrook, 'The Fijians and Physical Culture', *Physical Culture* (August 1907): 152.

90 'Fijians', 154.

91 Ibid., 155.

92 B. Macfadden, 'Editorial Department', *Physical Culture* (August 1901): 227.

93 Ibid., 'The Murder of Children by Parental Ignorance', *Physical Culture* (September 1899): 201.

94 D. Campbell, 'The Ancient Spartans as Physical Culturalists', *Physical Culture* (March 1913): 436–7.

95 C. R. Brady, 'A Maid of Sparta', *Physical Culture* (July–October 1916).

96 S. R. Jensen, 'Reception of Sparta in North America: Eighteenth to Twenty-First Centuries', in A. Powell (ed.), *A Companion to Sparta, Volume II* (Wiley-Blackwell, 2018), 712–13.

97 On fiction in *Physical Culture*, see P. J. Miller, 'The Imaginary Antiquity of *Physical Culture*', *Classical Outlook*, 93, 1 (2018): 21–31.

98 B. Macfadden, 'A Gladiator's Romance', *Physical Culture* (July–August 1900): 161.

99 Ibid., 163.

100 Ibid., 165–8.

101 Ibid., 161.

102 Ibid., 166.

103 Ibid., 171.

104 Ibid., 212–13.

105 Ibid., 215–16.

106 Ibid., 215.

107 As it did not with Pierre de Coubertin, who contrasts the Olympic athlete with the 'circus gladiator', N. Müller (ed.), *Olympism: Selected Writings*, (International Olympic Committee, 2000), 299.

108 H. Sandé-Stollnitz, 'The Athlete: What His Ambition Should Be', *Physical Culture* (September 1905), 219–20.

109 H. S. Eyre, 'A Gladiator of To-Day', *Physical Culture* (September 1902): 315–17.

110 'Inactivity Means Death', 80.

111 R. W. Walters, 'The Adventures of Trochilles', *Physical Culture* (February 1903): 137.

112 Ibid., 138.

113 Ibid., 140.

114 Ibid., 141.

115 Ibid., 142.

116 Ibid.

117 Ibid., 143.

118 C. Wood, *Bernarr Macfadden: A Study in Success* (Lewis Copeland, 1974), 2.

119 'Bernarr Macfaden', 6.

5 Arenas, Stadiums and Gyms

1 S. Leahy, *Yahoo Sports*, 'Here's What Hockey in a Roman Amphitheatre Looked Like (Spoiler: It was Awesome)', 17 September 2012, available online: https://sports.yahoo.com/blogs/nhl-puck-daddy/hockey-roman-amphitheater-looked-spoiler-awesome-181854444--nhl.html (accessed 26 May 2022).

2 On other military games, see C. Mann, 'Campaign *Agones*: Towards a Classification of Greek Athletic Competitions', *Classica et Medievalia*, 68 (2020): 99–117.

3 M. Scott, 'The Social Life of Greek Athletic Facilities (Other than Stadia)', in P. Christesen and D. G. Kyle, *A Companion to Sport and Spectacle in Greek and Roman Antiquity* (Wiley-Blackwell, 2014), 296.

4 'Social Life', 296.

5 D. G. Kyle, *Athletics in Ancient Athens* (Brill, 1987), 60–1.

6 E. Bevagna, 'Etruscan Athletics', in Christesen and Kyle, 406.

7 S. G. Miller, 'The Greek Stadium as a Reflection of a Changing Society', in Christesen and Kyle, 291.

8 'The Greek Stadium', 292.

9 Ibid., 292.

10 O. Van Nijf, 'Ceremonies, Athletics and the City: Some Remarks on the Social Imaginary of the Greek City of the Hellenistic Period', in E. Stavrianopoulou (ed.), *Shifting Social Imaginaries in the Hellenistic Period: Narrations, Practices, and Images* (Brill, 2013), 328.

11 P. Valavanis, *Hysplex: The Starting Mechanism in Ancient Stadia: A Contribution to Ancient Greek Technology* (University of California Press, 1999), 50.

12 *Hysplex*, 42–4. A version of the *hysplex* following Valavanis has been reconstructed and is in use at the revived Nemean Games.

13 M. I. Borer, *Faithful to Fenway: Believing in Boston, Baseball, and America's Most Beloved Ballpark* (New York University Press, 2008), 36.

14 B. D. Lisle, *Modern Coliseum: Stadiums and American Culture* (University of Pennsylvania Press, 2017), 105–6.

15 'Ceremonies', 316.

16 K. E. Welch, *The Roman Amphitheatre: From Its Origins to the Colosseum* (Cambridge University Press, 1998), 548.

17 H. Dodge, 'Venues for Spectacle and Sport (other than Amphitheaters) in the Roman World', in Christesen and Kyle, 568.

18 *The Roman Amphitheatre*, 565.

19 'Venues', 568.

20 K. Welch, 'The Stadium at Aphrodisias', *American Journal of Archaeology*, 102, 3 (1998): 558.

21 A. Papanicolaou-Christensen, *The Panathenaic Stadium: Its History over Centuries* (Historical and Ethnological Society of Greece, 2003), 25.

22 The base of a turning-post from the hippodrome of Delphi may still be *in situ* and preliminary research suggests that a man-made and levelled ground layer exists below modern topsoil. See P. Valavanis, 'Topographical Indications for the Site of the Hippodrome of Delphi', *Bulletin de Correspondance Hellénique*, 141, 2 (2017): 623–44. Vestiges of the hippodromes of Delos, Lykaion, Epidaurus, Athens, Messene, Larissa and Delphi are discussed in the recent collection, J.-C. Moretti and P. Valavanis (eds), *Les Hippodromes et les concours hippiques dans la Grèce antique* (Ecole française d'Athènes, 2019).

23 W. Petermandl, 'On the Length of the Greek Hippodrome', in Moretti and Valavanis, 133.

24 D. G. Romano, 'A New Topographical and Architectural Survey of the Sanctuary of Zeus at Mount Lykaon', in E. Østby (ed.), *Ancient Arkadia: Papers from the Third International Seminar on Ancient Arcadia, Held at the Norwegian Institute at Athens, 7–10 May 2002* (Norwegian Institute at Athens, 2005), 382.

25 D. G. Romano, 'The Hippodrome and the Equestrian Contests at the Sanctuary of Zeus on Mt. Lykaion, Arcadia', in Moretti and Valavanis, 40.

26 Ibid., 41.

27 'Topographical', 387. Romano has modified his earlier understanding of the location of the stadium and hippodrome. See 'The Hippodrome', 32–3.

28 For a detailed reconstruction of these gates, see B. Dimde and C. Fläming, 'The *Aphesis* of the Olympic Hippodrome: Dimensions, Design, Technology', in Moretti and Valavanis, 145–66.

29 J. H. Humphrey, *Roman Circuses: Arenas for Chariot Racing* (B. T. Batsford, 1986), 11.

30 *Roman Circuses*, 4.

31 Ibid., 68.

32 Ibid., 67.

33 Ibid., 70.

34 Ibid., 76.

35 Ibid., 79–80.

36 Ibid., 102.

37 Ibid., 255.

38 Ibid., 260–5.

39 Ibid., 266–89.

40 Ibid., 92.

41 *The Roman Amphitheatre*, 108–27.

42 Ibid., 18.

43 Ibid., 3–59.

44 Ibid., 309 n. 7.

45 Ibid., 156–7.

46 *Modern Coliseum*, 31–4.

47 Ibid., 114.

48 Ibid., 258.

49 G. Alföldy, 'Eine Bauinschrift aus dem Colosseum', *Zeitschrift für Epigraphik*, 109 (1995): 195–226; translation my own.

50 *The Roman Amphitheatre*, 160–1.

51 R. Rea, 'The Architecture and Function of the Colosseum', in A. Gabucci (ed.), *The Colosseum* (Getty Publications, 2001), 99.

52 'The Architecture', 128.

53 Ibid., 121.

54 Ibid., 140.

55 Ibid., 103.

56 Ibid., 119.

57 Ibid., 132–4.

58 Ibid., 104.

59 L. Lombardi, 'The Water System of the Colosseum', in Gabucci, 238–40.

60 R. Rea, 'The Colosseum through the Centuries', in Gabucci, 192.

61 Ibid., 197.

62 Ibid., 213.

63 *The Panathenaic Stadium*, 64.

64 A. Devitt, 'Spectatorship and Fandom of the Roman Circus' (PhD diss., McMaster University, 2019), 101–3.

65 'Spectatorship and Fandom', 144–8.

66 Ibid., 237–8.

67 Ibid., 264–5. See also, S. Forichon, *Les Spectateurs des jeux du cirque à Rome (1er siècle a.C. au VIe siècle p.C.): Passions, émotions et manifestations* (Ausonius, 2021), 166–71.

68 *Les Spectateurs*, 166.

69 'Spectatorship and Fandom', 357.

70 R. K. Barney and A. T. Berjkrek, 'The Genesis of Sacred Fire in Olympic Ceremony: A New Interpretation', *Journal of Olympic History*, 13 (2005): 17.

71 A. Kitroeff, *Wrestling with the Ancients: Modern Greek Identity and the Olympics* (Greekworks.com, 2004), 101.

72 See S. G. Miller, *Ancient Greek Athletics* (Yale University Press, 2004), 141–2.

73 M. Kiuri and J. Teller, 'Olympic Stadiums and Cultural Heritage: On the Nature and Status of Heritage Values in Large Sports Facilities', *International Journal of the History of Sport*, 32, 2 (2015): 684–707.

74 G. John and D. Parker, *Olympic Stadia: Theatres of Dreams* (Routledge, 2020), 25.

75 N. Müller (ed.), *Olympism: Selected Writings*, (International Olympic Committee, 2000), 389.

76 Ibid., 374.

77 *Olympic Stadia*, 34.

78 Ibid., 56.

79 IOC, *Olympic Agenda 2020: Closing Report* (International Olympic Committee, 2020), 13.

80 D. Hawhee, *Bodily Arts: Rhetoric and Athletics in Ancient Greece* (University of Texas Press, 2004), 113.

81 W. Petermandl, 'Growing Up with Greek Sport: Education and Athletic', in Christesen and Kyle, 238.

82 On these buildings, see R. Bertolín Cebrián, *The Athlete in the Ancient Greek World* (University of Oklahoma Press, 2020), 135–9.

83 On Jahn and the *Turnplatz*, see E. Chalin, *The Temple of Perfection: A History of the Gym* (Reaktion Books, 2015), 88–9. On a short-lived French

gymnasium in the 1820s, see ibid., 97–8. On early British gymnasiums, see ibid., 104–5.

84 Ibid., 123.

85 Ibid., 124.

86 Ibid., 128.

87 S. McKenzie, *Getting Physical: The Rise of Fitness Culture in America* (University Press of Kansas, 2013), 5.

88 *The Temple*, 135.

89 Ibid., 145. Muscle Beach in Santa Monica was an exception; it opened in 1934 (*The Temple*, 143–4).

90 *Getting Physical*, 99–100.

91 Ibid., 58–60.

92 Ibid., 150.

93 Ibid., 168–9.

94 Ibid., 170.

6 Olympic Art and Cinema

1 Posters of all Olympic Games are available at: https://olympics.com/en/olympic-games (accessed 26 May 2022).

2 K. R. Goddy and G. L. Freedman-Harvey (eds), *Art and Sport: Images to Herald the Olympic Games* (Amateur Athletic Foundation of Los Angeles, 1992), 12. See on this topic as well, J. Hughson, 'The Cultural Legacy of Olympic Posters', *Sport in Society*, 13, 5 (2010): 749–59.

3 Swedish Olympic Committee, *The Olympic Games of Stockholm 1912* (Wahlström & Widstrand, 1913), 264.

4 *Art and Sport*, 16.

5 See T. N. Edvinsson, 'Before the Sunshine: Organising and Promoting the Olympic Games in Stockholm 1912', *International Journal of the History of Sport*, 31, 5 (2014): 570–87.

6 'Before the Sunshine', 578.

7 *Stockholm 1912*, 266.

8 *Art and Sport*, 1992: 21.

9 *Stockholm 1912*, 267.

10 Ibid., 266.

11 M. Timmers, *A Century of Olympic Posters* (V&A Publishing, 2012), 30.

12 M. O'Mahony, 'In the Shadow of Myron: The Impact of the *Discobolus* on Representations of Olympic Sport from Victorian Britain to Contemporary China', *International Journal of the History of Sport*, 30, 7 (2013): 12–13.

13 International Olympic Committee, *Olympism through Posters* (International Olympic Committee, 1983), 24; *Century*, 31.

14 *Olympic Games Antwerp 1920 Official Report* (Belgian Olympic Committee, 1920), 17.

15 *Olympism through Posters*, 24.

16 *Jeux de la VIIIeme Olympiade Paris 1924: Rapport Officiel du Comité Olympique Français* (French Olympic Committee, 1925), 64.

17 Ibid., 64.

18 Ibid., 65.

19 *Century*, 35.

20 *Ninth Olympiad, Being the Official Report of the Olympic Games of 1928 Celebrated at Amsterdam* (J. H. de Bussy,1928), 218. The IOC today shows a different poster by Emil Ember on its website with a German title, *Olympische Spiele*, because they have not obtained copyright over Jos Rovers' original poster; see H. van Gelder, 'Die Spiele in Amsterdam', *NRC*, 30 July 1996.

21 *Century*, 42.

22 *Games of the Xth Olympiad, Los Angeles, 1932, Official Report* (Xth Olympiad Committee, 1933), 215.

23 *XI Olympic Games, Berlin, 1936: Official Report* (Wilhelm Limpert, 1937), 124.

24 *Century*, 47.

25 Ibid., 45.

26 M. O'Mahony, *Olympic Visions* (Reaktion Books, 2012), 132.

27 *Official Report of the Organising Committee for the XIV Olympiad* (Organising Committee for the XIV Olympiad, 1951), 112.

28 I. Jenkins, 'Patriotic Hellenism: A Poster for the 1948 London Olympics', *Print Quarterly*, 28 4 (2011): 453.

29 *Century*, 63.

30 *Official Report of the Organizing Committee for the Games of the XVI Olympiad, Melbourne, 1956* (W. H. Houston, 1958), 142.

31 *Century*, 63.

32 *Games of the XVII Olympiad, Rome 1960: The Official Report of the Organizing Committee of the Games of the XVII Olympiad* (Organizing Committee of the Games of the XVII Olympiad, 1960), 299.

33 *Olympic Visions*, 135

34 *Century*, 119.

35 Not to say that antiquity vanishes. 'In the Shadow of Myron', 21–3, shows creative reinterpretations of the *Discobolus* in the run-up to the 2008 Beijing Olympics.

36 P. Cowie and A. Wood (eds), *100 Years of Olympic Films 1912–2012* (Criterion Collection, 2017), 10.

37 B. Babington, *The Sports Film: Games People Play* (Columbia University Press, 2014), 3.

38 The film of the 1948 Winter Games at St. Moritz even makes such commentary part of the Olympic film. In its opening, the narrator comments on the strange outfits or practices of athletes in early Olympiads.

39 *100 Years*, 213.

40 M. Dahlquist, 'Stockholm Olympic at the Movies', *International Journal of the History of Sport*, 31, 5 (2014): 591–2. Approximately two-thirds of the original film survives.

41 'Stockholm at the Movies', 593–4.

42 In addition to the long documentary covering the Games, director Jean de Rovera and cinematographer Bernard Natan created a short film entitled, *The Olympic Games: As They Were Practiced in Ancient Greece, Shown in Living Pictures*. The eight-minute-long film shows actors/athletes posed in front of dark screens, sometimes as *tableaux vivants* and sometimes in motion.

43 *Sports Film*, 38. *Olympia* is composed of two parts: 'Festival of Nations' (discussed here) and 'Festival of Beauty'.

44 D. B. Hinton, *The Films of Leni Riefenstahl* (Scarecrow Press, 2000), 54.

45 *Leni Riefenstahl*, 54.

46 M. McKenzie, 'From Athens to Berlin: the 1936 Olympics and Leni Riefenstahl's *Olympia*', *Critical Inquiry*, 29 (2003): 312.

47 D. Wildmann, 'Desired Bodies: Leni Riefenstahl's *Olympia*, Aryan Masculinity and the Classical Body', in H. Roche and K. Demetriou eds., *Brill's Companion to the Classics, Fascist Italy and Nazi Germany* (Brill 2018), 71.

48 *Olympic Visions*, 72.

49 S. Bronwell, 'The View from Greece: Questioning Eurocentrism in the History of the Olympic Games', *Journal of Sports History*, 32, 2 (2005): 204.

50 On this sequence, see 'Desired Bodies', 68–71.

51 *Leni Riefenstahl*, 51.

52 'From Athens to Berlin', 333.

53 T. Downing, *Olympia* (BFI Publishing, 1992), 53.

54 Ibid., 54.

55 'Desired Bodies', 73–8. On the relay's ideological purpose, see J. Chapoutot, *Greeks, Romans, Germans: How the Nazis Usurped Europe's Classical Past* (University of California Press, 2016), 167–70.

56 Ibid., 77.

57 'In the Shadow of Myron', 18–19.

58 *XIV Olympiad*, 209.

Index